BEYOND GRAMMAR
LANGUAGE, POWER, AND THE CLASSROOM

Language, Culture, and Teaching

Sonia Nieto, Series Editor

For a complete list of LEA titles, please contact Lawrence Erlbaum Associates, Publishers, at **www.erlbaum.com.**

BEYOND GRAMMAR
LANGUAGE, POWER, AND THE CLASSROOM

Mary R. Harmon
Saginaw Valley State University

Marilyn J. Wilson
Michigan State University

Routledge
Taylor & Francis Group
New York   London

First published by Lawrence Erlbaum Associates
10 Industrial Avenue
Mahwah, New Jersey 07430

Transferred to Digital printing 2010 by Routledge
Taylor & Francis Group
270 Madison Avenue
New York, NY 10016

2 Park Square
Milton Park, Abingdon
Oxon OX14 4RN

Cover design by Tomai Maridou

Library of Congress Cataloging-in-Publication Data

Harmon, Mary R.
Beyond grammar : language, power, and the classroom / Mary R.
  Harmon, Marilyn J. Wilson.
       p. cm.
  Includes bibliographical references and index.
ISBN 0-8058-3715-9 (pbk.)
1. Language and languages—Study and teaching—Social as-
  pects—United States.   2. Sociolinguistics—United States.   3.
  Language policy—United States. I. Wilson, Marilyn J. II. Title.
P53.8H37 2006
418.0071—dc22   2006041253
                                                      CIP

Dedications

To my children, Amy and Chad, with whom I witnessed language acquisition;
To my students, who prove to me semester after semester that language lives
through change;
To Paul for friendship and support. M.R.H.

To my children, Tim and Ann, whose language examples have served me well
in my teaching and writing;
To my students, who inspire me to think about language in new ways;
To Stu for encouragement and support. M. J. W.

Contents

Series Foreword

Sonia Nieto
University of Massachusetts, Amherst

What does it take to be an effective educator in the United States today? It is becoming ever more clear that the answer to this question lies not only in knowing subject matter content or learning specific strategies. Teachers also need to know more about the students who currently occupy U.S. classrooms and, even more important, they need to challenge the conventional wisdom concerning the abilities and skills of these students. In addition, teachers in today's schools need to understand the sociopolitical context of education and how local, state, national, and global policies, practices, and ideologies influence education. The goal of the textbooks in the *Language, Culture, and Teaching* series is to help teachers do these things.

Long-held notions about cultural and racial superiority and inferiority have often found their way into teacher education texts. For much of our educational history, conventional wisdom held that students whose cultures and languages differed from the majority were functioning with a deficiency rooted in their very identities. Consequently, the thinking was that the sooner students assimilated to become more like the majority—in culture, language, appearance, experience, and values—the easier would be their transition to the mainstream and middle class. In the latter part of the 20th century, these ideas began to be repudiated, largely but not exclusively by people from the very backgrounds whose identities were being disparaged. It is no accident that educational movements in favor of ethnic studies, bilingual and multicultural education, and critical pedagogy all emerged at around the same time. These movements represented a denouncement of ideologies that had heretofore excluded large segments of the population from achieving educational success and that had viewed education as little more than filling students' heads with knowledge.

Contrary to this notion, the books in the *Language, Culture, and Teaching* series challenge traditional views of education as passive transmission of knowledge. They also confront head-on taken-for-granted assumptions about students' identities as mired in deficiency. Written by a range of educators and researchers from a variety of cultural backgrounds and disciplines, these books attempt to fill the gap that currently exists in preparing teachers for the schools and classrooms of the 21st century. The books focus on the intersections of language, culture, and teaching—specifically, on how language and culture inform classroom practice. At the same time, the series reframes the conventional idea of the textbook by envisioning classroom practice as critical, creative, and liberating. Rather than viewing the textbook as unquestioned authority, the *Language, Culture, and Teaching* series asks readers to reflect, question, critique, and respond to what they read through their thinking and practice. Using the "problem-posing" approach proposed by Freire (1970), the books in this series ask prospective and practicing teachers to think imaginatively and critically about teaching and learning, especially in terms of cultural and linguistic diversity.

Beyond Grammar: Language, Power, and the Classroom by Mary Harmon and Marilyn Wilson is the newest volume in the series and an exciting contribution to the field. Using a sociocultural approach to the study of language, the authors challenge readers to think about how power relationships shape our use of—and views about—language. With humor, everyday examples, and lively prose, they engage readers beyond the traditional aspects of language study to consider how larger social and political contexts inform language use. As a result, they broach issues of gender, social class, race, language, and others, to explore what it means to teach language in the postmodern era.

This book supports the Freirian idea that education is never neutral or objective. Like the other titles in the series, the authors do not claim to have all the answers, but they engage readers to question their beliefs and attitudes about their students, and to consider why and how they teach. By taking the intelligence of teachers seriously, Harmon and Wilson remind readers that, in the words of Freire (1985), "To study is not to consume ideas, but to create and re-create them" (p. 4).

REFERENCES

Freire, P. (1970). *Pedagogy of the oppressed*. New York: Seabury Press.
Freire, P. (1985). *The politics of education: Culture, power, and liberation*. South Hadley, MA: Bergin & Garvey.

Preface

We have long been concerned in our work with undergraduate pre-service teachers and graduate students about the quality of instruction being provided them regarding language. Too often our experience has been that we send teachers into elementary and secondary classrooms (and college/university, for that matter!) with limited information about language. We provide linguistics courses that focus on the structures of language but not courses that put language into larger social, cultural, and political contexts. Certainly, students should understand how verbs operate in English or how colons function differently from semicolons in written language, and they should know how dialect variations have arisen in the United States and how dialects differ from region to region. But we need to go beyond the mere facts of difference, interesting as those are, to look at deeper issues, for example, at linguistic prejudice, the social and political implications of language choices, and the power that resides in language use.

This book asks us to think about the power of words, the power of language attitudes, and the power of language policies as they play out in our educational and political institutions. Written with pre-service teachers and practicing teachers in mind, the book addresses how teachers can alert students to the realities of language and power so that existing language doctrine based on false assumptions and faulty logic is not perpetuated. Our goal is for teachers, as they learn about language and internalize and apply what they have learned, to become agents of change as they and their students deconstruct and undermine the inequities that unexamined language choices sustain. Such change can only occur when we begin to look more closely at the connections between language and the issues of power and dominance that permeate all use of language as they affect class, ethnicity, and gender.

The pedagogical imperative to address these issues arises from the following realities of language in use:

- The heavy-handed focus on prescriptive language use as the ultimate goal of language instruction.
- The increasing numbers of students in our school systems whose first language is not English.
- The resistance teachers find among some students to acquire and use standard English forms.
- The ways in which language instruction is sometimes used to restrict and control rather than to liberate and empower.

This book asks its readers to think beyond the grammar book and the vocabulary list, beyond prescriptive rules so glibly quoted, to the real issues of language use in society and in classrooms. What is the role of language in shaping as well as in reflecting culture? of advancing some persons and repressing others? of creating and maintaining—as well as reflecting—separations and hierarchies of race, gender, and class? How do language choices sanction hate, and how can they be countered? What are the dispositions and attitudes toward dialect variations that strip speakers of agency? What is the educational impact of dialect difference? Do educational policies and practices empower all speakers or only those with the "right" linguistic credentials? Do they actually diminish speakers' capacities and potentials rather than build on them? What can teachers do to foster attitudinal change about language use? How can classroom practices help empower all language learners? How do political movements like U.S. English and English Only impact national attitudes and our assumptions about language and people?

These questions begin to probe the politics of language, removing language study from a "neutral" corner to situate it within the context of political, social, and cultural issues. As linguist Geneva Smitherman asserts:

> Being a critical linguist means seeking not only to describe language and its socio-cultural rules, but doing so within a paradigm of language for social transformation .... Being a critical linguist means recognizing that all research is about power—who has it, who doesn't—and the use of power to shape reality based on research. (2000, 7–8)

In this book we hope to raise the critical consciousness of readers regarding language issues as they play out in communities, in educational institutions, and in their own lives as individuals, teachers, and participants in the larger community. Developing a critical pedagogy about language instruction can help educators understand that classrooms can either maintain existing inequity or address and diminish inequity through critical language study. Each of the following chapters provides extended discussions of critical language issues that directly affect students in classrooms: the political nature of language, the power of words, hate language and bullying, gender and language, dialects, and language policies.

A common framework directs the layout of each chapter.

- Each begins with an overview of the language issue in question and concludes with applications for classroom teachers.
- Interspersed throughout each chapter are references to current and recent events that illustrate the language issue's importance, cartoons that address the issue, and brief "For Thought" activities that illustrate the point being discussed and extend the reader's knowledge and awareness. Each chapter includes numerous references to the popular press and the breadth of language issues found therein to foreground current thought on sociocultural language issues, attitudes, standards, and policies found in the culture(s) at large.
- Each chapter includes suggested readings for further research and for classroom use, along with a series of explorations. Personal explorations ask readers to go beyond the text to develop further understanding; classroom explorations ask teachers to apply chapter content to teaching situations. Having used these activities successfully with our own students as a means of increasing their awareness, understanding, and critical perspectives, we urge readers to work through a number of them, learn from them, and try them in their own classrooms.

Chapter 1 provides an overview of the issues of language by considering six myths that permeate our society regarding language and its use, along with a theoretical framework for the book that suggests that language is never ideologically free nor politically neutral.

Chapter 2 raises questions related to what we mean when we say we "know" a language and its subsystems, how we come to acquire language, and what the implications of acquisition are for language study in classrooms. It considers shifting paradigms of language study and the political contexts in which these shifts occur.

Chapter 3 explores the power of words and investigates the sources of their power. After examining and exemplifying several uses and abuses of verbal power, it focuses on the language use of two kinds of professional wordsmiths whose efforts surround us every day and who cleverly manipulate language to influence our decisions: politicians and advertisers.

Chapter 4 zeros in on hate language and bully language, both destructive examples of the power of words. After defining hate language, distinguishing among types of haters, considering societal structures that underlie hate, and demonstrating the effects of hate language on users and targets, the chapter describes the language of bullying and offers teachers a wealth of suggestions for countering hate and bullying in their schools and classrooms.

Chapter 5 details the resistance that often accompanies the study of language and gender and suggests ways of countering that resistance and engaging students in thoughtful discussions of language and gender issues. It examines the pervasiveness of gender-biased language use on the semantic, syntactic, discourse, and culturally embedded levels and explores the inequities that can result from differences between women's and men's language choices and communication styles.

Chapter 6 considers linguistic variation as a social phenomenon, with all of its educational implications, and discusses the politics of language variation: who speaks a dialect; what we mean by "standard" English, and the issues of power inherent in the notion of standard; what the Ebonics debate means for the education of language minority students; and how teachers can help overcome restrictive language environments for linguistically diverse students.

The issues of language, power, and education coalesce in chapter 7 as we consider national language policies and their influence on educational policies and practices related to English language learners. Part of the discussion focuses on the English Only movement in this country and its attempts to limit and restrict the use of other languages in public and in educational venues. We address national and state laws that declare English as the "official" language and eliminate bilingual programs. Additionally, the chapter provides instructional strategies for English language learners and suggests several strategies for working with these students.

As pre-service teachers and practicing teachers read through these chapters, complete the "For Thought" and "Explorations" activities, and peruse and apply suggested resources, most will begin to notice language in new ways and begin to understand the power-fraught nature of language as they see it in action. Many will begin to hear language and to notice its complexities as they never have before. As they begin to make their own collections of articles, cartoons, literary pieces, and so on, we can predict that many of them will find themselves as addicted to language study as we are. We hope that that addiction will benefit both them and their students as they work together to construct a more equitable world.

WORKS CITED

Smitherman, Geneva. *Talkin That Talk: Language, Culture, and Education in African America*. New York: Routledge, 2000.

Acknowledgments

This book has been a labor of love. In the process a number of people made important contributions to our efforts. Our students gave us examples and generously allowed us to print them; their questions and developing curiosity about language inspired our work. They also read and critiqued many of these chapters, especially happy to tell us when we'd been too wordy. Throughout, their enthusiasm heightened ours. Dr. Paul Bruss and Stuart Wilson were valuable sources of language artifacts and provided encouragement, critique, and insight as our work progressed. We are also grateful for the careful reading and excellent suggestions from our reviewers Margo A. Figgins (University of Virginia-Charlottesville), Linda H. Goldsmith (Nova Southeastern University), and Judith Lessow-Hurley (San Jose State University), whose contributions have made this a stronger book. We wish to give special thanks to Saun Strobel, whose technical assistance with the manuscript was invaluable. And finally, we wish to thank our Lawrence Erlbaum Associates editors, Naomi Silverman and Sonia Nieto, Series Editor for the Language, Culture, and Teaching Series, whose faith in us was instrumental in this book's completion. Even when we struggled with deadlines, they gave us confidence, not only that we would finish the book but that the book was worth finishing. Their patience and encouragement challenged us to move beyond inception to final creation.

Chapter 1

Language Matters: Introduction to Language and Language Study

In an undergraduate language study class this past semester, we discussed several issues related to language and teaching, some of which resulted in heated debates. This course on language acquisition, language variation, and the politics of language and literacy generated wide debate and heated argument. This was the first time many of the students had been asked to think critically about language, language attitudes, and language teaching by addressing such questions as: Are there structures of English that are inherently sexist? Why shouldn't English be declared the official language of the United States? Is African American Vernacular a legitimate dialect, or is it street slang? Why are words used to label or identify people important and powerful? How does language get used as a vehicle for manipulation and control?

Language does matter. It is through language that we learn and come to understand the world we live in, adopt our world views, become socialized, and develop and maintain relationships. Through language we learn how to control our world and those in it, and through language we are, in turn, controlled and manipulated. This book asks teachers to think about language and the role it plays in all human endeavors. It asks them to think about the power of words, the power of language attitudes, and the power of language policies. And it asks how teachers can increase their students' awareness of issues so as to avoid perpetuating language misconceptions.

Contemporary educational philosophers argue that schools have a dual purpose: to reproduce the best of society and to enact social change. Embracing this dual role, educators agree, in theory, that schools should assist students to become critical, active, and productive learners and members of society. Educational theorist Alastair Pennycook maintains, however, that schools have tended to play a greater role in the reproduction and maintenance of the status quo, than in social change. Resistance to social change, he says, lies in language attitudes and policies (121).

Consider the importance teachers place on "standard" English usage. Citing French sociologist Pierre Bourdieu's discussion of cultural capital, Pennycook says that individuals have different kinds of cultural power—economic, linguistic, social, or symbolic—whose value or capital accrues to the holder of that power. One kind of cultural capital is linguistic capital, the value associated with certain forms of discourse within a language, with certain dialects of a language, or with certain languages themselves (123–124). Linguistic capital can turn into economic capital; speakers of some dialects or languages have greater access to employment and to positions of power. Pennycook claims that the language patterns of middle-class students afford them greater cultural capital than do the language behaviors of linguistically diverse working-class students. Majority students can use their more "legitimate" language patterns to achieve greater success in and out of school. Much of schooling is intent on perpetuating the language with the greatest cultural capital, empowering those who are already comfortable with its use, and using it to deny access to that power to those who aren't—in effect, reproducing the culture rather than working to change it. Even when schools, in theory, support the notion of empowerment through language and literacy, their instructional practices often contradict the intentions they espouse. Encouraging a basic skills curriculum for linguistically diverse students rather than the intellectually richer curriculum available to other students is just one example.

Myths about language, its acquisition, and its use are at the heart of the problem. As linguist Rudolph Troike bluntly states, "The literate public today knows more about plate tectonics and DNA than about its own speech" (B3). A fundamental ignorance about language issues not only endangers the educational progress of language minority students but also limits opportunities for real social change. As an introduction to the relationship between language and power, we will explore the *myths that contribute to major misunderstandings about language* and provide *alternative views of language* that underlie the rest of this text. This book asks teachers to look beneath the surface of language, to explore its deeper uses, and to discover the connections between speakers' intentions and the language they use within a particular social context, and then to interrogate the issues of language, power, and authority, in the classroom and out.

LANGUAGE MYTHS

Myth One: The transparency of language. Contrary to popular thinking, language is not a transparent system for communicating information. Speakers don't express ideas through objective, valueless language structures. The structure of the language, its organization, its specific words and pronunciations, its intonation patterns, its functions within the ongoing discourse, all carry a set of values that the speaker consciously or unconsciously conveys, as part of the "idea" itself. Words are not just sets of dictionary definitions. Highly nuanced and sometimes emotionally charged, words take on various shades of meaning depending on their cultural context, the individual using them, and the circumstances in which they are uttered. When Marilyn says to her husband, Stu, while eating breakfast, "I wonder if the paper is here yet," most of the time he doesn't just continue eating his cereal or give a simple "Yeah, I wonder, too" response. Instead he goes to the front door to see if it has arrived because he has understood the subtext of her comment—a request in the guise of a statement. When a textbook reads, "Over the past several centuries man has been able to use his powers of intellect to shape the world's economies, to control human behavior, and to create real worlds out of imaginary ones," despite what teachers have told students for years, the subtext subtly or not so subtly excludes the role of women in this attribution of progress. Language is full of emotional and semantic and sometimes diversionary intentions: subtexts that cannot be discerned from the words themselves but only from the language situated by speaker, listener, and situation and surface structures that often disguise the deeper levels of meaning. Most of the time, as speakers and listeners, we are not consciously aware of how we make and interpret meaning because meaning is never transparent.

Myth Two: Language equals the sum of its grammatical structures. Meaning as central to language use resides at various levels and cannot be discerned merely from words and their arrangement in sentences. Pragmatics, which is the study of language use within its social context, establishes the relationship between the structure of what is said (the *locution*, or the form of the utterance, such as statement or question) and what the utterance really does (the *illocutionary force*, or speaker's intention). When a stranger comes up to Marilyn on the street outside her office and asks, "Do you know where Bogue Street is?" she doesn't reply with a mere "Yes." Despite the fact that the stranger's comment is in the form of a yes/no question, Marilyn's knowledge of pragmatics—the underlying request for information in the question—leads her to ignore its yes/no question format and treat it instead as a request. Treating the question literally would be downright rude. The stranger has chosen to make the request in the polite form of a question rather than as a direct command. Both speakers operate with the implicit knowledge that the rules of language use are always situated in a particular social context and that accomplishing their goals requires them to play the language game.

Embedded in discourse patterns are rules that operate for turn-taking, getting and holding the floor, interrupting, and so on, that are sometimes violated by one or more participants in a conversation—frequently by the individual(s) with greater authority. Language used in these social contexts to wield power by controlling conversation has gender, class, and ethnicity subtexts and suggests that meaning and implication go far beyond mere words themselves. Linguistic analysis is incomplete without a context in which to study it. As sociolinguist Norman Fairclough describes it, "Linguistics proper," which focuses exclusively on the structures of language to the exclusion of the power relationships represented in language, becomes a study of language decontextualized, without the benefit of human beings who use it for political purposes (5).

Myth Three: The linguistic superiority of some languages, dialects, and patterns of linguistic behavior. Language is a system—highly structured at every level—that operates with intricate rules of pronunciation (phonology), rules for words and word endings (morphology), rules for sentence structures (syntax), rules for meaning (semantics), and rules for use within the context of human discourse (pragmatics). *Open the empty bottle* means something quite different from *empty the open bottle,* despite the fact that the words are identical. Speakers don't randomly string together words in a sentence but follow the constraints of word order (syntax) to indicate their intentions. Speakers mean something very different when they say *zip* rather than *sip,* even though the linguistic difference is a matter of a single phoneme (or distinctive sound). What makes the patterns and rules of a language describable is the fact that all languages are rule-governed. The grammar of a language is the set of internalized rules that govern our unconscious use of language—the knowledge that allows us to make sense of sentences we've never heard before and to utter sentences we've never said before, that differentiates the meaning of *open the empty bottle* from *empty the open bottle.* Most speakers understand that languages operate with a set of rules, although they may not be able to describe them.

Dialects, on the other hand, provide fertile ground for mythmaking. The serious misconception that some dialects of English are governed by a set of rules while others are not has obvious currency in the thinking of many speakers. English programs in schools have given the public a strong sense of the rule-governed nature of standard forms of English—as most grammar books are designed to do—and we've learned those lessons well: standard grammar rules are THE rules of a language, and any speech pattern that violates standard rules is not rule-governed at all. Nothing is further from the truth.

Every dialect, or linguistic variation of a language, is *rule-governed* because it *operates with a set of rules that its speakers adhere to.* The common misconception that speakers of some dialects use language randomly and haphazardly, use slang instead of "real" language, or use forms of language that prevent them from operating with complex concepts is simply false. All speakers of a language speak a fully rule-governed dialect of that language. An individual's speech community has a wide range of features reflecting geographic region, ethnic heritage, social class, occupation, and gender, manifesting themselves in every level of the linguistic system. These include phonological or pronunciation differences, such as how a speaker pronounces the vowel in *roof* or whether a speaker pronounces the *r* in *yard*; lexical or vocabulary differences, such as whether the speaker sits on a *couch*, a *sofa*, or a *davenport*; and syntactic or structural differences, such as *she is working* or *she be working*, or *he shouldn't do that* or *he hadn't ought to do that*.

Even though we are often judged by linguistic yardsticks, no dialect is any less capable than any other dialect of enabling speakers to express complex thoughts or of providing for a full range of linguistic functions and purposes. The deficit notion of language—that some dialects are less well-structured, incomplete, illogical, substandard, or impoverished versions as measured against some kind of ideal language system—is patently false. Dialects are simply *different, not deficient* systems of language, a point that is discussed in depth in chapter 6.

Myth Four: The passivity of language learning. The acquisition of language represents an intellectual feat that goes well beyond mere passive "learning." By the age of 6, children have already developed a set of language rules that are sophisticated, complex, functional, and developed without direct instruction. This phenomenon is possible only because, first, learners are active, creative generators of language rather than passive recipients of linguistic rules, and second, acquisition is more a matter of activating existing mental predispositions for acquiring language than merely imitating linguistic structures. Our assumptions of how language is used and how it should be taught implicitly reflect our understanding of how language is acquired in all its complexity. What we decide to do with language in our classrooms—to describe it, to teach it, to modify or change our students' use of it—directly relates to our understanding of the nature of the language itself and the process by which it is most easily learned and put to use.

The creativity of language acquisition is also reflected in speakers' inventions of new forms of language with new meanings. In Bill Watterson's *Calvin and Hobbes*, note the following example of language creativity:

Calvin: I like to verb words.
Hobbes: What?
Calvin: I take nouns and adjectives and use them as verbs.
           Remember when "access" was a thing? Now it's something you *do*. It got verbed. Verbing weirds language.
Hobbes: Maybe we can eventually make language a complete impediment to understanding.

While this may be an extreme example of language creativity, speakers regularly modify linguistic structures: note how often we hear *access* and *impact* as verbs rather than as nouns.

Language acquisition always operates within a sociocultural[1] context. Even though human beings have a biological predisposition for learning language, the actual event occurs only when children are immersed in language in their environment and become participants of social discourse by virtue of living in that environment. All language learners acquire the sociolinguistic rule system—the forms and structures used in particular social contexts—within their speech communities. Though the structures may differ from one speech community to another, the differences are not qualitative. Nothing is inherently or linguistically superior in the structure *I don't have a pencil* to *I don't got no pencil*. Both are rule-governed structures, even though one may be less socially prestigious than the other. All speakers operate with fully formed, rule-governed systems of language.

Being socialized through language suggests that issues of power and authority are present from the very beginning of the process. Caregivers often talk differently to baby boys than they do to baby girls. Baby cards portray baby boys as active doers, baby girls as sweet bundles of joy. And gendered conversational patterns in children's language use are often positively reinforced by caregivers; for example, boys are often allowed to use more boisterous or assertive language than girls. In this way, language use reinforces the patterns of authority and submissiveness that are played out and developed in social relationships.

Myth Five: Traditional, prescriptive grammar as the ideal basis of language study. Given our knowledge of language acquisition and its embeddedness in sociocultural situations, a redefinition of *grammar* in linguistics affects how language is now studied and analyzed. As a result of this paradigm shift in our views about language, linguists view *grammar* as the unconscious knowledge of the systems of rules, sociocultural as well as linguistic, that we operate with in our native language. The study of grammar, then, becomes a descriptive analysis of the rules underlying language use. This paradigm shift rejects more traditional uses of grammar as *prescriptive,* in which the "correctness" of the language we speak—the table manners of language that enable us to avoid social stigmatization by using *socially appropriate* language—becomes the central focus. We learn not to use double negatives, to avoid *ain't* in polite company, and to have our verbs agree with our subjects. Learning to use non-stigmatized language in formal situations is equivalent to learning not to lick the jelly from your knife at a formal dinner party. Sometimes, of course, we misuse the rule because we haven't fully internalized it; sometimes we forget the rule; sometimes we deliberately violate it for effect.

Refocusing language study as *descriptive* rather than prescriptive redirects our thinking away from linguistic judgments about language use to descriptions of how people actually use language. Implicit in this focus are three assumptions. The first assumes that acquiring a set of internalized rules of language occurs not through a conscious knowledge of the rules but by a natural process of acquiring those rules through communicative acts as infants and children. The second assumption suggests that being able to describe language rules consciously as adolescents or adults is not a prerequisite to using language effectively. As linguists suggest, learning the parts of speech of words or knowing how to diagram a sentence are not prerequisites for using language effectively, just as knowing the laws of physics is not a prerequisite for learning how to ride a bike. And third, language rules are not absolute but change from one speech community to another to reflect the sociopolitical[2] uses of language within speech communities.

Myth Six: Language as a neutral entity. George Orwell raised the issue of the myth of linguistic neutrality several decades ago in his classic essay, "Politics and the English Language": "Political language" he says, "… is designed to make lies sound truthful and murder respectable, and to give an appearance of solidity to pure wind" (126). While Orwell was referring specifically to language used by politicians, we are making the claim that all language is *political and always* imbued with power. Beyond conveying meaning, speakers' intentions operate in powerful rhetorical ways to shape listeners' perceptions and to control their behavior. That language can be manipulative is a fact not only understood by Sweepstakes companies who use language to increase their sales of magazines to gullible buyers with headlines that scream "MS. WILSON, YOU ARE THE MILLION DOLLAR WINNER … if you are the winning ticket holder," but also more insidiously by politicians who twist the truth by clever uses of rhetoric and word choice, as we will discuss in chapter 3. Orwell, we think, would approve that the National Council of Teachers of English (NCTE) annual Doublespeak Awards were given for a description of the Abu Ghraib torture as "the excesses of human nature that humanity suffers," and for attempts to disguise the reality of military deaths by changing the Vietnam era *bodybag* to *human remains pouches* during the Gulf War and to *transfer tubes* in the Iraqi War (NCTE Web site).

But language for manipulative purposes works not only for politicians and advertisers. It is used by everyone, including children, and it is learned early. Consider the following conversation recently collected in Mary's language and education class:

Son:	Dad, can we stop at the corner store on the way home?
Father:	Not this time, Bobby.
Son:	PLEASE! I just want to get one thing.
Father:	O.K. But only if you promise to behave while we're at Wickes?
Son:	I promise I'll behave.

Upon arriving at the corner store, the smile on the face of 4-year-old Bobby showed his excitement. After they entered the store, the following conversation took place.

Father:	What is the one thing you want, Bobby?
Son:	I want a candy bar and a pop.
Father:	But, Bobby, I said you could get just one thing. A candy bar and a pop are two things.
Son:	Whatdaya want me to do ... CHOKE?

Do you suppose this child was successful in his ability to use the power of language to negotiate what he wants?

Language and power inextricably intertwine. Language is not an autonomous entity apart from society or culture but an integral part of it, or, as Fairclough suggests, a strand of social constructs that cannot be separated out (11). The forms of the language we use are mostly determined by social convention (conversations between teachers and students, for example), so that discourse is a process of social interaction in which the social (conventional) rules of discourse operate by constraining the discourse, shaping it, and molding it. That is not to say that speakers have no free will to say what they want, in ways they want, but that their linguistic utterances are nevertheless shaped within the process of discourse by the demands of its social nature and by social convention. When speakers make linguistic decisions, conscious or unconscious, those decisions are to a large extent socially and culturally determined.

All speakers operate within discourse communities, the rules of which may vary from one discourse community to another. One acquires a primary discourse, largely family-oriented and generated, by participating in the speech community of one's immediate family or extended family as a child. As the child moves out into the world, she acquires a number of secondary discourses that involve, in many cases, a conscious effort to learn and acquire the features of those discourses. A discourse moves beyond language features to include, as sociolinguist James Gee suggests, "a sort of identity kit which comes complete with the appropriate costume and instructions on how to act, talk, and often write, so as to take on a particular social role that others will recognize" (127). Successful language use is as much a matter of understanding the nuances, the subtexts, the implicit assumptions, the appropriate styles and forms of language as it is of learning the syntax and vocabulary. Learning academic discourse is not only learning how to structure linguistic complexity into one's writing but also how and when to use particular features of writing or speech in order to accomplish specific purposes.

Speakers operate with various kinds of language ideologies that make language use highly political. As a sociocultural phenomenon, language is imbued with power that often goes unnoticed because it appears natural. As linguists Thomas et al. argue, our belief systems are "mediated by the language and system of signs" we use, which are not "unbiased reflection[s] of the world but a product of the ideologies of our culture" (38). Fairclough claims that "ideological power, the power to project one's practices as universal," occurs because power is exercised in naturalized discourse assumed to be "common sense" and the natural state of things (27). For example, the placement of *she* after *he* automatically reinforces a primacy for males which until recently was unquestioned and unexamined. It simply seemed the "normal" thing to do. Power, then, as Pennycook suggests, lies "at the heart of questions of discourse, disparity, and difference" (27).

MOVING BEYOND TRADITIONAL VIEWS

Traditional linguistics courses are largely descriptive of language in use. While important, this stance is not sufficient. Students must engage with language studies that move well beyond English structures to the political nature of language and how it functions contextually. Traditionally, teachers of secondary English have approached language study as vocabulary expansion, prescriptive knowledge of usage rules, or as a study of English sentence structure. This text calls for a more comprehensive and contextualized view of language through an examination of its use in sociocultural situations. In other words, even as we move from prescriptive views of language to more descriptive views, we must investigate how forms of language relate to forms of power and critique the social order that produces inequitable language attitudes and policies (Pennycook 51).

In increasingly multicultural classrooms, we find it important for teachers to address issues of language and power for the following reasons:

- Dialect variations are becoming the norm rather than the exception.
- English language learners are increasing in number.
- Teachers' language use and language practices often reveal gender, ethnic, and/or social class bias.
- Language is regularly used to suppress, cover up, sell, control, and distort.
- Textbooks still sustain, to some degree, social and political inequities.

As teachers we must counter what linguists James Milroy and Lesley Milroy describe as "a depressing general ignorance of the nature of language and the complexity of linguistic issues in society" (175). We must operate with a more sophisticated understanding of language so that we can make informed decisions about language study and about our responses to the language choices students make. We need to consider the following:

- The stance we take when working with varied dialects.
- Our treatment of "Standard English."

- Our attitude toward varied dialect features in the writing of students.
- Our own and our students' use of conversation and dialogue to exert power and control in and out of our classrooms.
- The invalidity of many "commonsense" notions about language.
- The destructive power of language to label, bully, and silence.

Our call for the study of language within a sociopolitical framework is supported by professional organizations. For the past 30 years, English language arts professionals have been calling for increased study about language, particularly the sociolinguistic, cultural, and political aspects of language use. In addition, state and national standards and documents of prestigious organizations such as NCTE (The National Council of Teachers of English), CCCC (the Conference on College Composition and Communication), MLA (Modern Language Association), and NCATE (the National Council for the Accreditation of Teacher Education) repeatedly speak to the necessity of teachers being aware of these language issues. NCTE, for example, in its resolution on language study, speaks to the need to integrate language awareness into classroom instruction and teacher preparation programs, including "how language varies in a range of cultural settings ... how oral and written language affects listeners and readers ... how 'correctness' in language reflects social, political, economic values ... and how the structure of language works from a descriptive perspective." (NCTE Web site).

This book, *Beyond Grammar: Language, Power, and the Classroom*, seeks to lessen language ignorance and to provide a framework not only for classroom discussion of these sociopolitical issues of language but also for ways to effect real change in attitudes, instruction, and policymaking.

ENDNOTES

1. By "sociocultural," we mean that the learning event occurs in the context of one's social community and in the context of the larger culture.
2. By "sociopolitical," we are referring to the social event that is imbued with issues of power and control.

WORKS CITED

Fairclough, Norman. *Language and Power.* 2nd ed. New York: Longman, 2001.
Gee, James Paul. *Social Linguistics and Literacies.* 2nd ed. New York: Falmer, 1996.
Milroy, James, and Lesley Milroy. *Authority in Language.* New York: Routledge, 1985. Retrieved 2 June 2005 <http://www.ncte.org/about/over/positions/category/lang/107490.htm>.
Retrieved 10 July 2005 <http://www.ncte.org/about/awards/council/jrnl/106868.htm>
Orwell, George. "Politics and the English Language." *What's Language Got to Do with It?* Eds. Keith Walters and Michal Brody. New York: Norton 2005. 114–126.

Pennycook, Alastair. *Critical Applied Linguistics: A Critical Introduction*. Mahwah, NJ: Lawrence Erlbaum Associates, 2001.
Thomas, Linda., S. Wareing, I. Singh, J. Stilwell Peccei, J. Thornborrow, and J. Jones. *Language, Society and Power*. 2nd ed. New York: Routledge, 2004.
Troike, Rudolph. (Letter) *Chronicle of Higher Education*, 29 Jul 1992.
Watterson, Bill. *Calvin & Hobbes*. Universal Press Syndicate, 25 Jan 1993.

Chapter 2

What We Mean by "Knowing" a Language and How We Come to Know It

Language consists of a series of well-organized, rule-governed structures and systems that operate interdependently with one other. We often speak of language as a "system" and its various components as "subsystems" consisting of phonology, morphology, syntax, semantics, and pragmatics. In natural, ongoing speech, speakers never operate at just one or two levels but instead weave together finely tuned structures within the full range of subsystems. This chapter begins with a discussion of *what it means to "know" a language and what we mean by "rules" of language.* We then move on to descriptions of the *subsystems of language, the nature of language acquisition,* and the *implications for the teaching of grammar* in elementary and secondary classrooms. We follow with a brief discussion of the *relationship between thought and language,* which becomes central to our view, and conclude with the *changing paradigms of language study* represented in this text. We frame our discussion with perspectives we have taken in chapter 1: the necessity of considering the political context as we study how language in use manifests forms of power.

LINGUISTIC COMPETENCE: WHAT IT MEANS TO "KNOW" A LANGUAGE

Are you aware that when you say, "I turned down the offer," you can put *down* at the end of the sentence, but that you can't do that when you say, "I turned down the street"? Do you know that 16-month-old children can already tell the difference between subject nouns and object nouns, even though they may have only one or two words in their productive vocabularies? That preschoolers already use language structures so complex that it takes a well-trained linguist to describe them? Speakers of a language have a phenomenal ability to acquire a highly complex set of rules at a very early age and to operate within the rule systems of that language, whether or not they have a conscious knowledge of those rules. Like bike riders who operate within the laws of physics without being able to articulate those laws, speakers operate with tacit language rules that are largely unconscious. Given our linguistic competence, we can even make sense out of nonsense. For example, we can make "sense" out of this string of nonsense words by rearranging them into some kind of logical order:

morked bliffles plony the ciptally the lampix

FOR THOUGHT 2.1: Before reading ahead, try to arrange these "words" in a sentence that makes "sense" by paying attention to the inflections (suffixes) and the forms of the words. Try to label the part of speech of each of the words and provide a rationale for each label.

Our intuitive sense of sentence structure and word structure might suggest that we assign the following specific linguistic functions to each of these words:

morked	bliffles	plony	the	ciptally	the	lampix
verb	noun	adj.	det.	adv.	det.	noun

Our sentence might read:

"the plony bliffles ciptally morked the lampix"

or

"the lampix morked the ciptally plony bliffles."

These are not the only two possibilities. *Bliffles* could be the verb, *morked* and *ciptally* modifiers: "The morked lampix bliffles the ciptally plony." But there are limits to how we can arrange them, given our intuitive knowledge of English words and sentence structures. Not just anything will work. The nouns *bliffles* and *lampix* will need to be in the subject or object position in the sentence, and the verb *morked* will need to follow the subject noun. If we consider *ciptally* as an adverb, there are restrictions on its placement in the sentence. We have this remarkable ability to order these sentence elements because meaning is a function of both word arrangement in sentences and of the morphological endings on words that carry grammatical information. This imperative to make sense of language and the ability to use linguistic structures are all part of our linguistic competence evolving from childhood and developing into adulthood. We achieve this tremendous intellectual accomplishment with little apparent effort, at an early age. Even though a significant amount of language acquisition continues during the elementary years, the majority of rules—phonological, morphological, syntactic, semantic and pragmatic—have been largely acquired by age six, and for the most part, unconsciously, without direct instruction.

A word about rules. We often think of a "rule" as something imposed from the outside: a restriction or a set of mandates from a parent to a child; from a teacher to a student; from a manager to her employees—restrictions imposed on individuals. When we use the term "rule" in the context of language development, however, we refer to the constraints or mandates that we operate with intuitively as speakers and writers—for example, the possibilities and constraints on our arrangement of the nonsense words above—not to rules imposed by an English teacher or a grammar book. We allow for certain combinations but reject others on the basis of a rule formed in our own thinking from our use of language over time. We can also think of these rules as conventions that the English-speaking community has developed over centuries.

FOR THOUGHT 2.2: What do young children already know about language rules, as evidenced by the following sentences of 2- and 3-year-olds? Try to provide some generalizations about the linguistic rules by which these children operate.

Daddy go bye bye Jeep	No want egg	What him see?
Allgone milk	Who not go?	Why me spilling it?

For example:

- They have a sense of English word order, putting the subject before the verb.
- They know how to form questions by using the interrogative pronouns *who, what,* and *why* and moving them to the front of the sentence.
- They are developing a set of pronouns (him, me) to reference themselves and others.

What are other generalizations or "rules" they have developed?

SUBSYSTEMS OF LANGUAGE

This chapter aims to help readers develop an appreciation for what humans know about language, to dispel the misconception that young adults "don't know their grammar" or "can barely speak the language," or that many "African American speakers don't have a grammar." Contrary to such misconceptions—based largely on a limited understanding of "grammar" or "language"—we claim that speakers know their native languages well, even if they can't articulate prescribed usage patterns or describe the rules that underlie their spoken and written structures; and all speakers, regardless of dialect or language, operate with a fully developed, rich, and complex set of rules for using language.

In the section that follows, we provide brief descriptions of each of the subsystems of language, along with a preview of the sociocultural political issues that are embedded in each of these subsystems.

Phonology

Phonology is the study of the system of sounds, or phonemes, in the language and the rules that underlie their use. The word *bit*, for example, has three distinctive phonemes, just as *beat* does. The only distinction between *bit* and *beat* is that the vowels are different. Linguists use the International Phonetic Alphabet to represent the 45 or so phonemes in English because the standard orthography of English contains only 26 letters of the alphabet that do not have a one-to-one correspondence with the phonemes of the language. Some sounds are represented by a range of letters. The "long e" sound can be represented by the following different spellings: b*ea*t, b*ee*t, am*oe*ba, mach*i*ne, b*e*, bel*ie*f, rec*ei*ve, q*uay*, funn*y*, mon*ey*, (and there are more!). Some letters can represent a variety of sounds like the *s* in *cats* (*s* is voiceless), *dogs* (*s* is voiced), and *horses* (plural is an additional syllable). Other letters have no phonemic value, such as the silent letters in "*k*night" and "com*e*." Other letters are digraphs (two consecutive letters representing one sound): *ph* in *phone*, *th* as voiceless in *thigh* or as voiced in *thy*. It is useful to say these words aloud to hear and feel the difference. This discrepancy between the sounds in English and their alphabetic representations accounts for the difficulty of standard spelling. Correct spelling in writing and correct word identification in reading are not always a matter of sounding out words "correctly."

Although most speakers of English share a consistent set of phonemes and phonological rules, phonological variants occur from one speech community to another, particularly among regional dialect speakers. How do you pronounce *park, high,* and *roof?* If you live in New England, you may *pahk* your car; if you live in Alabama or Georgia, you may give a *hah fahv*; and if you live in Michigan, you may disagree with your Kentucky neighbors about the pronunciation of *roof* because you prefer the vowel in *book* rather than in *goof*.

FOR THOUGHT 2.3: How might different speech communities pronounce the following words?

| garage | either | harassment |
| aunt | route | Caribbean |

These distinctions among users do not represent qualitative differences—that is, superior or inferior forms of the language—although they may carry greater or lesser degrees of prestige, which are social rather than linguistic judgments. For example, a speaker's choice of phonemes or deletion of phonemes can affect how the speaker is perceived by her listeners. "Pahk the cah" may be considered more prestigious than "Sit down at the des," yet both involve a simple phonological deletion rule—*r* in the first example, *k* in the second. *R* deletion by some east coast speakers is considered prestigious; deleting the *k* in *desk* is not. Clearly deletion itself is not the issue, only which phoneme is being deleted and who's deleting it.

Morphology

The subsystem of morphology is the study of words, word inflections, and the rules underlying their structure and use. Morphemes are the smallest distinctive units of meaning, different from "words," which can contain several morphemes. *Unhappiness* has three morphemes—the root morpheme *happy* plus a prefix and suffix. Suffixes and prefixes can be attached to other morphemes in order to add grammatical information, to change their meaning or to alter their function within sentences—the kind of word-ending information in the nonsense sentences that enabled you to put them into linguistic categories. Adding *ir* to *responsible* negates it; adding *ize* to *rational* changes its grammatical function from adjective to verb; and adding *s* to *cat* adds grammatical information about plurality.

Within this subsystem of language also lies the potential for lesser or greater degrees of prestige and power as morphological rules vary from one speech community to another. For example, the deletion of past tense, possessive, or plural inflections by speakers in some speech communities is socially stigmatized by many speakers of "standard English." The speaker who says "I work__ till midnight last night" or "I've gotta go see my son__ teacher" is making morphological choices that may be stigmatized by speakers outside his speech community. Ironically the deletion of the *s* possessive in *son__teacher* carries greater degrees of stigmatization than the deletion of the *s* plural in *breakfasts*, again, most likely because the former operates in African American Language communities, the latter more generally across a range of populations, including "standard" speakers. Although these dialect variations are fully rule-governed, the *s* possessive deletion signals a dialect that may suffer some stigmatization. In fact, many speakers of standard English are unaware of their own phonological and morphological deletions, which regularly occur in complex consonant clusters such as *sks*, *sts*, etc. Most speakers, regardless of their dialects, pronounce *west side* as *wesside*, deleting the *t*. Virtually no speakers articulate all the consonants in *this desk's scratches*. Instead they delete at least one *s* and one *k*. Consonant cluster simplification occurs in all dialects and in all speech communities, albeit with varying degrees of frequency. Language attitudes toward these features exist not because these variants represent qualitative differences but because they represent distinctions in class and ethnicity (Wolfram & Schilling-Estes), a point we return to in chapter 6.

Syntax

Syntax consists of the components and structures of sentences and the complex rules underlying their use. In their descriptions of English grammar, school grammars have greatly oversimplified English sentence structures. Traditional grammarians tend to focus on the grammatical relationships within the surface structures of sentences, such as the subject, verb, and object, as in "The man bit the dog"; on the eight parts of speech; and on types of sentences, phrases, and clauses. These descriptions, however, merely scratch the surface of English sentence structure and rarely focus on the underlying deep structures of language. Transformational grammarians, on the other hand, illustrate language structures at both the Deep Structure (the level of meaning) and the Surface Structure (the form that the meaning takes) by describing the transformations that operate on deep structure levels to create surface structures (Tserdanelis and Wong 532). Consider the two sentences, "She turned down the offer" and "She turned down the street." Despite the fact that their surface structures look very similar, the two sentences have different underlying structures. *Down* in the first sentence operates as part of the two-word verb phrase, *turned down*; *down* in the second operates as a preposition indicating direction in the prepositional phrase, *down the street*. What happens when we substitute a pronoun for *offer* in sentence one and for *street* in sentence two? The first sentence must be transformed by moving *down* to the end of the sentence. Only the second sentence can retain its original word order, "She turned down it, " even though it's a bit awkward.

FOR THOUGHT 2.4: What syntactic transformations must occur in the following structures to change these statements into yes/no questions?

1. Jill can run fast.
2. Sam ran fast.
3. They have left for home.
4. She seemed unhappy.

Sentences 1 and 3 merely need to move the auxiliary verb to the front of the sentence: Can Jill run fast? Have they left for home? What kind of changes and additions are needed to transform sentences 2 and 4 into yes/no questions?

Most of us are totally unaware of how complicated a series of linguistic moves this simple question requires, yet we do it all the time—effortlessly and unconsciously. Do we know language? You bet we do! Do our students know language? Absolutely!

Syntactic rules, like phonological and morphological, differ from one speech community to another and, as with phonological and morphological differences, some rules are socially stigmatized. The use of multiple negation, for example, (He *don't* have *no* common sense) or non-standard subject-verb agreement patterns (*they was* here, *she like* me), although rule-governed, are nevertheless stigmatized. Some bi-dialectal speakers who alternate between dialects as the social situation dictates may have a more conscious knowledge of the rules as they apply them. Others make the switch less consciously and rely on their intuitive knowledge of the rules in both dialect systems. But the point is that the use of multiple negation is as much a matter of following a rule as using single negation. They are merely different rules.

Syntactic Differences and Prestige

FOR THOUGHT 2.5: What image of the speaker comes to mind when you imagine hearing the following:

1. I'm a-workin' the night shift this week.
2. I asked her to whom I should address the letter.
3. I might could do that for you.
4. It don't make no difference to me.

Why do you think you have these images?

Each of the three subsystems described so far, phonology, morphology, and syntax, operates with rules that vary across a range of speech communities—from nonmainstream to "standard," from one social class to another, from region to region—with varying degrees of social acceptance or stigmatization. It is important to clarify the nature of this stigmatization. If regular use of consonant cluster simplification or multiple negation were part of the linguistic repertoire of stock traders on Wall Street, these features, rather than being stigmatized, would be considered standard. We all make judgments based on language, but it is usually those with the most economic or political power or authority, often related to their social class and/or level of educational achievement, whose linguistic judgments carry the most social influence; CEOs rather than Ford line-workers, middle-class Americans rather than working-class Americans, teachers rather than students are more likely to dictate social norms for language.

Social judgments based on linguistic features are regularly used as a means of gate-keeping—to deny people jobs, to categorize students, to classify people's worth—all judgments that have less to do with language patterns than with social class attitudes toward the individuals using those patterns. Just as we make judgments based on personal appearance, we judge on the basis of language. Like dress codes, language patterns change over time and vary from culture to culture. Having long hair, for example, is never inherently good or bad, but attitudes toward hair length, particularly for males, change over time. Deleting a phoneme or using a stigmatized grammatical structure is not inherently good or bad either, but attitudes toward phonological deletion can change over time as well, and like hair length, are unrelated to an individual's intelligence or worth.

Of course it's easier to approximate middle-class values by adopting hairstyles and clothing fashions than by modifying language usage because language patterns are not as subject to conscious control. Nevertheless, individuals often make efforts to change speech patterns to avoid the stigma associated with non-standard features. That's why some parents attempt to correct their teenagers' use of language, why job applicants are more conscious of their linguistic choices during an interview, why defendants standing before juries and judges use what they deem to be "appropriate" speech patterns.

FOR THOUGHT 2.6: Consider the following uses and rate them on a scale of 1 to 5, 5 being the most stigmatized, 1 the least. Who might use the feature? Why are these features stigmatized? Might speakers find value in using some forms that are stigmatized?

1. Me and Jim are going to a movie tonight.
2. I ain't never seen nothing like that before.
3. She be working there a long time.
4. I was so hungry I could have ate a horse.

5. I suppose I could go there anyways.
6. Just between you and I, I think you're right.
7. If youse guys aren't careful, you'll hurt yourselves.

Language prestige, however, is not always associated with social prestige. As a high school student, Marilyn's son often said, "Me and Costa are going to a movie" rather than "Costa and I are going" when talking to his parents, not because he didn't know the more prescriptively correct form but because the use of what he considered to be a hypercorrect form would detract from the identity he was establishing for himself at the time. For Tim there was greater value——a kind of "covert prestige" (Wolfram and Schilling-Estes 159)—in using the language that was respected by his peers rather than that expected by his parents. Many of the linguistic forms at issue in the "For Thought 2.6" exercise may be stigmatized by "standard" speakers but covertly valued by the speakers who choose to use them. Linguistic choices can become a form of resistance, influenced by peer group acceptance.

Pragmatics

Pragmatics is the study of conversational discourse patterns, including rules for turn-taking, for getting and holding the floor, for interrupting, etc. Pragmatics is also the study of locution—the surface forms of the sentence—and illocution—the underlying intention of the utterance. Because pragmatics concerns itself with the relationship between form and intention, it has perhaps the greatest potential of any subsystem for communicating power and authority. Indirect intentions, for example, are repeatedly demonstrated in gendered communicative styles, in asymmetrical conversational patterns among people with greater and lesser degrees of authority, and in classroom discourse among teachers and students whose differences in cultural backgrounds may play a significant role in conversational misunderstandings and miscommunications. Pragmatic rules are sometimes violated deliberately or ignored when it serves certain interests. Notice in Cartoon 2.1

CARTOON 2.1   Arlo and Janis © Newspaper Enterprise Associates, Inc.

how Gene deliberately misinterprets the indirect command given by his father, and how Arlo, in turn, deliberately misinterprets Janis's command.

FOR THOUGHT 2.7: Analyze the following conversation between a husband and wife in terms of each of the comments and their intentions. What is the subtext of their statements or questions?

H: Do we have any white thread?
W: Yeah, I suppose—in the sewing basket.
H: This button just came off.
W: You should be able to find a needle there too.
H: Well, will you at least help me thread it?

Different cultural expectations about interrupting other speakers and maintaining the floor in conversations, about appropriate responses to teacher questions, or about turn-taking and eye contact in conversations become potential areas for misunderstanding. Linguist Susan Philips, for example, reports that some Native American children fail to participate verbally in teacher-directed classroom discussions, not because they fail to understand the teacher's questions but because a verbal response is not required in their own sociocultural pragmatic system (380). Similarly, sociolinguist and educator Shirley Brice Heath, whose work in three communities in the Piedmont Carolinas have led to our understanding of linguistic and cultural differences between speech communities, suggests that African American children and white working-class children participate in their speech communities in somewhat different ways than middle-class children. The result is that the expectations of African American and white working class children about spoken and written language often differ from school expectations, and these differing expectations constrain their literacy learning (234–5).

Pragmatics also involves an understanding of the functions of language that include:

- Communicative, for conveying information: "There are five steps in the process."
- Regulatory, for controlling other people's behavior: "You can't leave the table until you've finished your dinner."
- Expressive, for asserting one's personal feelings: "I hate that attitude."
- Referential, for referring to people, things, ideas: "That man ate my bologna sandwich."
- Creative, for artistic expression: poetry, fiction, drama.

- Heuristic, as a tool for learning: writing out an explanation of a process in order to better comprehend it.

The reductive assumption that we use language primarily to communicate ideas and information overlooks the many personal, social, and educational functions of language. It also overlooks the fact that language is a powerful tool for concealing truth as well as for revealing it, for manipulating the behavior of others as well as for expressing one's own thoughts. Using *Peacemaker* as the label for an intercontinental ballistics missile (ICBM) sugarcoats its real function of killing people. Euphemisms abound across the political landscape, serving to soften reality or create a new reality.

Semantics

The subsystem of semantics, or the ways in which language structures meaning, is often discussed in relationship to words, as in the categories of content words and function words, connotation and denotation, and semantic properties of words, to name a few. We can also study semantics, like pragmatics, for its ability to influence, manipulate, and control. Hate language such as racist labels and sexist labels illustrates the power of language to demean or dominate. The chapters in this text on the power of words and hate language speak to these issues in considerable depth. But semantics and its manipulative power can be much more subtle than the hate language we're discussing. *Extraordinary rendition* ("Torture by Proxy" A22), the term used during the Iraqi war to name the process of sending suspected terrorists to countries that routinely allow for torture during interrogation, glosses over the real intention of the act—outsourcing torture because U.S. laws prohibit the use of torture during interrogation. The word *torture* never needs to be used, yet one more example of the Orwellian concern about thought control.

Manipulation of syntax as well as word choice, as will be discussed in chapter 5 on language and gender, also subtly conveys intended meanings. Passive constructions, for example, are sometimes used to avoid assigning a specific agent or source of action in the sentence. I could have written the previous sentence to read, "Speakers sometimes use passive constructions to avoid assigning …," but I chose to write it in the passive. The rhetorical choices and decisions speakers and writers make depend on what they wish that structure to accomplish. A press release reads, "Seventeen civilians were killed, including some women and children." Why doesn't it read, "U.S. troops killed 17 civilians, including some women and children"? Putting the sentence in the passive removes the agency. Active sentences point fingers; passive ones don't. And there's potentially a heap of semantic difference between the two when it comes to the world of politics. Certain kinds of rhetorical strategies help shape our thinking, help structure our interpretation of meaning.

Because these subsystems of language function only in social contexts, the sociolinguistic dimensions of language study become central to our analysis of language. For years linguists approached the study of language objectively and with critical distance, describing but not commenting on the social ramifications of its use. Currently, however, applied linguistics has taken a critical turn, focusing not just on the "object" but on the social and cultural framework of language, that has deepened our understanding of it. Decontextualized language study is less messy, but it's also irrelevant. People always speak within specific cultural contexts that relate their choices and intentions to issues of politics and power.

LANGUAGE ACQUISITION

How do children acquire language so effortlessly? How do they do it on their own, without a grammar book or an English teacher to teach them? Linguists agree that language is biologically determined and that its acquisition is an instinctive, natural process that is inevitable and certain, given normal intelligence and exposure to language. Steven Pinker says,

> Language is not a cultural artifact that we learn the way we learn to tell time or how the federal government works. Instead, it is a distinct piece of the biological makeup of our brains. Language is a complex, specialized skill, which develops in the child spontaneously, without conscious effort or formal instruction, is deployed without awareness of its underlying logic, is qualitatively the same in every individual, and is distinct from more general abilities to process information or behave intelligently. (18)

Although the degree to which language is biologically determined is vigorously argued, every linguist acknowledges the basic biological predisposition for language. Some linguists liken the process to the germination of a seed. When the conditions are right—the presence of sufficient sunlight, moisture, fertile soil—the genetic code in the seed is activated, and it grows and develops. When the conditions are right for language acquisition—when the child is in the presence of human language and is expected to be a participant—the language acquisition device is activated, and language develops.

In his early work, linguist Noam Chomsky described the process of language acquisition as the activation of the language acquisition device (LAD), genetically imprinted with language universals that need to be activated by human language input (30–33). Although this "little-black-box" theory has undergone transformations in its conception, the essential theory remains active. The genetic imprinting of language allows the learner to form a series of hypotheses about language structures that could never be learned from merely imitating or mimicking words or sentences. The behaviorist notion of imitation as the major means of language acquisition bears careful scrutiny because its status has been elevated to a piece of "common knowledge" in the lore of child language development. A theory of language acquisition based primarily on imitation posits the child as a relatively passive learner who acquires the language through a system of stimulus-response-reinforcement in which the child imitates a phrase, receives feedback, either negative or positive, and moves on to mimicking other structures. Acquiring a language, however, requires a much more complex cognitive act. While direct imitation may play a minor role, children's ability to hypothesize a set of rules and make generalizations about them is far more important. Their spontaneous utterances in any particular stage of development are often more syntactically complex than their imitated ones. Furthermore, many of their utterances are novel; i.e., they are based not on what they've just heard but rather on hypotheses about language that do not necessarily reflect adult syntax. Linguist Ray Jackendoff refers to these novel structures, however, as predictable ones because of the underlying rules of the language the child is in the process of forming (101). The child who refers to an eraser as an *unraser* is responding creatively with a set of hypotheses about the function of an eraser and his understanding of the prefix *un*—meaning to undo something, as in *undo, untie,* or *uncap.* When the 4-year-old refers to men as *mans,* the *rule* with which she is operating is based on her hypothesis that we use an *s* suffix to indicate plurality. Her hypothesis is accurate to a degree, but it is simply not extensive enough to embrace exceptions. Children develop various theories of language rules, test their hypotheses, modify them based on feedback over time, and gradually refine their hypotheses as they move closer to the rules of adult syntax. Of course this process of overgeneralization, particularly in the use of prefixes, occurs among adults as well. We know several people who speak of *unthawing* meat, when *thawing* would be adequate to express the idea of *unfreezing*; we also hear *irregardless* used frequently, even though the *ir-* morpheme is redundant with *less.*

Although nativists' positions on language acquisition argue that the process is genetically predisposed, they agree that language develops only in the presence of language itself. Kids don't learn language propped before a television set. Some linguists, such as the social constructionists, argue that the context for language learning is critical, that caregivers provide the environmental structures that nurture language development, and that they participate directly in the process by providing the scaffolding that facilitates language learning. These researchers cite "motherese" in caregiver speech evidenced by its simplified vocabulary and phonology, higher degrees of pitch, simple syntax, sentences that are structured for easier modeling, and the use of questioning to engage the child in verbal interactions. Using the Russian linguist Lev Vygotsky's concept of scaffolding, social constructionists describe caregiver speech as a careful, systematic orchestration of the speech event by the adult, always with a focus on the meaning but structured in such a way that the child can track the meaning mapped onto syntactic structures. When feedback is provided to the child in the course of natural language interactions, the feedback focuses on the meaning of the child's response, but the feedback is couched in linguistic structures that the child comprehends and can use as a model for linguistic development.

When the 2-year-old holds up a sock and asks, "Mommy sock?" the adult may provide a slightly more complex syntactic structure in response to the child's question such as, "Yes, that is Mommy's sock. Where's Annie's sock?" These conversational exchanges provide linguistic data for the child's developing repertoire of linguistic structures. The child's incomplete structure has not been "corrected," but the adult instead models a more linguistically advanced form. The adult's response is to the child's meaning, without direct correction, but couched in more sophisticated linguistic forms that provide a scaffolding for further development.

Steven Pinker counters the assumption of the universality of "motherese," however, by citing cultures in which parental scaffolding does not occur in the language development of children (39–40). He claims that linguistic scaffolding is a middle-class American experience that contrasts with the language learning experiences in many other speech communities, including African American communities. Whether the kind of scaffolding some parents provide actually promotes language learning or is merely coincidental to it remains uncertain. Whatever further research reveals about the need for formal scaffolding and "motherese," we do need language scaffolding that occurs naturally and more generally within social interactions, and scaffolding has proven to be a critical factor in the linguistic and cognitive development in classroom learning.

Linguist Breyne Moskowitz reports on Ron Scollon's research regarding a 19-month-old child, Brenda, who was able to use a vertical construction (a series of one-word or two-word sentences) to express a complex idea that she could not express syntactically in one sentence. Notice how the adult provides a scaffold for her to complete her idea (42–43):

Brenda:	Tape corder. Use it. Use it.
Scollon:	Use it for what?
Brenda:	Talk. Corder talk. Brenda talk.

Scollon framed a question to provide Brenda with the possibility of adding a structure to complete the complex thought.

When 3-year-old niece Kim was in her telegraphic speech stage, she used content words but few function words, and her utterances were limited to two or three words per utterance; yet, she was able to produce a complex concept involved several vertical structures. Here is a conversation between Kim and her uncle Stu:

> Kim: Stu go bye-bye. Kim go bye-bye.
> Stu: You want to go bye-bye?
> Kim: Go bye-bye Stu!

With help from her uncle, Kim was able to convey her desire to accompany him.

Scaffolding is less about direct instruction than about providing learners with a structure within which their language development processes can work more effectively. In the classroom, when teachers engage young students in conversation about recent events, the story-telling or recollection encourages them not only to talk about the event itself but to use past tense forms that help them internalize past tense structures. When teachers encourage young readers to predict what a story is going to be about from the pictures or the title, readers are increasing their facility with language at the same time they are increasing their reading comprehension. When teachers provide reasons and time for second language learners to talk about issues that they are familiar with, learners' experiences become the framework for their practice with English. As students talk, sometimes hesitantly, teachers should not overtly correct their English but model correct forms of English through the questions they ask and the comments they make. That is scaffolding and modeling at its best.

FOR THOUGHT 2.8: Think of other examples of scaffolding for the following scenarios: (a) a child who is language-delayed and who needs encouragement to speak; (b) a middle-school student who needs more practice with writing fluently; (c) a second language student who has considerable knowledge of world history but has a difficult time answering the teacher's questions in English.

The behaviorist view of language learning that assumes that direct instruction is required for learning contrasts sharply with the notion of scaffolding. In both first and second language acquisition, instruction based on a behaviorist perspective involves pattern practice, repetitious skill and drill, rote learning, and lots of correction, but little room for experimenting with acquisition through normal conversational discourse. The behaviorist approach gives the learner little credit or little opportunity for real-life language development and views learning as functioning in a teacher-controlled environment. However, all of the evidence in first and second language acquisition studies suggests a process driven by authentic reasons and purposes for developing language: for communicating with friends, for being able to play on a sports team, for collaborating with someone on a project, for ordering food in a restaurant. For young children it's being able to get the toy they want to play with, getting the juice they want to drink, making their needs and desires known. Language forms follow language need. The best language teaching provides scaffolds of support that enable language abilities to develop and flourish in normal conversational contexts.

THE RELATIONSHIP BETWEEN LANGUAGE AND THOUGHT

The language structures and patterns we each learn as children and continue to develop throughout adulthood clearly reflect the linguistic patterns of our speech communities, constructed by the social contexts in which we live, work, and play. It is a commonplace to discuss the obvious influences of thought and culture on language—how what we say and how we say it are largely a result of our cultural influences and experiences—but it is equally important to consider the reciprocity involved in language and culture—how language influences thought, reinforces it, and shapes it. The most well-known of the theories proposing that language influences thought is the Sapir—Whorf hypothesis, postulated by Edward Sapir and Benjamin Whorf (O'Grady et al. 184–186). These two linguists' work with Native American languages in the early 20th century led to their claim that the linguistic differences in vocabulary categories and grammatical constructions between those languages and English resulted in two different world views, or ways of perceiving the world, that made it almost impossible for speakers of the two different languages to construct reality in the same way. Since their work several decades ago, the theory has been tested in a number of ways, though none of these studies has supported a strong version of the theory. Having 20 vocabulary words in a language for various kinds of snow doesn't necessarily mean that only those speakers can perceive those variations in snow types. Neither does it mean that speakers of languages without grammatical gender cannot perceive the differences between males and females (O'Grady et al. 185). The strong version of the Sapir-Whorf hypothesis that grammatical structures control the speakers' world view seems not to be very credible.

While linguists no longer accept a strong version of the Sapir-Whorf hypothesis, many do accept the legitimacy of a weaker version. Linguistic patterns have the potential to constrain one's thinking and shape it in culturally significant ways. As will be discussed in later chapters, researchers suggest that language patterns can reinforce or create patterns of thought that, while not immutable, do, nevertheless, help to shape people's attitudes and belief systems. For example, diminutives used to describe women (referring to a woman as *the little lady* or to female college students as *the girls in my class*) can reinforce and reproduce stereotypes of powerlessness and diminished authority. Even more debilitating is verbal abuse, which diminishes self-concept and sense of worth because victims often begin to believe the abuser. Ethnic slurs reinforce negative cultural stereotypes, and terms of derision take on a life of their own.

CHANGING PARADIGMS OF LANGUAGE STUDY

Because of the complexity of language, and because so much of language is acquired before children go to school, we must consider how much impact teachers and school programs have on children's oral language development. If most of language is acquired before formal instruction, what content should students learn about language? Two traditions have prevailed for language study over the past several decades. The first describes structures of English, identifying parts of speech and types of sentences, even diagraming sentence structures to understand structures. The research over the past 70 years is overwhelming in its rejection of this kind of grammatical analysis for improving student writing or speaking. We know that having students do lots of writing with frequent feedback is more useful to their improvement as writers than is grammar study. If correction of sentence structure or writing conventions is necessary, it is more helpful and efficiently accomplished within the context of the student's own writing (Weaver 130). The second tradition is the direct teaching of English usage patterns and prescriptive forms of language in an attempt to instill the rules of "correct" grammar in students' speech and writing. The research, here again, shows no correlation between direct instruction and writing improvement. The political complexities of enforcing some kind of standard through direct instruction are discussed in greater depth in chapter 6.

APPLICATIONS FOR THE CLASSROOM

Paradigms of language study have shifted in the wider academic community regarding the nature and structure of language, but those same shifts have not fully occurred in elementary and secondary schools. So what are teachers to do to improve the study of language in the classroom—and particularly their students' writing—given the research that overwhelmingly denies the efficacy of direct instruction in "correct" usage and in systematic sentence analysis?

Increasing student awareness of effective sentence structures, helping students achieve clarity and precision in writing, helping them develop rhetorical structures that make effective arguments, and allowing time for frequent oral discussions in class all provide means of working with language and language structures within the context of students' own writing and speaking that will facilitate growth in language ability. Students develop increasing stylistic awareness by considering the ways in which language changes as audiences change, by comparing writing styles for various purposes, by workshopping their writing with their peers to determine the most effective ways of getting their points across, and by speaking in a variety of classroom contexts. Teachers who encourage class publications can contrast effective language structures for public audiences outside the school with language structures that may be more appropriate for peers. Language study in which the students' own writing becomes the material for discussions of language effectiveness is critical.

This text also argues for a shift in language study among elementary and secondary teachers away from a prescriptive approach to "correct" English to a more sociocultural approach grounded in language reality: what the various functions of language are, how it is used across speech communities, how it is a political phenomenon, and how it can and should empower students as language users. Such a shift will alter classroom instruction about language in positive ways by doing the following:

1. Broadening what we mean by "grammatical" in order to recognize the fundamentally complex language structures that all speakers use, regardless of dialect.
2. Reflecting the growing awareness of variation across speech communities.
3. Underscoring the negative impact of language bias and its tendency to silence people.
4. Suggesting ways of eliminating our own and our students' use of biased and intolerant language.
5. Providing ways of creating agency through language.
6. Setting aside linguistic prejudice about "correct" (grammatical) and "incorrect" (ungrammatical) uses of language and replacing it with the knowledge that the concept of *grammatical* is contextualized, personal, and relative.

Eliminating the dichotomous "correct" and "incorrect," "good" grammar and "bad" grammar from our teaching vocabularies will model for our students our beliefs that usage is more complex than these polarized categories imply, that the range of styles and forms of language that all speakers possess signals high levels of language flexibility and facility—and should be applauded rather than denigrated. We discuss these issues in greater depth in chapter 6.

Part of the paradigm shift involves developing awareness of negative judgments based on linguistic choices. Students may find it difficult to fathom that bloodshed has occurred over language issues in India and the Middle East, but they can surely come to understand the hurt that biased language causes in situations more immediate to them. Criticism of one's linguistic patterns can result in anger, in rebellion, or in silence. Children who struggle over writing "correct" English, who believe that correctness is more important than ideas, tend to write less or not at all. Speakers whose dialect is ridiculed frequently avoid ridicule by remaining silent. Language users who feel controlled and manipulated by others' use of language often remain submissive without developing agency.

Schools, never politically neutral institutions, attempt to mold and shape the linguistic attitudes, behaviors, and knowledge systems of students. As teachers of language we must understand the cultural and institutional pressure to mold students in certain linguistic images and to exert control through language policies and practices. It is our responsibility to mediate that kind of control by empowering students as users of language. At the same time, as teachers we have an obligation to alert students to the cultural fall out of stigmatized structures and to help them develop linguistic control as they move from context to context. Particularly in an era of global Englishes and rapid language change, we also have an obligation to engender in our students awareness of and appreciation for a range of language diversity and speakers. And finally, we need to help our students see language differences as enriching contributions to the chorus of human diversity. These are issues we'll be returning to in subsequent chapters as we come to understand the power and authority embedded in language use and language policies.

PERSONAL EXPLORATIONS

1. Listen to the speech patterns of a 2-year-old, a 4-year-old, and a 6-year-old and try to describe the patterns in terms of word order and complexity of structures:

   a. What rules do they use when forming past tense?
   b. How do they form questions differently as they develop linguistic maturity?
   c. Do you note any evidence of peer influence on their language development?

2. In those same speech patterns, identify any structures that appear to be "novel" utterances—phrases, words, or pronunciations that you would not expect to appear in the adult language in the child's speech community. Try to explain how the child has come up with this "rule" of language.

a. On what is the "rule" based?
b. What does it suggest about children's creative use of language?
c. What does it suggest about a child's rule-governed use of language?

3. Given our definition of "grammatical" as consistency between oral language use and our internalized rule system, which of the following sentences would you consider to be grammatical for native speakers of English in general? Which ones are unlikely to be grammatical for any speaker of English? Which ones would be grammatical for speakers of some dialects of English? On what basis are you categorizing them?

a. Ate the soup I.
b. Leaves she tomorrow at 3:00?
c. Will she leave tomorrow at 3:00?
d. I don't like him doing that.
e. Who did you go with?
f. I might could drive you to school tomorrow.
g. He ain't had nothing to eat yet.
h. She's a wicked good tennis player.

Survey people in an older generation to see if there are differences between your responses and theirs. If so, what does this suggest about language change?

4. Find examples of language in the media that serve to conceal rather than reveal; that gloss over harsh realities; that attempt to create a change in people's perceptions or attitudes through language. You might start with the editorial page of your local newspaper or with phrases used in political speeches. Look for word choice used to influence readers; passive constructions that remove agency, etc.

TEACHING EXPLORATIONS

1. Ask your students to bring in newspaper headlines from three different newspapers, some of which can be obtained online. You might suggest *The Miami Herald*, the *New York Times*, the *Washington Post*, the *San Francisco Chronicle*, *The Houston Gazette*, and there are many others. List the headlines of each of the papers as they report on identical news stories. How do the headlines suggest different perspectives on the stories? Are there headlines that seem to suggest a biased perspective? Do any of the headlines use "loaded," value-laden language as a way of presenting a particular perspective on the issue?

2. Ask your students to look at different grammar books that you bring in to the classroom and do an analysis of the perspectives on linguistic variation in each of the texts. How does each one present information on language variation and dialect variation?

Do any of them move beyond a simple description of "correct" and "incorrect"? What are the specific labels used? Do any of them acknowledge the legitimacy of dialect variation? If so, in what way?

3. Modify any of the "For Thought" or "Explorations" activities used in this chapter in such a way that your own students might use them for mini-research projects on language use.

WORKS CITED

Chomsky, Noam. Aspects of the Theory of Syntax. Cambridge, MA: MIT Press, 1965.

Heath, Shirley Brice. *Ways With Words: Language, Life, and Work in Communities and Classrooms.* Cambridge: Cambridge UP, 1983.

Jackendoff, Ray. *Foundations of Language: Brain, Meaning, Grammar, Evolution.* Oxford: Oxford UP, 2002.

Johnson, Jimmy. "Arlo and Janis." Cartoon. Newspaper Enterprises Associates, Inc. 7 Jan. 1999.

Moskowitz, Breyne Arlene. "The Acquisition of Language." *Linguistics for Teachers.* Eds. Linda Miller Cleary and Michael D. Linn. New York: McGraw, 1993. 35Œ66.

O'Grady, William, Michael Dobrovolsky, and Mark Aronoff. *Contemporary Linguistics: An Introduction.* New York: St. Martin's, 1989.

Philips, Susan. "Participant Structures and Communicative Competence: Warm Springs Children in Community and Classroom." *Functions of Language in the Classroom.* Eds. C.B. Cazden et al. New York: Teachers College Press, 1972. 370–393.

Pinker, Steven. *The Language Instinct: How the Mind Creates Language.* New York: HarperPerennial, 1995.

"Torture by Proxy." *The New York Times.* Editorial. 8 Mar. 2005: A22.

Tserdanelis, Georgios, and Wai Yi Peggy Wong, Eds. *Language Files: Materials for an Introduction to Language & Linguistics.* 9th ed. Columbus, OH: Ohio State UP, 2004.

Vygotsky, Lev. *Mind in Society: The Development of Higher Psychological Processes,* Ed. Michael Cole, Vera John-Steiner, Sylvia Scribner, and Ellen Souberman. Cambridge: Harvard U.P., 1978.

Weaver, Constance. *Teaching Grammar in Context.* Portsmouth, NH: Boynton/Cook, 1996.

Wolfram, Walt, and Natalie Schilling-Estes. *American English: Dialects and Variation.* Malden, MA: Blackwell, 1999.

Chapter 3

The Power of Words

In the beginning there was the Word. John 1:1

But I've gotta use words when I talk to you. T.S. Eliot

CARTOON 3.1   Nancy © United Features Syndicate, Inc. Guy and Brad Gilchrist, 16 May 1995

Nancy knows better.

That words have the power to hurt is common knowledge today, despite old adages that tell us "words will never hurt us." In fact, the widespread currency of the old saying attests to the power of words. Words can inflict pain or deepen insecurity just as they can uplift, inspire, and encourage. While words and their meanings serve to link people, forging strong emotional, social, national, and political connections, they also serve to separate people. Words categorize; they erect and strengthen barriers between people; they establish boundaries and bar some people from full participation

in the society in which they live even while they serve to enhance the privileges others enjoy. In this chapter, we will explore the constructive and the
destructive power of words, with emphasis on *words as weapons*. *Words and
their sources of power* will follow as we define *words as signs* and consider *words
as meaning: semantics*. Next, we detail *five axioms which scaffold our discussion of
meaning*. Then we focus on critical *uses and abuses of verbal power*, including
names and labels, *euphemisms and doublespeak*, *jargon*, *charged language*, *taboo
words*, and, finally, *the language of advertisers and politicians*. We will close the
chapter with *applications for teachers* that assist them as they engage their students in thinking about words and alert them to words' power.

WORDS AS PLOWSHARES AND WORDS AS WEAPONS

How many of us recall flushing with pleasure when special words of love or
praise were spoken to us and feeling the joy, satisfaction, and security such
words gave us? For many of us who were fortunate enough to hear such
words often, empowerment followed, and we were enabled to confidently
construct our lives. That verbal pat on the back or word of endearment
strengthened us. For us, words were a means of self-cultivation and personal growth. However, how many of us can recall wincing from the wounds
caused by words used as weapons, these wounds sapping our confidence?
And how many of us have fenced with words, the look of pain on our victim's
face telling us that we had scored a hit? Words have the power to heal or to
hurt. Often words confuse; sometimes they are deliberately chosen to do
just that, to obscure meaning and to mislead their hearers. Some words are
invested with magical or religious powers; others act as codes known only to
insiders; still others are taboo in some social contexts or altogether.

Occasionally, words and their pronunciations mark their speakers for
death. Poet Rita Dove's "Parsley" recalls the 1937 execution of 20,000 Hai-
tians who were seen as a political threat by Rafael Trujillo, dictator of the
Dominican Republic, because they could not pronounce the *r* in *perejil*, the
Spanish word for parsley. Their pronunciation of the test word condemned
them to death as it separated them from those Trujillo saw as loyalists, all of
whose phonological systems contained the *r* sound (Dove 501). The Bible's
Old Testament tells a similar story in Judges: 42,000 Ephraimites were slain
by the Gileadites because they pronounced the word *Shibboleth* without the *h*
sound as *sibboleth* (cited in Andrews: 200-01). While not marked for death,
English teacher Cissy Lacks was surprised in March 1995 to be fired from
the school district near St. Louis, Missouri, where she had taught successfully for 21 years. She'd allowed her students to use taboo language, language commonly referred to as "profanity," in their creative writing.
Following the firing, in a nearby district, a drama teacher was told to excise

all the "damns" and "hells" from her high school production of *Oklahoma* (Diegmueller 24–29). In September 1998, the Eighth Circuit Court of Appeals refused to rehear Lacks' case. As a result, Lacks lost her bid to be reinstated in her teaching position, as well as the $750,000 awarded her by Federal District Court Judge Catherine Perry, who had previously ruled that Lacks' school board had violated her First Amendment rights (Harris 1, 8).

Like Lacks, Timothy Boomer of Arenac County, Michigan, found himself embroiled in a dispute over words and their power. After falling out of a canoe on the Rifle River, Boomer shouted a volley of words at the friends who had overtipped him. Under Michigan's 101-year-old obscene-speech law, which prohibits cursing or using vulgar or insulting language in the presence of women and children, Boomer was prosecuted for his language use. The case attracted considerable attention: CBS television interviewed Boomer ("Profanity has man battling in court over freedom of speech", Argus Press, p. 3) and NBC examined his case on the news program *Dateline* in early 1999. In 1999, Boomer received a 3-month-long community service sentence. However, in 2002, Michigan's century-old law was found to be unconstitutional, and Boomer's conviction was overturned (Tucker B-1). In another case in Kentucky, Circuit Court Judge Dennis Foust let stand a lower court's ruling that a woman was guilty of harassment for wearing a T-shirt with profane language quoted from a Marilyn Manson song. Because the words were constantly in view, the court ruled that that equated to the woman's repeating them again and again ("Profane shirt" B-8). Public profanity has continued to be an issue. The year 2004 saw major television networks called to task for not screening out the obscenities of talk show guests, award recipients, and sports figures. Besides profanity, other words have been banned. In the 2004 Presidential campaign, persons wearing T-shirts that protested then-current administrative views or supported John Kerry were banned from political rallies for presidential candidate Bush, or they were asked to turn their shirts inside out if they wished to remain.

Words have political implications; hence the current international dispute over whether the present carnage in the Sudan is "genocide." By international agreement, labeling the killing "genocide" obligates world nations, through the United Nations, to take direct and overt action in the Sudan to stop the violence. Words not only have direct power; they have an indirect power as well. If politicians adopt the slogan "Moral Values" or "Pro-Life" to encompass their set of values or their views on the abortion issue, and if those slogans gain wide public use even by those in opposition to the political/ethical stances the sloganeers espouse, the implied, or subliminal message to many listeners is that people who have values differing from the sloganeers' are either immoral or "pro-death." Both are, of course, untrue. Nonetheless, those who differ are placed in an almost defensive posture in the war of words that surround political campaigns and legislative hearings. Politicians know that whoever controls the rhetoric of a situation—whoever's slogans, metaphors, and word choices catch on with the public and become a part of common parlance—has an edge on his/her opponent. Language choices from 2004–2005 efforts to change Social Security—*private accounts* and *personal accounts*—serve to illustrate. Knowing that *personal accounts* sounds less threatening to the electorate, Republicans have begun to use that term when they speak of a key component of proposed Social Security reform, and they have urged news reporters to do so. However the term *private accounts* and the phrase *the privatization of Social Security* are those used by Democrats when the issue is under discussion, because they say that historically those have been the terms employed by persons on both sides of the argument, and because they know that to voters, these terms imply fewer government guarantees and greater personal risk (Toner A1, A16). The unwise choice of words can cause a politician or a political group to lose favor in the public eye. If a police chief publically refers to politically popular members of the council governing her/his city as "morons" or "idiots," the chief may lose a great deal of public support. Amnesty International was recently under fire in some quarters for referring to the U.S. Federal Prison at Guantanamo, Cuba, as a "gulag," a word that brings to mind the harsh labor camps of the Soviet era with their attendant disregard for human rights. Amnesty's use of the word was said to "politicize" their work, despite their claims to being a non-political organization.

Contemporary writers frequently feature the power of words. A *Newsweek* article, "The Wounds of Words," reminds readers that "verbal abuse is as scary as physical abuse" and describes the verbally abusive person as one who uses words "to punish, belittle and control" (Seligmann 90). Tim O'Brien in a *New Yorker* story, "Faith," asks, "Are we bruised each day of our lives by syllabic collisions, our spirits slashed by combinations of vowel and consonant? Do verbs destroy us? Do proper nouns kill and maim? … Can a word stop your heart as surely as arsenic?" (67). Fanny Flagg's Evelyn, in *Fried Green Tomatoes,* having been verbally assaulted by an adolescent boy who snarled "You stupid cow," "You fat, stupid cunt," and "Fuck you, bitch" (232-33), felt "raped by words" and "stripped of everything" (236). As a writer who regularly moves back and forth between Spanish and English in her works, Sandra Cisneros is especially sensitive to the power of words. As one of our students pointed out in her written response to *Woman Hollering Creek*:

> Cisneros depicts her belief in the power of language. Ines in "The Eyes of Zapata" says that "Words hold their own magic. How a word can charm, and how a word can kill" (105). Ines and her mother have both been called *perra*

(bitch) and *bruja* (witch); Ines states that people hurled these words. Cisneros' use of the word *hurled* lets readers know just how much the words hurt. When remembering having been called *mujeriego*, Ines says, "the word is flint-edged and heavy, makes a drum of the body, something to maim and bruise, and sometimes kill" (105). Clearly Cisneros recognizes the harm words can cause. My mother used to say something that really sums up what Cisneros knows about the power of language. She said, "Sticks and stones may break our bones but words will break our hearts." (Hendricks)

On the first day of her Language and Education class, Mary asks her students to introduce themselves and to recall a language usage they had found particularly distasteful as well as one they had especially liked. Many report words of praise they've been given or the special nicknames their friends and families have called them in affection. But most also recognize the downside of words used as weapons as they recall taunts directed their way such as "hillbilly," "blackie," "dumb-Indian," "crazy," "freckle-face," "queer," "slant-eyes," "chick," "bitch," "slut," "flat-face," "Bucky-Beaver," and "chub-tub." One told a story about her son at age five who, when told that "words cannot hurt you," said, "Mama, why do you say that? They do *too* hurt; they hurt my feelings." Another, an African American woman whose elementary schoolmates had called her "Blackie," summed up that downside: "The pain of words is more than a sharp, quick sting. It's a persistent pain that lasts and lasts."

FOR THOUGHT 3.1: Recall a time when you were the victim of words which stung you. How did you react? Why did you react as you did? Was it the words, the tone or volume in which they were spoken, the speaker of the words, the situation in which they were spoken, or a combination of these that caused pain? Recall a time when you felt uplifted or empowered by words. Who was the speaker? What was the situation? What did the speaker say?

WORDS AND THEIR SOURCES OF POWER

Given their power to hurt as well as heal and to suppress as well as express, words merit much closer examination. What are words? From whence do they derive their meanings and their power?

Words as Signs

As was stated in the previous chapter, language, as the term is consistently used in this book, consists of sounds (phonemes), their arrangements into meaningful units (morphemes), the meanings of these units (semantics), their arrangements in utterances (syntax), and the systematic ways these arrangements function in actual discourse (grammar and pragmatics). Words are meaningful arrangements and units of sound that signify meanings; they are signs of meaning. In her essays on linguistics as collected, edited, and mediated by Toril Moi, Julia Kristeva argues that functioning as signs of meaning and the basic elements of discourse, words are the site of contested definitions and political struggles as diverse political interests seek to determine their meanings (Kristeva 72; see also Moi 158). The past contested definitions of "impeachable offense" and "sexual relations" can serve to illustrate as can "schools of choice," "back to basics," "literacy education," "values," "inclusion," "no child left behind," "proficiency testing," and "core curriculum." Words, as signs, do not, says Kristeva, "refer to a single reality, but evoke a collection of associated images and ideas." Signs are distanced from their referents; they are arbitrary. Their meanings are the result of interactions with other signs (Kristeva 72). Thus, no necessary correlation exists between words and the things and emotions they signify; nor are their meanings absolute and unchanging. Nothing about a dog demands that the English word for that animal be "dog," just as nothing about the affection we feel toward another person demands that it be labeled "love." The relationship between a word's referent and the sounds of the word itself, except in the cases of onomatopoeic words like *buzz*, *hiss*, and *bow-wow*, is also arbitrary. The arrangement of sounds in *chair* does not make a chair a chair, whether we are referring to a comfortable seat or to the head of a committee.

Words as Meaning: Semantics

The power of words derives from their meanings and the societal values attached to their use. It derives as well from their users, from the positions their users occupy in societal hierarchies, and from their definers, that is, those who possess the power to name, the power to determine definitions, the power to enforce definitions and names, the power to prescribe "correct" usages and pronunciations. Lewis Carroll's Humpty Dumpty in *Through the Looking Glass* knows well that those who define, who label, and who name wield power. He tells Alice that he is "master" because "When I use a word, it means just what I choose it to mean—neither more or less .... I can manage the whole lot of them" (1969, 143). In occupying the position of Master (or teacher, president, police officer, pastor, parent, etc.) Humpty Dumpty plays out what Norman Fairclough, in *Language and Power*, refers to as "the exercise of power through the manufacture of consent or at least acquiescence to it" (1989, 4). Humpty Dumpty relies upon his exercise of linguistic power, the power to define, as a natural and commonsense outcome of culturally determined relationships of power and authority. Fairclough argues that the "nature of language conventions depends on the power relationships which underlie those conventions ... they are a means of legitimizing existing social relations and differences of power simply through the recurrence of ordinary and familiar ways of behaving which take these relations and power differences for granted" (1989, 2). Jennifer Coates, well aware of the connections between power and language, writes of the "vicious circle" which results when "social distinctions are reflected in linguistic distinctions which, in turn *reinforce* social distinctions" and argues that language has the power in a secondary way to perpetuate the social distinctions it names and defines (160).

In Figure 3.1, Harmon graphically depicts her interpretation of a weak version of the Sapir—Whorf theory discussed in chapter 2 as it applies to the cyclic and reciprocal nature of cultural dominance and language use (20). A complex reciprocity exists between dominant culture institutions which have the power to legitimize language norms, that is, to name and to define. Language reveals the political and social attitudes of the dominant culture. Language use, which voices the attitudes and states the names and labels assigned by those with the power to define others, helps perpetuate that power as those names, labels, and definitions are widely subscribed to by the general public, often even by those adversely affected by such language use.

Conversational styles and discourse modes as well as various media serve as transmitters of dominant cultural definitions and attitudes, and, in doing so, reinforce them. The diagram is not closed; closure would deny the possibility of change and would render futile any efforts to resist or to alter the linguistic choices and cultural power of the dominant culture; it would, in

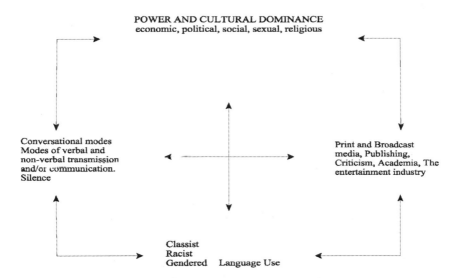

FIG. 3.1. Cultural dominance and language.

effect, freeze both in place. Language is, in Raymond Williams' terms, both "constitutive and constituting" (*Marxism and Literature* 43). Accordingly, the openness of the diagram posits an active "social language ... living evidence of a social process, into which individuals are born and within which they are shaped, but to which they also actively contribute in a continuing process" (37). If that were not the case, the efforts of those who propose gender-fair language guides and who advocate elimination of ethnic slurs would be in vain. And we all would be condemned as ignorant for saying "ice cream" instead of the formerly preferred "iced cream." Despite its openness, the diagram does indicate pervasive pathways and directions. Julia Penelope points out that Sapir "suggested that language is a prepared road or groove into which our thoughts slip. Language guides and limits the options available for describing our perceptions" (*Speaking Freely* 203).

As stated in chapter 1, Fairclough labels the power to successfully promote one's ideas and practices as *universal and common sense "ideological power"* (2001, 27). He adds that such power at times is maintained by coercion as in the legal actions against Lacks and Boomer above. At other times, ideological power is maintained by consent as occurs when Alice acquiesces to Humpty Dumpty's dictum, or when students and many of their teachers acquiesce to the idea that a so-called nonstandard pronunciation of a word (*cain't* for *can't*) or the inclusion of so-called nonstandard vocabulary (in Scotland *lugs* for *ears*) marks speakers as ignorant. The authority invested in words and the link between language and power is clear in the New Testament of the Bible where the Word is equated with the ultimate divinity: "In the beginning there was the Word ... and the Word was God" (John 1:1). The dictionary granted similar authority to official versions of words' meanings. The relationships between power, language, and social hierarchy are apparent in Holt, Rinehart and Winston's 1993 American literature anthology (*Elements of Literature*), which dubs Noah Webster's first dictionary "Noah's Ark"—like an ark it saved the newly language-conscious, rising middle class from drowning in "lower class dialects," mispronunciations, misused words, and misspellings. Holt adds that many early American households placed their copies of Webster's *Dictionary* "next to the Bible," a telling comment granting almost divine authority to Webster's book (172–176).

FIVE AXIOMS THAT SCAFFOLD OUR DISCUSSION OF MEANING

Before proceeding further in our discussion of the power of words and their meanings, we must detail five basic axioms which scaffold it.

1. Meaning is arbitrary. There is no necessary relationship between an arrangement of sounds and its referent or the meaning people ascribe

to that set of sounds. As was noted previously the relationship between a dog and d-o-g is arbitrary just as in French and in Spanish the connection between *chien* and *perro* and the animal that both words name (dog) is arbitrary.

2. Meaning is not fixed. Meaning changes as time passes, as people age and change; as cultures, speakers, and listeners vary; as structures of power evolve; and as events and people transform cultures and ideologies. Forms of the slang word *piss* (from the French *pisse*) may refer to urine, anger, or drunkenness depending on who uses the word and where and how the word is used. In fact, context will not only determine the word's meaning but also whether the word is used at all and what listeners' reactions are to its use and user. *Bad* means "good" to some of its users; *gay* may refer to homosexuality or to lightheartedness. At one time, *culture* meant "to cultivate" or "to grow" and was associated with tilling the soil; today, the word is associated with a much wider range of meanings as is readily apparent as one reads the word's entry in any reputable dictionary or peruses theorists' explications of the term (see Raymond Williams' *Keywords* and his *The Sociology of Culture*).

Calvin of *Calvin and Hobbes*, always the cagey language user, has caught on to both numbers 1 and 2 at a young age.

CARTOON 3.2 CALVIN AND HOBBES © (1992) Watterson. Dist. By UNIVERSAL PRESS SYNDICATE. Reprinted with Permission. All rights reserved. (Watterson 1 Sept. 1992)

Totally spam!

3. Meaning comes from people who draw upon institutional practices, conventions, and power relations as they communicate with each other; thus, meaning is constructed socially. Language users functioning

within their varied social and cultural contexts validate, extend, or change words' meanings as they read, speak, and write them in communication with other language users. In "'Nigger': The Meaning of a Word," novelist Gloria Naylor states, "the spoken word, like the written word, amounts to a nonsensical arrangement of sounds or letters without a consensus that assigns 'meaning.' Building from the meanings of what we hear, we order reality. Words themselves are innocuous; it is the consensus that gives them true power" (527). In her narrative, she recounts the first time she ever really heard the word *nigger* used as hate-language. A boy seated behind her in math class "spit out" the word at her from "a small pair of lips that had already learned it could be a way to humiliate" her. She recalls, "I didn't know what a nigger was, but I knew whatever it meant, it was something he shouldn't have called me" (527). Naylor adds that people can claim a word employed by others to degrade them. Through using the word themselves as they renegotiate its meaning and ascribe their own meanings to it, they can "meet the word head-on" and render it impotent (529).

4. Meaning is multiple and metaphoric and, thus, ambiguous. Words are polysemous; their meanings are multiple and varied. *Love* can serve to exemplify. We may say we love ice cream; we love our mothers; we love our friends; we love some of our classes; we love our spouses; we love sunny days, and we love our cats; we make love. Surely *love* does not have the same meaning in each of these phrases. In fact, the word *love* is used in so many ways that it has become overdetermined; that is, the word has no readily definable meaning. *Cat* may name any domestic cat, our own cat, a tiger, a leopard, a woman, or a man. Forms of *dog* may signify a domestic animal, a worthless person, our feet, an unattractive person, tiredness, or determined pursuit. When Marilyn and Mary take their dogs out for a walk, observers' (especially children's) tones of voice let us know that the word *dog* when applied to Marilyn's Dachshund and Mary's Great Dane has very different meanings to its speakers. In addition to their polysemous nature, words have both denotative and connotative meanings. The denotative meaning of a word, its referential and intentional meaning, consists of its direct and specific meaning as found in a dictionary or as objectively defined. A word's connotative meaning, that is its extensional meaning, includes the emotional, social, and cultural implications associated with word. Although *dog, cur, doggie, pooch, canine*, and *mutt* all refer to a dog and are synonymous with *dog*, most of us would agree that each word has a different set of emotional or cultural meanings associated with it. Public safety officers, pigs, cops, bobbies, police, and law enforcement officers all are names given to the police; yet, each synonym carries with it a different set of connotations.

FOR THOUGHT 3.2: List all the synonyms you can think of in common usage for each of the following words. Compare your list with several classmates. How are the connotations different for each of the words you have listed? Who might be most likely to use each of your synonyms? In which situations? What social or cultural opinions or judgments are contained in each word you list? *Woman, man, sexual encounter, home, car* (avoid brand names), *a good time, a bad time, a disabled person.*

To add to the ambiguity of words and their meanings, some words, like *lead, wind, lie, cleave, die, may,* and *mine,* are really two words; some words such as *spare* (extra and thin) and *blue* (Blue skies versus I feel blue) have embedded meanings that nearly oppose each other; some words are used both literally and metaphorically (*green, red,* and *dog*), and many words (homophones) which sound the same are spelled differently and differ in meaning, as do *knew, gnu,* and *new.* Cartoonists seem particularly aware of the slippery nature of a word's meaning. "Wiley's Dictionary," a feature of the *B.C.* cartoon, delights in the ambiguity of language as it offers daffy definitions: A "bassoon" is defined as a tropical storm which rains fish; to "determinate" means "to rehire the guy you just fired" (Hart 9 Mar. 1996). *Frank and Ernest*'s cartoon humor depends often on words' similar sounds and multiple meanings. The dialogue below is between the two featured characters, Frank, a newspaper editor, and Ernie, a writer.

Frank:	Ernie, what's your headline for this item about the jail with creative writing courses for inmates?
Ernie:	A story of prose and cons!
Frank:	And the monarch who cancelled his trip because of a blizzard?
Ernie:	Reign and snow don't mix!
Frank:	And this guy who bought his pet turtle a toupee?
Ernie:	The tortoise and the hair, Part 2!
Frank:	Confound it, Ernie, I could strangle you, you depress me so much!
Ernie:	Writer causes editor piques and valleys!
Frank:	I pay you big bucks and you're a complete fool.
Ernie:	Stop the Presses! I have the page one headline. "Editor says writer has lots of dollars but no sense!!" (Thaves 15 May 1994)

The children in *The Family Circus* are hardly the first to confuse the meanings of words that sound the same but are spelled differently in such phrases as "Ted's secretary is a dear (deer)," "Bear to the left," and "The three of you are to stick together." The pictures in the children's minds are quite different from those their parents meant to impart as they spoke (Keane 14 Apr. 1996). These few examples illustrate that the comics provide a ready resource for teaching about—and having fun with—the multiple and slippery nature of words.

Celeste Branachek, a former student and a teacher's aide, devised a series of language explorations into the metaphoric and ambiguous nature of language using several of the *Amelia Bedelia* books by Peggy Parrish. Amelia, a literal minded woman, seldom takes into account the metaphoric and ambiguous nature of language. When asked to pitch the tent, Amelia throws it away; when asked to put the baby's bib on, she wears it herself. Celeste's students had fun predicting what Amelia might do if asked to bake a marble, sponge, or coffee cake; to buy a blazer to wear; to shake a leg; or to punch the clock. And they came up with many of their own examples of metaphoric or ambiguous words and phrases. Students of all ages enjoy word play, and that enjoyment can serve as an introduction to the more serious examples of word manipulation discussed later in this chapter: doublespeak, euphemisms, jargon, labels, charged language, and the language of advertisers and politicians.

FOR THOUGHT 3.3: In Wiley's Dictionary style, construct meanings for the following words. Then check their meanings as recorded in a recent dictionary. Retire, polyunsaturated, disinclined, pork barrel, piebald, retreat, dogmatic, disgruntled, lambaste, degrade, unimpressed, designed, distressed, serial killer, pigment, inverse, catatonic.

---

5. Meaning is contextual. The above examples and illustrations demonstrate vividly that the meaning of a word depends on its context. A word's context includes that word's speaker, listener, and their attitudes toward each other; their specific situation and relationship to each other; all the denotative and connotative meanings both speaker and listener associate with the utterance; the other words which surround or frame the word when used; the speaker's implied intent as the word is uttered, and the cultural milieu in which the utterance occurs. Words' power lies in their contextual, metaphoric, culture-laden, and emotion-laden meanings. From these, rather than from anything inherent to their sound arrangements, words derive their power. What follows will consider some specific kinds of words that work to empower or diminish their speakers and listeners.

USES AND ABUSES OF THE POWER OF WORDS

Names and Labels

Most of us like our names or gradually come to like them; if we don't we change them to something we like better, as did our friends Cookie and

Corky, who became Aurelia and Charles as they dropped childhood nicknames. Liz became Elizabeth; Lorie, Lorraine. How many of us in dreamy moments have traced elaborate monograms of our names or of our initials? Alleen Pace Nilsen (1999) reports that Ernest Hemingway was "so fascinated" with his name as a high school newspaper reporter that he used six bylines with six different name variations (10). Edite Cunha recalls that as a child in Portugal, she loved her name, María Edite dos Anjos Cunha, and adds that she would recite it at the least provocation, enjoying its melodious beauty. Her name told her exactly who she was (117). We may feel hurt if others find our names peculiar. In *My Name is Johari*, Johari loves her name and loves to repeat it, reveling in its rhythm, until one of the children at school tells her it's a "funny" name and everyone laughs. Suddenly her name embarrasses her, until she learns from her parents that her name is African and that it means "jewel." When she reports this new knowledge at school, her classmates learn her name's origin and declare it a great name. Now, Johari feels both happy and accepted (A. O'Brien). To avoid a student's being in Johari's predicament in classes where students may not be aware of a wide diversity of names, Johari's story might be shared with students along with Esperanza's commentary on her name in Sandra Cisneros' *The House on Mango Street* (i). Both invite discussion which explores the meanings and histories of students' names and queries why people like or dislike their own names or make fun of others' names. Johari's story is hardly confined to the world of small children. Mary recalls an episode from her high school days when an 11th grade woman, new to Mary's town, was teased unmercifully as "Brewster, the Gobles' rooster," by several of her male classmates. Brewster was her surname; Gobles, Michigan, was her hometown and the name of a then-popular beer (a brew). Rooster rhymed and, to her detractors, referenced her aristocratic, slender, and tall stature as well as her Roman nose.

We often feel annoyance when others misspell or mispronounce our names or take uninvited liberties with them. Michael, Itabari, Jennifer, and Charles may cringe each time someone calls them Mike, Jenni, Ita, or Chuck. Many people experience displacement when their names are insensitively altered without their consent. At the age of seven, Edite Cunha moved from Portugal to Peabody, Massachusetts, where she found her name changed to Mary Edith by her teachers. At home she "cried and cried"; at school, she struggled to pronounce her new name. And, in the process, she recalls, "I never knew quite who I was …" (117). Unfortunately, her experience is not unique; in the recent past it was common for teachers to change a student's "foreign sounding" name to an anglicized version of that name.

Our names tell us who we are and where we have come from. As we sign them, our names become signs of our honor, our promises and pledges, our seals of approval. Both Lorraine Hansberry and Arthur Miller clearly reveal the importance attached to a person's name and to a person's signature. In *A Raisin in the Sun*, Walter Younger appears to be about to accept Mr. Linders' racist demands and move from an all-white neighborhood until he recalls that his father was a man proud enough to almost kill another who had called him a bad name. To accept Linders' money and sign his name to the racist contract would be to dishonor his father, himself, his family, and his son. Miller's John Proctor (*The Crucible*), while willing to make a false confession to witchcraft to save his own life, will not sign a paper implicating others: "I like not to spoil their names" (135). Nor will he actually sign the false confession. In agony, knowing he will die as a result, he refuses to sign and cries: "Because it is my name! Because I cannot have another in my life! Because I lie and sign myself to lies .... How may I live without my name? I have given you my soul; leave my name!" (138).

FOR THOUGHT 3.4: Do you like your name? From where does your name come? Are you named after someone? What does your name mean? What are the origins of your surname? What does your name tell others about your ethnic and/or cultural heritage? Check a list of names to find out what your first, middle, and last names mean (for example, Paul Samuel Bruss means "little, name of God, woods"). Have you changed your name in any way? Why? What, if any, choices have you made to make your name your own?

Because the relationship between language and culture is reciprocal, "naming is power, which is why the issue of naming is one of the most important in bias-free language" says Rosalie Maggio (252). In his well-known book, *The Language of Oppression*, Haig Bosmajian states: "the power which comes from names and naming is related directly to the power to define others—individuals, races, sexes, ethnic groups. Our identities ... are greatly affected by the names we are called and the words with which we are labeled" (5). Adds Toril Moi, "to impose names ... is not only an act of power, an enactment of Nietzsche's 'will-to-knowledge'; it also reveals a desire to regulate and organize reality according to well defined categories" (160). Thus while some names and labels can empower us, others and the categories they place us in can serve to objectify, degrade, disenfranchise, and, hence, control us. Gordon Allport, in "The Language of Prejudice," points out the power of what he calls labels of primary potency, labels whose use in reference to a person blinds others to all the other qualities the labeled person may possess. *Cripple, retard, feminazi, squaw, Mexican, neo-con, fundamentalist, communist,* and *Jew* exemplify labels which have been used to define people in such a one-dimensional fashion, both negatively charged and culture-laden. Such naming or labeling "magnifies one attribute out of all proportion to its true significance and masks other important attributes of the individual" (288), thus serving to erase individuality through categorization and generalization, and to dehumanize or reductively cast the individual. Terms once thought favorable can become negatively charged labels of primary potency as the words *liberal, feminist,* and *conservative* illustrate. Cartoons can serve to bring the topic of pejorative labels to light for classroom discussion. April Patterson, from the comic strip *For Better or For Worse,* as she hears her friend, Becky, labeling schoolmates "doofus, hunk, nerd, hottie, foob, hotbed, porko, zombie, airhead," declares rating and labeling people to be a game "where everyone loses" (Johnston 22-24 Mar. 2005). Becky's use of labels of primary potency blinds her to all other qualities of the students she rates except for their personal appearance.

Regularly we ask our students to list all the names (including nicknames) and labels, other than their own name, which have been applied to them. They share their lists in small groups and decide which of the names and labels are of primary potency. Then, they create categories for and categorize the words on their combined lists. They find that nearly all the negative labels they've been called fall into the categories of ethnicity, body types or parts, intellect, physical strengths or handicaps, sexual practices or orientation, social class, and gender. Students respond intensely to this exercise and recognize that the categorized words have been used to dehumanize them, to "disparage and reject" (Allport 290) them, while giving their users power over them. Names and labels hurt, as Curtis, at some risk to himself, points out to his father below.

CARTOON 3.3   Curtis by Billingsley May 26, 1995 © King Features Syndicate.

FOR THOUGHT 3.5: Make a list of all the positive and negative names and labels you can remember being called. Include nicknames. Next to each item on the list tell who used it. How did you react to the name or label at the time? How do you react as you recall the name or label now? Which of the names/labels are of primary potency? Now list all the names and labels (both positive and negative) you can recall giving others. Were any labels of primary potency? Do the names and labels you have been called or you have called others fit under the categories identified above? Can you add any categories (for example, religion)?

Our reactions to the names we have been called and the reactions of those we have labeled testify to their power. As we explore issues of language and gender, social class, and ethnicity in chapters 4 and 5, dialects in chapter 6, and the labels given to immigrants in chapter 7, we will examine further the issue of power-laden labels and names.

Euphemisms and Doublespeak

A quick look in nearly any dictionary shows that *euphemism* comes to English via Greek and means speech which sounds pleasant, or "the substitution of an agreeable or inoffensive expression for one that may offend or suggest something unpleasant" ("Euphemism" 400). We may say *get sick* or *vomit* rather than *throw up,* or *pass away* rather than *die.* Engaging in sexual intercourse becomes sleeping together; using the toilet is visiting the women's (or men's) room. Euphemisms like these usually do not interfere with communication; most speakers, Amelia Bedelia aside, know the code and are not misled by their use. In fact, euphemisms such as those conventionally used for death when comforting the bereaved, sometimes assist communication and make the truth easier to bear. It is when euphemisms obscure meaning, when they camouflage it or suppress it, that they become doublespeak. Says William Lutz, the foremost chronicler of doublespeak in the United States, they become "language that pretends to communicate but really doesn't ... that avoids or shifts responsibility, language that is at variance with its real or purported meaning ... language that conceals or prevents thought" (*Doublespeak* 1). Users of doublespeak knowingly choose words and phrases that "mislead, distort, deceive, inflate, circumvent, obfuscate," adds Lutz (*Doublespeak* 2). In a *U.S. News and World Report* column, John Leo declares this sort of euphemizing to be "tongue violence" and "gassy" (15 Apr. 1996, 23). He points out current doublespeak euphemisms such as "swimmer nullification program," the name of a program to teach U.S. "frogmen how to kill other countries' frogmen," and "gender illusionists" for drag queens. He says sex [*sic.*] alteration surgery has become "gender reassignment"; and pedophilia is named "intergenerational intimacy."

Other examples abound as even a quick reading of Lutz' *Doublespeak* reveals. Elsewhere, Julia Penelope cites an insurance company's letter which substitutes "mortality experience" for death rate (*Make Money* 173). What some dismiss as "political correctness," and others regard as sincere attempts to use the language sensitively and empathetically, has spawned its own collection of euphemisms and doublespeak. Mort Walker's *Beetle Bailey* comic strip spoofs this sort of doublespeak when the general tells his wife that he is not an alcoholic, he is "merely sobriety deprived" (Aug. 26,

1995)". Marilyn and Mary are not short; we are vertically challenged. We are not far-sighted; we are visually challenged. As we advance into our golden years, should we find ourselves pleasingly plump, we will not resort to girdles; we will buy shape wear.

Doublespeak abounds during war and presents a real danger to honest communication when it is used to obfuscate war's realities for political intent. During the 1991 Gulf War, euphemistically referred to as *Desert Storm*, the *Detroit Free Press* (Bruni F1+) detailed that war's doublespeak lexicon. Among the terms listed were:

Bouncing Betty	a land mine
Amazing Grace	a 63 ton tank
candymen	bomb assemblers
collateral damage	civilian casualties
cleansed	cleared of Iraqi troops
KIA	killed in action

Clearly doublespeak permeates military language. Nearly everyone has heard of Hitler's *final solution,* and the use of *ethnic cleansing* in Bosnia, Kosovo, and the Sudan. Genocide stood masked behind these seemingly bland words. The current war in Iraq has fostered doublespeak such as *regime change* and *pre-emptive strike,* and *shock and awe.* On a November 14, 2004, news broadcast, a military spokesperson proclaimed "We have *liberated* (my italics) Falluja." As the news camera roamed the scene, what viewers saw was a city in rubble with corpses lying in the streets. Not a new term, *friendly fire* has resurfaced; the euphemism refers to military personnel's being killed accidentally by fighters from their own side. *Extraordinary rendition*, as discussed in chapter 2, points out the dangers of doublespeak. Few would guess that a practice many would consider immoral has been hidden under an obfuscating word.

However, as Lutz convincingly argues in *Doublespeak*, the military stands in the company of a host of other doublespeakers. Business CEOs downsize rather than fire; educators assess and evaluate meaning making strategies rather than grade papers; medical personnel speak of "negative patient care outcomes" rather than deaths (192), advertisers regularly sprinkle ads with weasel words, as will be discussed below, and politicians enhance revenue, offer the public the chance to make a contribution, or legislate a down payment on the deficit rather than raise taxes. Says Lutz, such doublespeak contrives deliberately to mislead: "It is language designed to distort reality and corrupt thought" (19). Thus, doublespeak works not only as "tongue-violence," but also as mind-violence.

FOR THOUGHT 3.6: The human activities of death, sex, pregnancy, and excretion have a great many euphemisms associated with them. List those you have used, read, or heard. Why do you suppose so many euphemisms exist for those activities? How will you speak of these in your classroom? How will you suggest that your students speak of them?

Jargon and Inflated Diction

Jargon or specialized language often serves useful purposes as a shorthand means of communication among its users. Members of professions, trades, sciences, and sects routinely use vocabularies among themselves that may seem incomprehensible to outsiders. Computer users and Internet travelers may seem to be speaking or writing in code to those unfamiliar with their jargon. In the world of academia, terms such as *hermeneutics* and *heuristics* speed communication between literature professors even as they may intimidate students new to the discipline. *High-stakes assessment*, *mainstreamed classrooms*, and *integrated, whole language approaches* are commonplace phrases among educators but may confuse or intimidate parents. Alexandra Day's delightful book *Frank and Ernest* (not to be confused with the comic strip of the same name) introduces its readers to restaurant jargon via the two protagonists, an elephant and a bear, who take a job at a diner. An order for apple pie and milk becomes "Eve with a lid and moo juice"; ham with a potato and cabbage becomes "Noah's boy with Murphy carrying a wreath." Understanding the jargonized phrases and their roots poses puzzles for readers of all ages. Technical jargon creates few problems for its in-the-know users; however, when jargon is used to confuse, to exclude, to inflate, or to deceive, it becomes what Philip Howard terms "gobbledygook" or the "pompous use of long words, circumlocution, and other linguistic flatulence in order to impress the hoi polloi" (232). For users of this "pretentious gibberish" (232), housekeepers are domestic engineers, teachers are instructional advisers, and the awareness of one's surroundings inflates to "the multiformity of environmental apprehension" (233). Cartoonists love to mock pretentious jargon and those impressed by its use. In *Hi and Lois*, the son, stymied while composing a speech, resorts to jargon and cliches when he pens: "In the course of human events, there comes a time when a man must cast off the shackles of conformity …. He must batten down the hatches of his ego and dive into the waters of uncertainty … swim to the shores of stoicism across the seas of ostracism and plant his feet in the sands of sincerity." "Marvelous! Outstanding!" proclaim Hi and Lois as the son walks away bemused. "I only wish I knew what it meant," he says (Walker et al. 25 Feb. 1996).
Young Calvin is onto the jargon loved by academia:

CARTOON 3.4 CALVIN AND HOBBES © (1993) Watterson. Dist. By UNIVERSAL PRESS SYNDICATE. Reprinted with Permission. All rights reserved.

FOR THOUGHT 3.7: What effect does the diction in the following statements have on its readers? Translate the proverbs from inflated diction and gobbledygook to their more familiar form:

A rotating lithoidal fragment never accrues lichen.

It is not proper for mendicants to be indicators of preference.

Pulchritude does not extend below the surface of the derma.

Precipitancy creates prodigality.

An aged canine cannot be educated to innovative attainment.

Do not scrutinize the masticating apparatus of a donated equine.

Slanted and Charged Words

She has short, blond hair worn brushed back; with a smile on her face, she greets people as they enter the hall. She is dressed in jeans, a plaid shirt, and sandals.

Stylishly cut natural blond hair feathers back from her face. Her friendly smile warmly sets folks at their ease as they enter the hall as does her relaxed dress: a plaid shirt, blue jeans, and sandals.

Her brassily bleached hair, stiffly sprayed back from her face, her absurdly wide grin, and her peasant garb—faded plaid shirt, frayed jeans, and beat up sandals—tell the hall's visitors that she is out of her league here as she extends them forced greetings.

The above descriptions, all about the same person and situation, demonstrate that our emphases, the number of words we allot, our diction, and the analogies and images we choose can slant the message we present and persuade listeners to share our positive or negative biases. Politicians, advertisers, media personnel, and speakers of all ages know well how to manipulate messages and charge them positively or negatively. Someone who likes Jane and supports her for public office may describe her as a complex thinker and a thoughtful person who examines all sides of an issue before rendering a decision. Someone who supports her opposition may say that she is wishy-washy and flip-flops so many times before coming to a decision that by the time it is made it has little meaning or its time has passed. Similarly, someone who admires Jacob may praise him as an insightful leader who is skillfully adept at convincing others to accept his views, while one who distrusts him may reject him as a conniving manipulator.

FOR THOUGHT 3.8: A list of details which describe a dog named Fezzik follows. Using these details construct a positive passage about him. Then, using the same details, construct a negative passage about the dog. Be sure to use only the details provided and rely on word choice, comparisons, imagery, emphasis, and/or space in words to provide the positive and negative charges. *Named for the giant in* The Princess Bride, *black with a patch on his chest, five years old, a 140 lb. male Great Dane, likes to go for outside walks, energetic, wags tail, deep bark, a house dog, sleeps in the family room, likes to climb on the couch, short haired, likes to greet people, large unclipped ears, about 45 inches tall when standing on all four feet, nearly six feet tall when standing on his back legs.* What is the value of this activity or one like it that you construct for your students as they explore slanted and charged language?

Fighting Words and Taboo Words

A few words, such as some racial and political epithets, carry such a powerful charge or excite such charged responses that they have been declared "fighting words" and do not enjoy First Amendment free speech protections (Chapalinsky v. New Hampshire 315 US 568 in Bosmajian 4). As we will discuss in more detail in chapter 4, others carry a charge potent enough to be declared taboo, sometimes officially, but more often unofficially by cultural norms. Other words are taboo in some contexts, but not in others. "Dirty words" or "bad words" fall into this category. Washing out an offender's mouth with soap for using taboo language, as Larry Andrews points out, is to confuse "a word with the word's unspeakable referent" (242). Clearly it is not the sounds of the words themselves that make them offensive enough to be taboo; rather, it is the meanings people ascribe to them. Thus verbal taboos are culturally determined by social and religious norms and are subject to change. The potency of their charge, their shock value, varies from person to person and place to place. In the United States, taboo or "bad" words include those commonly referred to as swearing, cursing, or blasphemy; those which refer to sexuality and excretion; and those which slur another's ethnicity and/or race. While some people dismiss the idea of language taboos as unnecessary or unsophisticated, others, aware that language both reflects and shapes cultures, voice concern over what they see as the increasing violence and incivility of public discourse. Both Dr. Joyce Brothers and Barbara Lawrence object to "dirty" sexual words, not because they are sexual, but because "they imply a narrow, mechanical, master and victim concept of sexuality" (Brothers 376). Many of the most extreme words describing sexual intercourse have origins in brutality and violence (*screw*, for example). Naming people with sexual words associated with women's and men's genitalia (*cock, cunt*), robs persons of individuality, thus depersonalizing them (Lawrence 335–336).

Concern about profane language can be easily found in the popular news media. Carey Goldberg dubs New York "the capital of profanities" and links what she sees as the increased use of public profanity to the increased pressures, anonymity, and stresses of urban life, to the decreased shock value of taboo words' use and to feminism's giving women more access to here- to-fore "unlady-like" language (B1+). Over the past several years, television networks have faced controversy and fines as athletes and performers have used taboo language on the air. In her *Newsweek* discussion of Vice President Cheney's loudly advising Senator Patrick Leahy to "F— himself" in response to a question from Leahy, Anna Quindlen states that Cheney, rather than apologize, justified his use of the word by arguing that his integrity had been challenged. She suggests that such public usage from a high-ranking political figure, while it may promote "macho posturing" and a" hard-guy" image, "brings out the worst in everyone" (76). John Leo's "Foul Words, Foul Culture" asks, "Does language really matter?" Leo concludes it does, decries the increased public use of "in-your-face messages that shed social norms," and suggests that within the United States, "our levels of political, social, and commercial discourse are so low that it is surely time to restore civility from the bottom up. The alternative would seem to be an increasingly stupid and brutal culture" (26 Apr. 1996 73).

Newspaper cartoonists offer similar commentary. In *Jump Start*, Marcy and Joe express alarm at adults' and children's use of "garbonics," or "filthy language" (Armstrong, 1-3 Oct. 1997). And *Dilbert* featured a series of strips about "women who like to swear at work" (Adams 2-5 Nov. 1998). Teachers, too, voice concern at the taboo language spoken openly, in school, by their students. *Washington Post*'s Valerie Strauss states that teachers throughout the United States worry about the pervasiveness of foul language in schools and argue that it coarsens the school climate and speaks to a "decline in language skills." While many school systems ban profanity, "not much happens to most offenders," thus, teachers do not report students who use it. Parents, many of whom use foul language themselves, "exacerbate the problem by defending their children caught swearing in school" (A12). One of our students reported that a seventh grader told his teacher she was a fucking cunt. Another recalled a recent incident in which a three year old shouted at a classmate at her preschool, "You mother-fucker."

While we certainly do not want to be in the business of making social or moral pronouncements and while we, like Larry Andrews, recognize that prescriptive measures toward taboo language seldom are desirable or of lasting value, we do think the topic of offensive language is worth examination in classrooms, particularly if Andrews' comments on Robert Pooley's definition of "good English" are kept in mind. "Good English is appropriate to speakers/writers' purposes ... appropriate to the context ... comfortable to both speaker and listener" (135–136). Open class discussion about taboo language—why users choose it and how it affects listeners—as well as the collaborative production of a class set of rules and consequences regulating in-class language will help protect both students and teachers from offensive language, as will enlisting the aid of colleagues, administrators, and students to formulate a school policy on taboo language on school grounds. Literature can open discussion of taboo language. After reading Terry McMillan's *Waiting to Exhale* and after being somewhat shocked by what seemed to them to be an abundance of taboo language spoken by the four main female characters, three of our students began to examine when the characters used such language. They found the four women spoke most often in unrestrained fashion in intimate and friendly conversation with each other. The women chose when and where to use "offensive" and taboo language, and in doing so, did not violate Pooley's definition of "good English." Our students next made a list of all the words they considered taboo or offensive in the book and asked other students in the class to assess each word as to its offensiveness to each of them under the headings "always," "usually," "sometimes," "seldom," and "never." One student tallied the results and found that the most offensive words were those that refer to women by naming genitalia. The least offensive were the "swear" or "curse" words *hell* and *damn*. In the ensuing discussion, students talked about *why* they found specific words offensive or demeaning. As students described just how reductive or insulting they found some words and how relatively inoffensive they found others, we saw students listening and responding to each other with genuine interest and intensity. Our student-devised activity was far more effective in prompting a thoughtful examination of taboo language than anything we might have constructed.

Taboo language poses particular problems for literature teachers. One of the most common reasons for censorship challenges to school materials is "objectionable language" or "offensive language." Problems arise not only from authors' inclusion of "objectionable" words but also from the fact that the degree of offensiveness of specific words varies from person to person and context to context. Often those who challenge books wish to keep them out of classrooms, even if the entire class is not reading the book, and out of school libraries. Among books that have come under fire for "offensive language" are *Fallen Angels* by Walter Dean Meyers, *I Know Why the Caged Bird Sings* by Maya Angelou, *Of Mice and Men* by John Steinbeck, *Blubber* by Judy Blume, *Catcher in the Rye* by J.D. Salinger, and *Huckleberry Finn* by Samuel Clemens (American Library Association Web site). Both the National Council of Teachers of English (NCTE) and the American Library Association (ALA) websites contain valuable background information on intellectual freedom, First Amendment rights, and book challenges. Both offer procedures to follow and other practical assistance to teachers whose materials have been challenged. NCTE provides access to rationales for the defense of frequently challenged books. ALA details its annual autumn Banned Books Week, lists books and authors who have been frequently challenged, and offers activities, posters, and tool kits for teaching about censorship or for teaching banned books. Because censorship is a topic critical to teachers and their careers and because we do not want teachers to fall victim to self censorship and, thus, fail to use important literary works out of fear of reprisal, each year we assign our students to produce a rationale for the classroom use of a banned book of their choosing. In their defense of the book, geared to an audience of interested parents and school board members, they include the following:

1. An acknowledgment of the charges against the book.
2. The overriding aesthetic, literary, and/or social values of the book.
3. Their plans for the book's use.
4. Precedent for using the book with its intended audience.
5. Other critics' appraisal of the book.

Students are reminded of the importance of tone and diction as they address their parent and school board audience. They compose their defenses, peer-critique them, and distribute polished copies to their classmates. Those who choose to—usually about half the class—deliver their defenses orally as well. In short, they use the power of words to defend the power of words.

THE LANGUAGE OF ADVERTISERS AND POLITICIANS

Advertisers and politicians are well aware of the power of positively and negatively charged words, and they capitalize on the deceptive nature of what William Lutz calls "weasel words" (*With These Words* 394). Among those he lists are *help, virtually, new, improved, acts fast, works like, up to*. With these weasel words, advertisers make claims much like the following: A skin care product helps make (helps make, not makes) the face virtually free (not free, virtually free) of wrinkles; it works fast (how fast is fast?); it's new (is new better? What makes it new—a new bottle, a new formula?). Using a diet plan, we will lose up to 20 pounds (1 pound is "up to 20") in just 20 days. A fast acting weed killer will make a lawn look like a golf course (which part—the rough?). Or advertisers may use meaningless metaphors—a product cleans like a white tornado—or empty slogans—"Mid-Michigan, the right place for you" (why? who is you?). They carefully choose words and images that appeal to persons' desires for acceptance, for friends, for good health, for success, for greater comfort, for escape, for a better life, for affluence and social prominence, for the nurture of themselves, their children and their pets. Both advertisers and politicians play on our fears, inflate language and make exaggerated claims, and create faulty analogies. Advertisers use the desire for sexual encounter and the desire to be thought sexually attractive to sell their products. Additionally, according to Charles O'Neil, advertising "encourages unhealthy habits, sells daydreams and fantasy, warps its audience's views of reality, downgrades the intelligence of the public, debases English, and perpetuates racial and sexual stereotypes" (415). To exemplify, while reading the ads in popular magazines in May of 2005, we found: "Introduce your legs to four play," as an ad for a four-blade razor made for women. Zantrex is the "hottest selling" "amazing new super" diet pill "with a kick" that results in "incredible energy." Diamond nail polish delivers "diamond strength, diamond shine, diamond wear." Inefficient computers are as bad as "bad to the bone" convicts, a Toshiba ad would have its readers believe. And Jessica Simpson promotes Dessert Treats, a cosmetic line, which will make its users "deliciously flavored, irresistibly sweet and scented" with its "body-beautifying yummies."

Like advertisers of a commercial product, politicians are in the sales business—selling themselves and their programs. They pitch us for our support and our votes. Like commercial advertisers, they slant language and they choose words, symbols, and pictures carefully for their campaign ads. "Careful re-evaluation" based on changing circumstances may become "flip-flopping," a much more negative sounding term. A bill which grants industries the right to raise their industrial waste emissions may be called "The Clean Air Act," its proponents contending that the increased levels of emission do not cause additional harm to air quality; thus, the air is still "clean." Another bill which diverts water from the Great Lakes or from farmlands to industry may be called a "Water Resources Act," the term masking the law's intent. Under a slogan like "The Great Society" or "No Child Left Behind" sweeping changes in policy may occur, the positive sounding slogans working to obfuscate the implications of the bills which underlie the slogan. Other means through which politicians often persuade the unwary include those that follow.

The Appeal to Patriotism and/or Religion. Invoking patriotic principles or religious belief during a campaign or as a piece of proposed legislation is promoted as proof of merit, including references to a candidate's religiosity or military service and/or photos of the candidate at church or at prayer. Ending speeches with "God bless America," depicting the candidate saluting the flag, referring to french fries as Freedom fries and discouraging the use of French wines following France's non-support of the invasion of Iraq are all examples.

Name-Calling. Labeling people, countries, or ideas with words that have a negative connotation: tax and spend liberal, reactionary conservative, neo-con, the Evil Empire, an Axis of Evil, terrorist.

Glittering Generalities. Using positive terms that have no specific meaning: The American way, Christian values, Fighting For Families, American values, our democratic heritage.

Oversimplifications, Overgeneralizations, and Partial Truths. Making statements which do not address the complexities of an issue or making broad statements that do not apply to everyone included in the statement, and, thus, are only partially true. "Just say no" as a solution to sexually transmitted diseases or to illegal drug use is seen by many as an oversimplification which fails to take the complexities of both problems into consideration. "Drug Free School Zone" signs likely express only partial truths. "Senator X always stands with you" and "We all support free speech" are overly general, partial truths.

Red Herring. Bringing in an unrelated issue to divert attention from the real issues: the discussion of both 2004 Presidential candidates' Vietnam War experience struck some voters as use of the red herring.

Plain Folks Appeal. A speaker presenting himself/herself as a person just like the listeners—"I know what it's like to have to work hard; my parents were working people." The speaker often dresses and acts the role as well—eating potato salad and fried chicken at supporters' picnics, wearing denim or flannel and cowboy boots or work shoes.

Argumentum Ad Populum (stroking). Praising the audience. When Professor Harold Higgins of *The Music Man* fame begins his pitch to sell instruments to the parents of River City by saying, "I know all you folks are the right kind of parents," he is stroking them.

Argumentum Ad Hominem. Attacking the person rather than addressing the argument: "Only leftists and lesbians support non-discrimination laws." "Feminazis are behind the proposed Equal Rights Amendment." A local politician recently attacked the age and, by implication, inexperience of his candidate by picturing children's alphabet blocks on the front of his brochure and stating inside "When X was playing with blocks, I was working for you."

Transfer. Transferring negative or positive associations that accompany another person, object, or idea to oneself: "Like Ronald Reagan (or John Kennedy), I support …"; "In keeping with our nation's proud democratic heritage, I propose …"; using the symbols of religion or patriotism like the flag, a cross, a church as a backdrop for a speech; calling those who disagree with one's policies terrorists.

Bandwagon. Pressuring listeners to go along with the crowd or to join the side that appears to be winning. As an idea, action, or opinion becomes popular, many people, eager to be on the winning side, jump on the bandwagon—move to support it. Children use the bandwagon appeal when they say, "But Mom, everybody has a Vespa; why can't I have one?" Politicians desire positive poll ratings, because they know that persons are likely to jump on the bandwagon of a candidate with high poll figures.

Non Sequitur. Coming to a conclusion based on faulty cause and effect or an illogical or incorrect premise; the conclusion "does not logically follow" from the premise. For example, "The best beauty salon around is Allure because they give the best pedicures" or "My rottweiler is sleepy; she must be sick."

Post Hoc Ergo Propter Hoc. Assuming that just because one event precedes another, a causal relationship exists between the two. An example: "Governor X was elected in 2000. By 2001, the crime rate began to rise. Therefore, Governor X and her policies are responsible for the rising crime rate."

Testimonial. Gaining and using the endorsement of someone in power or of great popularity. When advertisers procure the endorsement of a famous sports figure for their shoes, they are using the testimonial. The sports figure "testifies" to the quality of the shoes. Political candidates often enlist the testimonials of other popular politicians or of well-known entertainment figures.

Either/Or–Faulty Dilemma. Posing two opposites as the only alternatives: "You are either with us or against us." The either/or thinker and propagandist does not allow for subtleties, ambiguities, complications, or shadings. The situation is wholly black or white.

False Analogy. Making an illogical or misleading comparison. Two examples are "If we can put a man on the moon, surely we can solve earthly environmental problems" and "If we can teach dogs through patience and reward, so can we teach children."

Slippery Slope. Asserting that one instance will inevitably lead to many or that one action will lead to others with widespread negative results. "If we allow researchers to clone animals, soon we will have a controlled society where people are cloned to inhabit specific castes or a society in which prospective parents will special order their children" and "Convicting X for repeatedly and violently threatening his neighbors restricts free speech. Soon no one will be able to object to anything he or she finds disagreeable" are examples.

Begging the Question. Two kinds of begging the question are often found. 1. Creating A=A arguments; that is, repeating the proposition rather than giving substantive support for one's position or stance. 2. Assuming the point to be proven as true rather than proving its truth. "Governor X's misguided and mismanaged environmental policies threaten us all. They are obviously unpopular; few people support them." Who is threatened? How? In which ways are the policies mismanaged? By whom? Is it the policies themselves or their mismanagement that constitutes a threat? The second statement in this example—They are obviously unpopular; few people support them—is an example of the first kind of begging the question.

Card Stacking. Using all the propagandistic tools in tandem with symbols, music, slogans, placards, the gathering of huge supportive crowds, and showy displays. Political rallies and product promotions often employ card stacking.

We have devoted considerable space to the propagandistic strategies above. Because they affect national and international policy and the political, social, and economic choices the public makes, deep understanding of the charged and manipulated language they entail is critical not only to public and personal choices, but to the continuation of language as a meaningful medium of communication. In conversations, for successful communication to occur, speakers have an obligation to be honest—to honor the conversational principle of quality (Andrews 177). If politicians successfully persuade people using combinations of the tactics above; if their words are doublespeak or outright deception and their logic faulty; if they engage in generalizing, sloganeering, and name-calling rather than in detailing their positions in a straightforward manner, political systems and political policies invite distrust and cynicism with resultant voter non-participation. As people find they have been deceived, a more general cynicism may prevail and the statements of us all become suspect. Genuine democracy demands honest conversations so that voters can make informed choices. And voters have an obligation to carefully examine the statements of their leaders and would-be leaders to ensure that verbal manipulation is minimal and that honesty prevails. Thus, after reviewing and discussing the language of advertisers and politicians, we ask pairs of students to choose from the large stack of political brochures we have collected and to identify the propagandistic devices they find in the political advertisements. We are careful to save brochures from candidates from both major political parties as well as non-partisan candidates. The conversation becomes especially interesting when pairs of students work with opposing candidates. Next, in election years, we ask each student to find a political ad—brochure, radio spot, Internet, television—and to lead the class in an analysis of the ad for its propagandistic devices. In non-election years, we use ads we or former students have videotaped.

APPLICATIONS FOR THE CLASSROOM

Our readers cannot help noticing that we make frequent reference to discussions and depictions of language use in popular culture, for example, news articles, cartoons, and literature, including children's picture books. We do so for several reasons. First we wish to demonstrate that the power of language is much on the minds of "real world" people and is featured in many venues. It is not just a dry classroom topic of concern only to linguists. Secondly, we find our own students more open-minded in regard to language issues once they have seen that these issues are of genuine concern to the "real world" and have read about them from a variety of perspectives. Finally, excited by the wealth of material readily available for language study in cartoons and comics, in films, online, in news media and on television, our students have been motivated to make their own collections for use in their own classrooms.

As our students become increasingly aware of the power of words, we ask them to search popular print news media to find their own articles and cartoons. They participate in "show and tell" sessions where they share their finds with class members, apply them to student and classroom contexts, relate their pieces to our ongoing classroom discussion of language, and predict how they will use them with their own students. Each of our students is responsible for two "finds" each semester. Many continue to bring in items of interest long after they have already shared their required two. One student was even prompted to send a letter to his local newspaper debating Ebonics issues he'd read about there and proudly showed us that his letter had been printed. Others have gone on to engage in funded independent research using the articles they have collected as a starting point. In short, our students not only learn about the power of words, but they become active participants in the conversations which determine how this power is played out. Most tell us that they will use a similar activity in their own classrooms.

In this chapter we have presented an overview of the power of words as well as activities through which we have fostered our students' awareness of their power, all of which can be adapted to their own classrooms. In addition, we have included "For Thought" sections which invite readers and, by extension, their students to engage with the power of words as do the Personal and Teacher Explorations which close the chapter. In the chapters that follow, we will return more specifically to many of the topics introduced here as we consider hate language, dialects and dialectal speakers, language policies, bilingualism, and issues of language as they relate to gender, ethnicity, and social class.

PERSONAL EXPLORATIONS

1. Compare and contrast a few pages of a recent edition and an older edition of the same dictionary. What changes in entries and their definitions do you find? What remains unchanged? Compare and contrast entries and definitions in dictionaries published by different publishers. How can you account for the differences you find?

2. Research and examine the names of U.S. military offensives in the years 2001–2004 in Iraq and Afghanistan. What connotations are associated with each? Which, if any, of the tactics used by advertisers and/or politicians do you find at work in each title you find? (Operation Enduring Freedom is one example.) During the war in Iraq (2003–2006), all of the following words might be used to describe the same person. Who might use each word? How do the connotations of each differ? Which are slanted or charged words? An insurgent, a terrorist, a freedom fighter, a defender of democracy, a defender of the nation's sovereignty, a hero, a fighter, a resister, a soldier, a sniper, a sharpshooter.

3. Make a list of all the specialized words you can find used in connection with a sport, music, computers, or any other pastime with which you are familiar. Now, try writing a short piece which features the jargon of the profession or pastime you have chosen (reading Day's book and its accompanying lexicons of words and phrases might be both enjoyable and useful to you in completing this activity). What problems would your piece pose for readers unfamiliar with its topic?

4. Read James Finn Garner's "Little Red Riding Hood" in his *Politically Correct Bedtime Stories*. What are the effects of Garner's so-called "politically correct" language choices? In causing us to laugh at some of his exaggerated choices, is he also, indirectly, causing us to laugh at the efforts of those who try to use language in a less exaggerated but sensitive manner (e.g., saying "handicapped" instead of "crippled," or "Chair" instead of "Chairman"), thus undermining their efforts?

5. Create a series of three advertisements for the same product, each of which targets a different age group, perhaps male teenagers, women aged 30–35, and both men and women in their late 50s. How will your pitch and the words you use to sell your product differ from ad to ad?

6. Find a minimum of four political ads from each of the major political parties (the internet and the local party headquarters will be useful here). Which advertising and propaganda strategies does each use? Review a presidential speech from the last 10 years—newspapers such as *The New York Times* often carry and archive the full text of presidential speeches. Which of the propagandistic devices listed above can you find? What effects might each have upon listeners/readers?

7. List any taboo words that you have used. Where, when, with whom, and under what circumstances did you use them? Were there any repercussions for their use? When, where, with whom, and under which circumstances do you refrain from the use of taboo language? Why? Which taboo words are especially offensive to you? Why? Investigate the origins of several taboo words. What do you find? How, if it is, is the current meaning and usage of the word related to its origins and previous usages?

TEACHING EXPLORATIONS

1. What names, labels, and categories do students give one another ("Dude" and "a tool" are two we remember hearing our sons use)? What positive purposes, if any, do these names and labels serve? What negative purposes, if any? What positive and negative effects might such labeling have?

2. In both informal conversational and in more academic situations, what are some of the labels and categories teachers give to students? *Jock, reading readiness student, AP student* are some examples. What positive or negative purposes do these serve? What positive or negative effects might such categorization have?

3. How will (or do) you deal with taboo or offensive language used in the literature you teach? With attempts to censor a book you use in class due to

its containing taboo or offensive language? Visit the American Library Association's website www.ala.org/ala/oif/bannedbooksweek/bannedbooksweek and the National Council of Teachers of English website www.ncte.org/about/issues/censorship for help. How will you deal with taboo language as students use it in the halls? In classroom discourse? As students wear it on their clothing? As students use it in the pieces they write? If it is directed at you by a student in the hall?

4. A 12th-grade student has called you, the teacher, a "fucking bitch" in class, just loud enough so that you and the six students near her can hear. What do you think you would do in the absence of an established school-wide policy which provides procedures to be followed in situations similar to this one? Below are several possible actions that our students suggested in their initial discussion of the situation. What are the pluses and minuses of each? What others might you suggest? Would you respond differently if the student was a 1st grader? If so, how?

a. Ignore the incident.
b. Directly and angrily address the student and send her out of class to the principal's office.
c. Confront the student directly in class and assign the student a paper on offensive language.
d. Calmly tell the student you wish to see her after class and carry on with the lesson. After class, talk with her and tell her such language is not acceptable.
e. In class, take the student to the telephone and tell her to call a parent and reveal what she has just said.
f. After class, take the student to a telephone and tell her call a parent and reveal what she has just said.
g. Look directly at the student for a moment. Say nothing at the time and proceed with class. Just before the class is dismissed tell the student you wish to see her, so that the whole class knows that you will be talking with her. Privately, tell her what you heard, give her a chance to speak, then take her to the principal's office.
h. Directly in class, tell the student that she will receive a detention.
i. Bring the student to the front of the class and ask her to explain what she said and why she said it to the class. Then, seeing this as a teachable moment, facilitate a short lesson on taboo language with the whole class

5. The Association of American Editorial Cartoonists at http://nieonline.com/aaec/cftc/cfm and the *Newsweek* Education Program at http://school.newsweek.com/extras/pol.cartoons4.php both advocate the

inclusion of political cartoons in school curricula and provide teachers with lesson plans and activities for analyzing the words and images in political cartoons. Investigate these Web sites. What do you find that you could include in your classroom to teach about the power of words?

WORKS CITED

Adams, Scott. "Dilbert." Cartoon. Scott Adams, Inc. 2–5 Nov. 1998.

Allport, Gordon. "The Language of Prejudice." *Language Awareness*. Eds. Paul Eschholtz, Alfred Rosa, and Virginia Clark. 6th ed. New York: St. Martin's Press, 1994: 287–296.

American Library Association. <www.ala.org/ala/oif/bannedbooksweek/bannedbooksweek>.

Andrews, Larry. *Language Exploration and Awareness*. Mahwah, NJ: Lawrence Erlbaum Associates, 1998.

Armstrong, Robb. "Jumpstart." Cartoon. United Features Syndicate, Inc. 1–3 Oct. 1997.

Billingsley, Ray. "Curtis." Cartoon. King Features Syndicate, Inc. 26 May 1995.

Bosmajian, Haig. *The Language of Oppression*. Washington: Public Affairs Press, 1974.

Brothers, Joyce. "What Dirty Words Really Mean." *Exploring Language*. Ed. Gary Goshgarian. 8th ed. New York: Longman, 1998: 375–378.

Bruni, Frank. "Troops use words to mask the danger." *Detroit Free Press* 10 Feb. 1991: F 1+.

Carroll, Lewis. *Through the Looking Glass*. Chicago: Children's Press, 1969.

Cisneros, Sandra. *The House on Mango Street*. New York: Vintage, 1991.

Coates, Jennifer. *Women, Men, and Language*. New York: Longman, 1986.

Cunha, Edite. "Talking in the New Land." *Language Awareness*. Eds. Paul Eschholtz, Alfred Rosa, and Virginia Clark. 7th ed. New York: St. Martin's, 1997: 116–125.

Day, Alexandra. *Frank and Ernest*. New York: Scholastic 1988.

Diegmueller, Karen. "Expletives Deleted." *Teacher Magazine* Sep. 1995: .

Dove, Rita. "Parsley." *New Worlds of Literature*. Eds. Jerome Hunter and J. Paul Beatty. 2nd ed. New York: Norton, 1994: 289–290.

"Euphemism." *Merriam-Webster's Collegiate Dictionary*. Springfield, MA: Merriam. 10th ed. 1994: 400.

Elements of Literature. Fifth Course. Literature of the United States. Chicago: Holt. 1993.

Eliot, T. S. "Sweeney Agonistes." *Collected Poems 1909–1963*. New York: Harcourt, 1963.

Fairclough, Norman. *Language and Power*. New York: Longman, 1989.

Fairclough, Norman. *Language and Power*. 2nd edition. New York: Longman, 2001.

Flagg, Fanny. *Fried Green Tomatoes*. New York: McGraw, 1988.

Garner, James Finn. *Politically Correct Bedtime Stories*. New York: MacMillan, 1994: 1–4.

Gilchrist, Brad and Guy. "Nancy." Cartoon. United Features Syndicate, Inc. 16 May 1995.

Goldberg, Carey. "Welcome to New York, Capital of Profanities." *New York Times* 19 June 1995: B1, B3.

Hansberry, Lorraine Vivian. *A Raisin in the Sun. The Heath Anthology of American Literature*. Ed. Paul Lauter. 3rd ed. Vol. 2. New York: Houghton, 1998: 2462–2522.

Harmon, Mary Rose. *A Study of Sociolinguistic Texts and Subtexts as Found in Five High School American Literature Anthologies*. Diss. Michigan State University, 1993.

Harris, Peggy. "Court Appeals Rules Against Veteran Teacher." *The Council Chronicle* Nov. 1998: 1, 8.

Hart, Johnny. "B.C." Cartoon. Creators Syndicate, Inc. 9 Mar. 1996.

Hendricks, Nancy. "Response to *Woman Hollering Creek.*" 1995. Used with permission.

Howard, Philip. "The Two Sides of Jargon." *About Language*. Eds. William H. Roberts and Gregoire Turgeon. 3rd ed. Geneva, IL: Houghton, 1992: 231–236.

Johnston, Lynn. "For Better or For Worse." Cartoon. Lynn Johnston Products, Inc. 22–24 Mar. 2005.

Keane, Bill. "The Family Circus." Cartoon. King Features Syndicate, Inc. 14 Apr. 1996.

Kristeva, Julia. "From Symbol to Sign." *The Kristeva Reader*. Ed. Toril Moi. New York: Columbia UP, 1986: 62–73.

Lawrence, Barbara. "Four Letter Words Can Hurt You." *About Language*. Eds. William H. Roberts and Gregoire Turgeon. 5th ed. Geneva, IL: Houghton, 1995: 335–337.

Leo, John. "Foul Words, Foul Culture." *U.S. News and World Report* 26 Apr. 1996: 73.

_____. "Who's for a Little Tongue Violence?" *U.S. News and World Report* 15 Apr. 1996: 23.

Lutz, William. *Doublespeak*. New York: Harper, 1990.

_____. "With These Words I Can Sell You Anything." *Exploring Language*. Ed. Gary Goshgarian. 10th ed. New York: Longman, 2004. pp. 393–406.

Maggio, Rosalie. *Guide to Non-Discriminatory Language*. *Language Awareness*. Eds. Paul Eschholtz, Alfred Rosa, and Virginia Clark. 7th ed. New York: St. Martin's, 1997: 245–256.

McMillan, Terry. *Waiting to Exhale*. New York: Pocket Books, 1992.

Miller, Arthur. *The Crucible*. New York: Bantam, 1959.

Moi, Toril. *Sexual/Textual Politics: Feminist Literary Theory*. New York: Routledge, 1993.

National Council of Teachers of English. <www.ncte.org/about/issues/censorship>.

Naylor, Gloria. "'Nigger: The Meaning of a Word." *Exploring Language*. Ed. Gary Goshgarian. 10th ed. New York: Longman. 2004: 526–529.

Nilsen, Alleen Pace. *Living Language*. Boston: Allyn, 1999.

O'Brien, Anne Sibby. *My Name is Johari*. Newbridge, 1994.

O'Brien, Tim. "Faith." *The New Yorker* 12 February 1996: 67.

ONeil, Charles. "The Language of Advertising." *Exploring Language*. Ed. Gary Goshgarian. 10th ed. New York: Longman, 2004: 407–417.

Penelope, Julia. "Make Money, Not Sense: Keep Academia Green." *Beyond 1984*. Ed. William Lutz. Urbana, IL: National Council of Teachers of English, 1989: 165–178.

Penelope, Julia. *Speaking Freely: Unlearning the Lies of The Fathers' Tongues*. New York: Pergamon, 1990.

"Profane shirt is harassment, judge rules." *Lansing State Journal* [Michigan] 3 Apr. 1999: B-8.

"Profanity has man in court battling over freedom of speech." *Argus Press* 24 Dec. 1998: 3.

Quindlen, Anna. "A Foul Mouth and Manhood." *Newsweek* 12 July 2004: 76.

Seligman, Jean. "The Wounds of Words." *Newsweek* 12 Oct. 1992: 90

Strauss, Valerie. "More and More, Kids Say the Foulest Things." *Washington Post* 12 Apr. 2005: A12.

Thaves, Bob. "Frank and Ernest." Cartoon. Newspaper Enterprise Associates, Inc. 15 May 1994.

Toner, Robin. "On Bush Plan It's 'Private' Vs. 'Personal.'" *New York Times.* 22 Mar. 2005: A1, A16.

Tucker, Daryl O. "Vulgar talk not a crime." *Saginaw News* [Michigan] 2 Apr. 2002: B-1.

Walker, Brian, Greg Walker, Chance Browne. "Hi and Lois." Cartoon. King Features Syndicate, Inc. 25 Feb. 1996.

Walker, Mort. "Beetle Bailey." Cartoon. King Features Syndicate, Inc. 26 Aug. 1995.

Watterson, Bill. "Calvin and Hobbes." Cartoon. Universal Press Syndicate. 1 Sept. 1992.

_____. *Homicidal Psycho Jungle Cat.* Kansas City, MO: UPS, 1996: 62.

Williams, Raymond. Keywords. New York: Oxford UP. 1983.

_____. *Marxism and Literature.* New York: Oxford UP. 1977.

_____. *The Sociology of Culture.* New York: Schocken. 1981.

Chapter 4

Hate Language and Bully Language: The Language of Destruction

---

FOR THOUGHT 4.1: Recall instances when you have called others demeaning names or when you have engaged in teasing others. What do you think motivated your behavior? Now recall instances in which you have been teased or called demeaning names by others. What do you think motivated their behavior? Recall instances of when you have seen or heard others demeaned verbally. What do you think motivated the behavior of those who demeaned others? What did you do? Why?

CARTOON 4.1 CALVIN AND HOBBES © (1993) Watterson. Dist. By UNIVERSAL PRESS SYNDICATE. Reprinted with Permission. All rights reserved.

Calvin shares with many the feeling of having his past and present denigrated by the use of a reductive label. When we planned this book several years ago, we did not envision a separate chapter on hate language; rather we thought the topic could be covered adequately, if briefly, in the previous chapter on the power of language. Since then, we have reconsidered. Recent emphases on bullying and so-called teasing and the personal harm and public explosions they create; more careful attention to music lyrics and to the media; the rhetoric surrounding recent events, including the aftermath of the attacks on September 11, 2001, the war in Iraq, the 2004 presidential election; and the experiences of our students and other persons we read about convinced us that special attention must be paid in this book and in all teachers' classrooms to the widespread use of hate language, its power, and its harmful consequences. Because the school, too often, is one of the environments in which hate language thrives, yet one in which teachers can provide safe spaces where hate language can be studied and discussed, teachers must include such study in their classrooms, and they must develop strategies and help their students develop strategies to counter hate language and its effects. This chapter will assist teachers to do just that. First we will answer two questions: *What is hate language? Who are the haters?* Then we will examine *structures that undergird hate,* including *media* and *institutions. Verbal manifestations of hate*—slurs, derogatory labels, and bully language—all of which abound in schools, will follow. The chapter will close with *applications for teachers: what can teachers do?*

WHAT IS HATE LANGUAGE, WHO ARE ITS TARGETS, AND WHO ARE THE HATERS?

Hate Language

We will define "hate language" as that which demeans another person and as that which reveals hostility to difference, whether that difference be of ethnicity, age, religion, gender, social class, physical appearance, or a variety of other characteristics. While that definition may seem broad, we suggest that it is difficult to distinguish where intolerance stops and hatred begins and that intolerance always underlies hatred. Targets of hate language are many; among the most frequent are ethnic minorities, gays and lesbians, religious groups, women and girls, the poor, the disabled—anyone haters categorize as the "other." Hate language permeates contemporary society, its use often undergirded by any number of seemingly neutral groups and social institutions, such as schools, religion, government, and the media, including music lyrics, television news and programs, talk radio, and film. Hate language has profound effects upon its users, its targets, and society as a whole when its methods—name calling, bullying, harassment, sloganeering, and mockery—are used as tools to enhance the power of their users and as weapons of ridicule to diminish and dehumanize others or to silence and control them. Before our discussion of what teachers can and should do about hate language and one of its most visible forms, bullying, we will take a closer look at who the haters and their targets are, as well as what their motives and the results of their efforts may be.

Janis L. Judson and Donna M. Bertazzoni, in *Law, Media, and Culture: The Landscape of Hate*, assert that

> we are living in an era in which hatred has become a part of our national ideology, a subtext of our national conversation. Hatred against the "other" is an endemic and unforgiving aspect of our popular culture. It can be found in contemporary cinema, in television news and entertainment programs that reinforce racial and ethnic (we would add age, social class, and gender) stereotypes, on talk shows that rail against affirmative action, in schools that are reluctant to allow children to read books about alternative life styles, and on web sites that assert that "God hates fags." (7)

They add that politicians and activists on both the right and the left help weave a national fabric of hate whether through a rhetoric of so-called "moral traditionalism and traditional family values—anti-gay, anti-Hollywood, anti-abortion, pro-Christian, pro-white patriarchy" on the part of the political right or through the violent sloganeering and demonstrations "by protesters at World Trade Organization meetings, members of radical environmental groups, and radical animal rights activists" (7–8) on the political left. What follows summarizes their review of Levin and Paulsen's typology of haters (14–19) and adds examples we have found of persons and groups who exemplify each type.

Haters and Their Targets

The Hatemonger or the Mission Hater.   These persons, uninterested in civil and informed debate, populate hate groups such as the White Aryan Resistance or the World Church of the Creator. Because they are on a mission to eliminate or disempower those groups of people whom they see as threatening to their personal and their collective way of life, hatemongers actively "proselytize"—they "pass out leaflets, recruit, and produce programs to air on cable access television stations" (14). *Newsweek*'s "The Hot Sound of Hate" profiles Bryon Calvert, the director of Panzerfaust Records, who in late 2004 distributed 100,000 CDs with lyrics like "Hang the traitors of our race. White Supremacy! White Supremacy! White Supremacy!" to kids 13–19 as a part of his Project Schoolyard. His Web site asserts: "We don't just entertain racist kids, we create them," as it tries to lure kids into hate and feed their anger at "blacks, Jews, homosexuals, immigrants." His CD label, state authors Sarah Childress and Dirk Johnson, is "likely to surpass its influential rival, Resistance Records" (32). Although, as of March

2005, Panzerfaust appears to have morphed into Free Your Mind Productions, its CDs are still available ("Panzerfaust Apparently Out of Business"). Closer to Mary's home, *The Bay City Times* recently featured a front page story on James P. Wickstrom who, according to the *Times*, is a "white supremacist preaching the gospel of hate ... [and] anti-Semitism" from Bay County's Marquiss Quality Furniture store (Kark).

In February 2004, Mary was disturbed to find a leaflet at the end of her driveway—she later learned these were distributed at many west side Saginaw addresses—which states in bold letters "Love Your Race" and features the picture of a pale, long-haired, blond, white woman on the front along with "National Alliance" and www.natall.com. Attached was a front and back article responding to an ABC News feature on the National Alliance, defending the organization from accusations that it is a hate group, and stating that it has been gaining membership among young people. Said an Alliance member that the leaflet identified as Chuck, "We're white separatists ... we want our own country, our own homeland, our own defensible borders ... We can stay in our country and they can stay in their country." In the leaflet readers learn that the National Alliance targets affirmative action, immigration, and the war in Iraq, which it contends was initiated to defend Israel. The organization has also distributed leaflets in Colorado warning white women that they can get AIDS if they have sex with black men, after which distribution the group experienced rapid growth gains according to the flier. The back lists eight addresses for contact, further information, or financial contribution. Unfortunately, hatemongering is alive, well, and local. Although one can still access its Web site as listed above, some former members of the National Alliance state that the organization "has reconstituted under a new name—National Vanguard"; this new Web site (www.nationalvanguard.org) assures its readers that as a "new forward-looking organization" it "will use proven principles to uncompromisingly stand for white people" (National Vanguard: Our Cause Reborn).

Dabblers.   These haters, often young males who have trouble getting along with their parents, teachers, bosses, fellow employees, are those most likely to commit overtly violent crimes against blacks, Asian, Latinos, and Jews to gain "bragging rights" (Judson and Bertazzoni 14). Both dabblers and hatemongers, extremist haters, are most likely to belong to organized hate groups. Hatemongers, organizers, and savvy propagandists who give dabblers a "home" and a cause, need them to carry out hate terrorism. Increasing multiculturalism and globalism, international conflicts involving the United States, and economic woes are among the catalysts for their violent hatred and their scapegoating of the "other." They share common beliefs: "the natural rights of whites in a 'Christian' nation, the dangers of Jewish dominance ... the breakdown of the family that would result if 'special rights' were given to gays and lesbians, the unfairness of affirmative action programs ... and the fear of race-mixing" (16). Judson and Bertazzoni contend that some of these beliefs have entered the U.S. political mainstream and have been "embraced by the right wing of the Republican Party, which over the past several decades has been willing to use race, homophobia, and opposition to affirmative action to appeal to white conservatives during presidential election campaigns" (17). The political strategy of placing anti-gay marriage propositions on the ballots of several key states in the 2004 election seems to lend credence to their argument.

Dabblers have been active. In May of 2005, three crosses were burned in various locations in Durham, North Carolina, and Ku Klux Klan fliers were found at one site ("North Carolina: Cross Burning in Durham"). Despite assertions that the Ku Klux Klan was a long time ago, and "we are a long time past that as a country," (Gershman and Maher) spoken by a spectator/bidder at a 2005 auction of Klan paraphernalia in Howell, Michigan, only two years prior, in 2003, Third Reich flag bearers, Confederate flag bearers, men in KKK garb, and members of the World Church of the Creator converged in Lewiston, Maine, to demonstrate against the 1,100 Somali immigrants who had moved there. A World Church member, David Stearns, stated "They're doing the same things as African Americans are doing here ... leeching off the system ... eating up subsidized housing ... spreading diseases" (Gates). In fairness to both Lewiston and Howell, it must be stated that at both the auction and the anti-immigrant protest, many citizens gathered to publically protest what they saw as the racism and hatred.

Sympathizers and Spectators. *Sympathizers* do not usually act out their hate violently. But they speak it using derogatory slurs, symbols, slogans, or code words, and they vote for proposals that tend to suppress those they quietly or not so quietly hate. Ample evidence exists that sympathizers make their presence known. One need not look far from home. In Saginaw, Michigan, a frequent council critic publically used a racial slur at an August 2003 city council meeting and refused to apologize for it. More recently, Councilwoman Roma Thurin was pelted with racial slurs by a citizen during a minor traffic encounter. Teachers are likely to encounter the verbal acts of sympathizers whose hate can lead to violent repercussions. In 2004, Saginaw area schools saw several instances of students bringing arms to school to counter racial slurs, causing widespread alarm among parents who feared for their children's safety from both arms and racial taunts. Saginaw Valley State University recently featured the topic of racial intimidation at a President's Open Forum, following the Student Association President's comments that he had been approached by a student who was the target of racial slurs on campus. Slurs against gays and the mentally handicapped also became a part of the forum as participants began preliminary plans to counter prejudice. *Spectators* are not necessarily filled with hate themselves; in fact, they may support the rights of the "other" in principle, but, often, not in fact. Although they are often appalled by overtly violent acts against the "other," and may speak out against individual acts of violence, they do not speak out against the hate rhetoric that underlies violence. They unthinkingly sit quietly and passively as the blatantly negative, venom-filled, often knee-jerk pronouncements of haters on issues such as immigration, affirmative action, welfare regulation, and gay rights and marriage gain mainstream acceptance, and, in doing so, they indirectly become supporters of hate (18). They may display symbols of hatred such as the Confederate flag or the swastika unthinkingly, without investigation; buy into slogans and code phrases like "tough on crime," "reverse discrimination," "welfare queens," "traditional family values"; or use the language of overt hatred (faggot, queer, spic, trailer-trash, feminazi, nigger); and yet may state they "don't mean anything by it"—they are not prejudiced. In classrooms, teachers must alert students to the role of the spectator who fails to acknowledge the damage caused by hate language and bullying and who fails to counter them, thus, permitting them. Unfortunately recent research reveals that too often teachers and administrators, themselves, play the role of spectator.

FOR THOUGHT 4.2: Have you ever played the role of spectator as you heard hate language directed at another person? If you answer yes, why did you not intervene? What prompts spectators to remain silent and/or passive?

STRUCTURES THAT UNDERGIRD HATE

Both overt and covert hate in the United States are buttressed by the media and a number of institutions, some of which we have already referred to but wish to discuss in more detail. If language and culture have a reciprocal relationship, and if language and institutions not only reflect the culture but shape the culture, it is critical that we do so. Do music lyrics only reflect hate, or do they also shape and create hate? Do narratives, whether printed, filmed, personally performed, or televised merely reflect the culture, or do they also shape the culture? Bryon Calvert of Panzerfaust Records, quoted above, clearly believes his messages of hate create haters as well as reflect existent hate. One of hate's strongest supports is the persistent refusal to admit it exists. Those who use derogatory slurs will often contend they mean nothing by them, or they will dismiss their use of slurs by saying that they were just being funny or blowing off steam; they are not prejudiced, they'll add. The torture of Iraqi prisoners at Abu Ghraib Prison and Guantanamo had little to do with hatred; it was just the work of a "few rogue guards" we've been told. Matthew Shepard's murder in Laramie, Wyoming, was not an instance of gay-hatred but the work of the misguided. The humiliation, beating, rape, and murder of Brandon Teena, the real-life subject of the recent film *Boys Don't Cry*, were not acknowledged as crimes stemming from a culturally reinforced hatred of transgendered persons or from sexual bias, but were cast as the actions of miscreants. Dismissal of hatred's pervasive reality allows it to thrive.

MEDIA

Judson and Bertazzoni argue that the Internet, popular music, the news, and other media all provide a venue for hate mongers. Below, we summarize their contentions, add ours, and exemplify both with evidence from popular culture.

The Internet

A wealth of hate sites and hate blogs can readily be found on the Internet. We hesitate to publish their addresses here as doing so merely gives them more publicity. In fact whenever a news story on hate organizations airs, hits on their Web sites increase dramatically. Nonetheless, we find it critical that teachers and students know that such sites exist and that there be classroom discussion of them for three reasons:

1. To show students the problem of hate is real, alive, and widespread.
2. To reveal the fallacies in haters' logic.
3. To counter the messages such sites present.

Among the many Web sites are those of the National Alliance, now the National Vanguard, already referred to above; the Klu Klux Klan; The World Church of the Creator, now functioning under the title "Creativity Movement," which along with its hate discourse offers outreach to women and games and puzzles for children; The Nation of Islam; and a number of Neo-Nazi groups. The World Church of the Creator has made savvy use of the Internet as has the National Alliance, both with sophisticated, multi-link Web sites. Google's Orkut Web site, created as a members only site that allows people to join many on-line communities, has become a home for hatemongering, with "Death to Jews" and "Death to Blacks" sites (Rivlin). E-mailed messages of hatred and hate blogs thrive on the Internet and are rarely punished, as courts, including the Supreme Court, have determined that unless imminent violence is advocated and threatened toward specific individuals, most Internet hate discourse is protected by the First Amendment. Courts have sometimes ruled against hate symbols. In a 6-3 ruling in April 2003, the Supreme Court proclaimed cross burning an act of terror and upheld the constitutionality of Virginia's law—11 other states have similar laws—that bans cross-burning ("Cross burnings"). Speech, however, is privileged. With court protection as free speech, haters' Internet sites, blogs, and e-mails can defame and advocate violence toward their targets: Blacks, Jews, Asians, Latinos, abortion providers, and others. Pornographic sites which depict hatred and graphic violence toward women abound, available for viewing by anyone, including children. Yet hate does not reign unchecked. Organizations that monitor, counter, and challenge hate sites include the Anti-Defamation League, The Jewish Defense Organization, the Southern Poverty Law Center, and the Prejudice Institute.

FOR THOUGHT 4.3: Should all speech, including hate symbols, be court protected as free speech? Support your answer. Free speech, the right to privacy, and the right to equal protection under the law are all central, if sometimes conflicting, values most Americans hold dear. Can they be reconciled in regard to verbal harassment and hate language? If so, how?

The News

Too often, news coverage of the underlying issues surrounding hate is scant or missing, or its coverage reflects "society's fascination with hate and hate crimes" that "may end up glorifying the perpetrators of crimes, giving them the notoriety they crave, while ignoring or marginalizing the victims" (Judson and Bertazonni 83–85). In televised or press interviews, hatemongers such as the leaders of the National Alliance or The World Church of the Creator often are given considerable media exposure which they see as an opportunity to promote their message; sometimes press stories turn them into cultural icons. Indeed David Pringle, National Alliance Membership Director, was delighted with an ABC News feature on the National Alliance entitled "The Racist Next Door: White Separatists Say Professionals Hear Their Message." Stated Pringle, "This is without a doubt one of the best articles I have seen on the National Alliance." In short, National Alliance leaders were confident that the news piece, though intended to expose the Alliance as a hate group, would bring them new members and reveal that "there is substance in the National Alliance's message" (The National Alliance, "Love Your Race" leaflet). In a later chapter we will address a specific instance of press-related hate: a cartoon that appeared in the midst of the Oakland, California, Ebonics controversy.

Yet the effect of the press cannot be seen as wholly negative. Careful reading and viewing of a variety of news sources can alert readers to the prevalence of hate in America, the forms it takes, its targets and victims, hate crime's legal implications, and current legislative and court debates over hate-laws and speech regulation. Articles like "'Gooks to Hajis'" in *The New York Times* ask readers to confront hate. Bob Herbert exposes "the growing rage among coalition troops against all Iraqis (known derisively as 'hajis,' just as the Vietnamese were known as 'gooks')." He quotes Sergeant Camilo Mejia as stating, "You just sort of try to block out the fact that they are human beings and see them as enemies. You call them hajis, you know? You do all the things that make it easier to deal with killing them and mistreating them." Syndicated columnist Clarence Page argues that Shaquille O'Neal's use of racist trash talk about Yao Ming tarnished O'Neal's image, infuriated Asian groups, and alerted the Select Committee on Hate Crimes in California to call for NBA sanctions against O'Neal (A5). An advertisement by the Indigenous Language Institute in *Men's Health* reminds readers of the hatred toward Native Americans that prompted the attempted eradication of indigenous lifestyles and languages (45). And Christine Rook's "No offense, but some words do offend others," a June 2004 article in the *Lansing State Journal*, educates readers to "avoid mutations of ethnic or racial names ... avoid words or phrases that mock groups ... if a word is monosyllabic, exercise caution (since so many ethnic slurs are of one syllable, i.e., "Spic") .... know the difference between in-group and out-group" use of ethnic language. She reminds readers "that American English is riddled with ethnic and racial slurs" (1D+). Thus, while the press can, indeed, scaffold hate, with articles that teachers and their students find and bring to class and discuss, the press can be a means to undermine and disarm hatred.

Popular Music

Hate lyrics that target women, Blacks, Asians, and gays are easily found in popular music. One need not resort to the non-mainstream hate artists like the SS Bootboys and Das Rich or recording companies like Panzerfaust Records and Resistance Records; the latter functions under the ownership of the National Alliance. Rap lyrics readily available for purchase and easily found on the Internet at www.azlyrics.com or at sites readily accessed through any of the popular search engines often feature the language of hate. Though he may wish to shrug them off or state that he is only joking, Eminem's lyrics are notorious for savagely ridiculing gay men. Nekesa Mumbi Moody describes one of Eminem's Grammy-winning albums as "riddled with derisive or violent references" to gay men that "joke about stabbing them." Moody quotes recording Academy President Michael Greene's defense of Eminem's right to "say things that anger people," even while Greene depicts the artist and his work as "'truly some of the most repugnant things we've heard recorded this year .... He hates everybody'" Moody adds that "women's groups also have criticized the rapper for violent lyrics" (A8). Well known past and present rappers such as Ice-Cube, Tupac Shakur, and 50 Cent denounce women as bitches, hookers, and "hoes"; threaten them with violence; and blatantly depict then as little other than sexual receptacles. Popular rap albums that demean and degrade their targets and promote violence are listened to again and again, memorized, repeated by countless people—and internalized. Eminem's and other rappers' music and lyrics are sanctioned by the recording industry, despite its disclaimers as exemplified by Greene, above, when it repeatedly awards them top prizes. Do those rappers and other recording artists who foreground hate into their music reinforce and/or create haters? Ask Bryon Calvert of Panzerfaust Records. Clarence Page wonders what Martin Luther King Jr. "would think if he were alive today" to hear current rap. He suggests that Black rappers' hate-lyrics can be best challenged not by censorship, but by dialogue which persuades "both rappers and producers that they are degrading the image of African Americans" (11A).

Not only rap artists mouth hate. Reggae star Beanie Man, who records for Virgin Records and who collaborates with well-known stars such as Janet Jackson, fills his work with anti-gay lyrics in which he refers to gays as chi-chi men or batty boys. Samples from his work include: "We burn chi-chi man and then we burn sodomite and everybody bawl out, say 'Dat Right!'" and "Hang chi-chi gal wid a long piece of rope." The virulence of his anti-gay message has prompted the cancellation of some of his concerts throughout Europe and in Miami, Florida. Virgin Records "put out a contrite statement" which later "was disavowed by his (Beanie Man's) manager" and, to some extent, by Virgin Records, themselves (Sanneh B1+).

Country music sometimes features hate lyrics. Recently Mary's students alerted her to the 1970s lyrics of David Allan Coe's "unabashedly offensive" X-rated albums, that are currently enjoying a resurgence of popularity and whose lyrics are accessible on the Internet. Although he sold them through *Easy Rider* magazine and still sells them at his Web site, and although some of them have been criticized for racist or misogynist content, Coe states that *these* X-rated albums were not intended to be racist but to be humorous and controversial and adds that he never intended these songs to become so well known. He denies he is a racist; he contends that his X-rated pieces were recorded with the help of Shel Silverstein simply "to be funny" (Wikipedia "David Allan Coe"). We find it imperative that teachers know the extremism that permeates lyrics readily available to their students for purchase or perusal; thus, we suggest that readers go to http://www.officialdavidallancoe.com to find listing of Coe's X-rated albums and songs and then to www.sing365.com to locate and scroll through some of the X-rated lyrics they find, not for shock value nor to suggest the songs for classroom use, but to allow readers to decide if those they deem controversial or offensive can be defended as humorous.

FOR THOUGHT 4.4: Would you use any of the lyrics referenced above in your classroom to teach about hate language? Why or why not? If you would, how could you do so without angering students, their parents, or your principal?

Radio, Film, and Television

Films, television programming, and media news stories that disproportionately emphasize crimes committed by minorities or present stereotypes of minorities reinforce the biased attitudes of hate spectators and sympathizers. Media stories that consistently show recipients of welfare to be female, unmarried, and Black, and films and television programming that underrepresent women and minority persons also feed bias, as do those that include them primarily as secondary sidekicks or, in the case of minority persons, clowns. Are *South Park* and *Politically Correct* popular because they feature spokespersons for spectators and sympathizers in the guise of humor? Talk radio makes no pretense of presenting unbiased or rigorously substantiated views. Listened to by millions of Americans daily, it all too frequently feeds the hatred felt by *sympathizers* toward liberals, assertive women, minorities, welfare recipients, abortion-rights persons, immigrants, minorities, and anyone perceived as an enemy of so-called "American values" or "America." Yet, like the news media noted above, all media can also serve to counter hatred. *The Laramie Project* and *Boys Don't Cry* can painfully awaken viewers to homophobic hatred and foster discussion of its results as well as ways to counter it.

FOR THOUGHT 4.5: List films and television programs that target persons for ridicule and hate. Who is targeted? How: Specific language? Stereotyping? Slogans? Visual images? Now list films and television programs that might be used to either counter or expose hate. How could you use these in your classroom?

INSTITUTIONS

Education, religion, and government also can provide underlying structures that support hate. We have already included commentary from Judson and Bertazzoni that makes it clear that they consider government and education to scaffold hate. So do we, and to that list we would add religion. Evidence for our contentions abounds. One example is schools, colleges, and professional sports teams' insistence on keeping their Native American team names and mascots, often depicted in caricature fashion. Eighty-one percent of Native Americans regard these team names and mascots as offensive, as do Native American organizations, the NAACP, the ACLU, The National Education Association, and a number of church organizations. They find the portrayal of Native Americans by these mascots, often in stereotypical dress and crudely and inaccurately enacting war chants and dances, to be demeaning, to promote the idea that Native Americans were always violent, and to violate sacred traditions (Grotelueschen 5A).

Government and government leaders also provide a wealth of examples both historically and in recent times. In the past, the U.S. government sanctioned slavery and the extermination or isolation of Native Americans. Throughout the first half of the 20th century, Congress repeatedly refused to pass an anti-lynching law, school segregation was legal, and Jim Crow laws remained on the books of many states. The U.S. government internment of Japanese citizens during World War II exemplifies government sanctioned xenophobia. More recently, in 2002, then-Senate Leader Trent Lott stated that the United States would be better off today if Senator Strom Thurmond, a man who ran for President on a segregationist platform in 1948, had been elected. Although he apologized, his comments were in keeping with his record of consistently voting against civil rights legislation. He, however, was hardly alone in his lack of support for Civil Rights Restoration Act and a 1998 bill "to guarantee minority participation in highway construction projects" (Raspberry A7). Many other politicians voted against these measures as well. The 2004 Bush Campaign's and Governor Arnold Swarzenegger's derision of women will be documented in the chapter that follows. And chapter 7 explores the xenophobic traces that underlie state and national English-Only initiatives.

Among other minorities targeted by leaders in the Federal Government are Muslims and gays. Republican Senator Rick Santorum recently stated publically that he considers "gay sex to be immoral—though not as heinous as 'man-child' or 'man on dog' sex. If the Supreme Court creates a zone of privacy to protect gay sex, he said, the legal precedent is tantamount to protecting 'bigamy, polygamy, and incest'" (Fineman 47). More recently a federal agency under the aegis of the Department of Health and Human Services demanded that the words *gay, lesbian, bisexual*, and *transgender* be removed from a title listed in the program for a federally funded conference on suicide prevention (Weiss). The U.S. military's anti-gay stance is well known. Some persons argue that the ban on gays in the military has eliminated linguists from the armed forces, who as translators, would be valuable in the nation's "war on terror." Since the attacks of 9/11, at least 20 Arabic and six Farsi linguists have been discharged from the military because they are gay, at a time when the United States is desperately short of persons who speak those languages ("Military Has Discharged 26 Gay Linguists"). Government's refusal to pass laws that protect gay persons from harassment underwrites that harassment. A *New York Times* editorial states that "84% of gay, lesbian, bisexual, and transgender students, primarily in high school, are exposed to antigay comments from students or faculty over the course of a year." It also tells the story of Thomas McLaughlin, who when it became known he was gay, received a letter from a teacher telling him he would go to hell and whose family received a call from the school counselor. "A main reason," the *Times* contends, "that antigay discrimination continues in the schools—and on the job and in the streets—is that the law has not been emphatic enough about protecting gay Americans" ("The Rights of Gay Americans" A24).

Governmental and religious scaffolding of hate have become intertwined as U.S. leaders label the "War on Terror" a crusade, bringing to mind the medieval crusades of Christians against Muslims, and as persons like Lieutenant General William Boykin, the nation's top uniformed intelligence officer, contend that radical Muslims hate the United States because "we're a Christian nation." He adds that "the enemy is a guy named Satan" and presents the war in Iraq as a Christian mission (Thompson 30). Many Muslims citizens object to the U.S. description of its values as Judeo-Christian, and according to Mark O'Keefe in *Ann Arbor News*, declare "it's time for Americans to stop using the phrase" and to find an alternative such as Judeo-Christian-Islamic, a more inclusive term which recognizes the more than 7,000,000 Muslims in the United States (E1–E2). Religious leaders, like governmental and military leaders, prop up hate. Since 9/11 several well-known clergymen and leaders of large religious organizations, including the Christian Coalition and the Southern Baptist Convention—Jerry Falwell, Jerry Vines, Pat Robertson, and Franklin Graham, who delivered a prayer at George W. Bush's 2001 Presidential Inauguration—have asserted that "Muhammad was a 'terrorist'" (Zakaria 40), an "absolute, wild-eyed fanatic (Kristof A27), "a robber and a brigand"(Kristof, Zakaria) and "a demon possessed pedophile" (Kristof) and have declared Islam a "monumental scam" and a "very evil and wicked religion" (Zakaria). Additionally, Falwell blamed the 9/11 attacks on the United States in part on "the pagans and the abortionists, and the feminists, and the gays and the lesbians ... the ACLU, People for the American Way, all of them who have tried to secularize America." Pat Robertson concurred (Zakaria). In light of such commentary, Fareed Zakaria proposes that besides confronting extremism abroad, President Bush should do more to confront extremism at home.

Space prevents more exhibits, so our final one comes from mid-Michigan. There, in 1998, Rol Jersevic, campaigning for the Michigan legislature, tapped sympathizer and spectator hatred by depicting racial and social class stereotypes in a campaign leaflet he sent to westside Saginaw addresses. In the guise of a traffic ticket, the leaflet targeted "Willie Welfare," who drives a Cadillac on a suspended licence, whose license plate number is "tax cheat," who is on welfare, and whose address is located on the east side of the Saginaw River, the side of Saginaw predominately inhabited by African Americans. The charges on the ticket are drunk driving, reckless driving, and parking in handicap parking. The back of the flyer records Jersevic's previous experience as a state representative, as an assistant prosecutor in Saginaw County, and as a member of the Saginaw Township School Board. It is the role of teachers, when they receive pieces of campaign literature that contain either blatant or subtle hate messages, to bring them to the attention of their students, to discuss and expose the hate strategies involved, and to, we hope, undermine them.

FOR THOUGHT 4.6: Many people like to think of the United States as a classless society. Yet pejorative social class labels pepper too many persons' discourse, and social class commentary features in political campaigns. In a mainstream news magazine, we found a book reviewer who referred to one of a novel's characters as trailer-trash. Make a list of all the social class related labels you can think of. Why do you think so many negative social class labels exist? Are they examples of hate language? Why or why not? How does "offensive language" differ from "hate language"?

SLURS AND SYMBOLS

The most common forms of hate language teachers are likely to encounter in schools are slurs that target ethnic minorities, girls and women, and homosexuals. Words like *fag, faggot, bitch, whore, gay* (as in the pejorative "that's so gay"), *slut, dick, dyke, chief, nigger, squaw,* and *spic* are so commonly spoken that persons who use them sometimes fail to see the depths of hate they convey and the damage they do, especially when, as stated earlier in this chapter, so many of them appear so commonly in popular music's lyrics. At other times, slurs and symbols (swastikas, pictures of a burning cross, the burning cross itself, a noose) are used deliberately to demean, threaten, hurt, and/or to silence; for example, the case of students from an elite private school in New York City who chanted anti-semitic slurs at a rival basketball player while those who did not chant stood by and "giggled and snickered" (Gross). Regardless of their users' intent, an examination and investigation of derogatory slurs, their users, their targets, and their effects must be a part of all classrooms. Students should never be able to say honestly, as we have heard them say, "I was just kidding around; I don't mean anything by it."

In their "Some Theoretical Notions and Preliminary Research Concerning Derogatory Ethnic Labels," Jeff Greenberg, S.L. Kirkland, and Tom Pyszczynski state that "no utterance can convey hatred for an individual based on his or her membership in a group as quickly or vividly as a derogatory ethnic label." Despite the generally taught taboo on the use of such words and despite the fact that their use often leads to anger and violence, the authors note that derogatory ethnic labels (DELs) "occur with disturbing frequency in the United States in graffiti, books, television, and films" (74). To their list we add on the street, in school halls, on the Internet, in popular music, and on the playground or sports field. Native Americans, African Americans, Asian Americans, Latinos, and Jews have all been frequent targets of ethnic slurs as have, more recently, Muslims, and inhabitants of the Middle East, who have been labeled A-rabs, rag heads, diaper heads, and hajis.

Prior to recounting their research on the effects of DELs, the three authors delineate the motives of DEL's users and the effects of DEL use on both users and targets. We suggest that their comments often can be generalized to include those derogatory labels (DLs hereafter) that target women, the poor, the elderly, the physically or mentally handicapped, etc. What follows is a list-like summary of Greenberg, Kirkland, and Pyszczynski's work.

DELs and DLs

Encourage the categorization of people, which can provide an initial basis for hatred—the label directs and focuses the hatred.

Symbolize all the negative stereotypic beliefs associated with the target's group; a single word communicates all the negative beliefs about an out-group.

Allow the out-group to be referenced without acknowledgment of their national or cultural affiliation or heritage—they become subhuman creatures: chinks, frogs, wops, micks, kikes.

Why do people use DELs and DLs to target others?

To convey contempt, anger, fear, hostility as they dehumanize the target.

To provoke violence or hostility from the target to justify the speaker's negative attitudes.

To ridicule (in literature either the speaker or the target).

To portray prejudice accurately in literature.

To maintain or enhance the user's sense of self-worth and self-esteem.

To release tension—cathartic effect.

To encourage group solidarity.

To win approval and social acceptance from others.

To encourage listeners to experience heightened prejudice.

In addition, we find that DELs and DLs are sometimes used out of ignorance or in imitation of others.

Effects of DELs and DLs
Immediate effects on targets

Denies the target's existence as an individual.

Denigrates the target as sub-human.

Causes the target to feel rejection, dejection, anger, rage, helpless-ness, self-deprecation.

Insults the target's entire group.

Long-term use effects on targets

Implies a culturally sanctioned view of out-groups (present in music, literature, films, television).

Creates oppositional hostility toward and distrust of the in-group.

Promotes out-group members' acceptance of the negative views con-veyed by DELs and DLs.

Effects on in-group users of DELs and DLs

Boosts self-esteem.

Increases prejudice and promotes violence.

Provides cathartic effects when venting without the target present.

Creates anxiety and fear of retaliation (possibly) if the target is present.

Effects on in-group members who hear DELs and DLs used

Increases prejudice.

Prompts and encourages listeners to use DLs themselves.

Produces the effects on in-group users listed above vicariously.

Activates negative stereotypes.

Encourages negative behaviors toward targets.

Why do out-group members use DELs and DLs directed at themselves?

Indicates out-group acceptance of others' stereotypes and negativity.

Creates camaraderie and community—through victimization, one has earned the right to use these labels—a right not granted to major-ity in-group speakers.

Reduces the sting of such terms.

Provides for semantic inversion—a negative term acquires a positive meaning.

Changes the power structure between out-groups and in-groups; out-groups can engage in linguistic behavior forbidden to in-groups (74–86).

After giving this list to students, we ask them to apply it to pieces of literature such as Countee Cullen's "Incident," Ann Petry's "Like a Winding Sheet," or Gloria Naylor's "Nigger: The Meaning of a Word." Additionally we ask them to compare and contrast this list with the one generated through group compilation of the responses to for thought 4.1 which begins this chapter.

Because the list deals with both in-group and out-group use of DELs and DLs, it is particularly helpful in answering a question we find students often ask: "Why can't I call someone a_____, when I hear_____ call each other that all the time?" Members of groups have privileges not granted to members outside the group. This phenomenon is especially true of minority out-groups, whose members gain a sense of power and solidarity by denying majority in-groups the right to use terms to disparage them but who may use the terms themselves, their suffering at the hands of the in-group having given them the right to claim the word and infuse it with positive meaning. In a somewhat analogous manner, an in-group/out-group phenomenon can operate in families. Mary and her brothers sometimes called each other "stupid" as children; sometimes they used a derivative of the word—stupido, pronounced stupeedoe—affectionately. Should they have done so? Probably not, but they did. However, if a child outside the family called any in-family child "stupid," that child had the immediate defense of his or her siblings. Randall Kennedy in his *Nigger: The Strange Career of a Troublesome Word* reviews the DEL's pejorative use in a wide variety of situations and contexts. Then, he details many instances in which Black people, who largely regard the word as off-limits to whites, use *nigger* among themselves, including those in which Black comedians and Black rap artists such as Richard Pryor, 50 Cent, and Dave Chappelle make the word a part of their routines. Kennedy understands the arguments of the eradicationists who, since they see such use to encourage racist whites to speak the word, would eliminate the word from all entertainment, even when black people use the word themselves. Yet he argues that the word works for African Americans who wish to show defiance of racial subjugation or spur others to action. Use of the word claimed and revalued can "throw the slur right back in their oppressors' faces," can promote solidarity, and can "rope off cultural turf" (47–49). Speaking the word by African Americans ropes off linguistic turf, giving linguistic privilege to persons who have historically been linguistically disparaged and politically oppressed, and makes, if briefly, a former out-group an in-group.

However, as in any other language situation, social context, speaker intent as perceived by both the speaker and the listener, and delivery–including expression, intensity, volume, and tone of voice–determine what is and is not appropriate. Gloria Naylor's piece, previously referenced above and in chapter 3, lists several uses of *nigger*, some very positive, she'd heard as a child in her African American community and contrasts them with a white child's venomous use as he targeted her in school. Naylor adds that she disagrees with those who see Black persons' use of the word as internalized racism; rather, she argues that the close-knit network of friends and kin who used the word in her home setting had transformed the word "to signify the varied and complex human beings they knew themselves to be" (529). However, the use of DELs in most contexts may brand users as racist, ignorant, or self-hating, may provoke anger and violence, or may evoke conscious or unconscious racism in those who hear them. Ann Petry's "Like a Winding Sheet" clearly reveals that the word's use can have destructive effects, even if used among African Americans who love each other, when it arouses the suppressed rage felt at previously experienced racial hatred. Greenberg, Kirkland, and Pyszczynski's research found that "overheard DELs can encourage derogation of targets by listeners" (88), including listeners who insist they are not racially biased. They add that DELs not only "promote access to prejudiced attitudes and behaviors," they may do so "without the listener's conscious knowledge" (89). DEL's they conclude, "are verbal expressions of prejudice with psychological impact that can encourage negative behavior toward out-groupers" (90).

BULLYING

DELs and DLs, sexual slurs among them, play a major role in the hate language laced power dramas that occur daily in school when children become targets of verbal harassment and bullying. In fact, power determines who defines the terms *verbal harassment*, and *bullying* as something different from *teasing* and *flirting*. Rachel Simmons and James Garbarino and Ellen deLara observe that only in the past few years have bullying and harassment in schools become topics of serious consideration, much of it prompted by the recent wave of school shootings and threatened shootings, largely by persons who named themselves the targets of relentless "teasing" and name-calling. Too often both are still dismissed or ignored by teachers and principals. Even parents, who should be their children's primary advocates, have been unaware of the degree to which bullying occurs in schools, involving, according to National Institute of Child Health and Human Development (NICHD), almost one third of students: 10 % as bullies, 13% as targets, 6% as both. Because these figures do not include bullying by peers, and only address the frequency of that done by someone older than the target, the number of bullied children is likely much higher. The U.S. Department of Education states that "77% of middle and high school students in small midwestern towns have been bullied" (Garbarino and deLara 1). Often the victim of verbal harassment and bullying is blamed for the actions of the aggressors: s/he is a nerd, a hick, a greaser, a loser; s/he should just ignore it; s/he should "take it'" since "that's the way the real world is out there." Targets are many and varied: she or he may be unpopular; new to a school; smaller, more overweight or poorer than others; an immigrant; a person unable or unwilling to dress or wear his/her hair as others do; a person from an ethnic or religious minority; a person with a dialect or with a speech impediment; or a physically or mentally handicapped person. If female, due to power struggles and jealousies in groups of "friends," she may be the victim of other girls wanting to solidify their power base and unity, as they make one of the group the "odd girl out" by passing notes which disparage her, spreading false sexual gossip about her, or simply refusing to talk to her.

Words often escalate into violence as bullying plays itself out in halls and school grounds. Syndicated columnist Jane E. Brody cites the research of Dr. Tonja R. Nadel and her colleagues at NICHD, who found as they interviewed 15,686 6th-10th grade students that "children who bully are at risk for engaging in more serious violent acts." Of the boys surveyed who said they had bullied others frequently, 52.2% had carried weapons; 43.1% had carried them to school, and 38.7% said they fought frequently as compared to 13.4, 7.9, and 8.3% of the boys who said they had never bullied. Thirty percent of the girls who reported that they had bullied others carried weapons. Girls and boys who had bullied and who had been bullied themselves were 16 times as likely to carry weapons than those children who had not engaged in bullying as either bullies or targets (C7). Bullying has profound effects on its targets, who are sick more often than their peers, are absent from school more often, tend to receive lower grades, and often become depressed and withdrawn (Lemonick 144–145). Two consistent themes run throughout all researchers' accounts of bullying:

1. Teachers are ignorant, uncaring, or ineffectual in regard to harassment and bullying.
2. Principals are unaware of much of the bullying that occurs in their schools and/or are reluctant to take steps to stop it.

Thus teachers and administrators often take the role of spectator haters when bullying takes place on school grounds.

Derogatory sexual language plays a major role in bullying. Among the sexual slurs used to bully girls are *slut, cunt, whore,* and *bitch.* Boys as well as girls are denounced and harassed as *fags, faggots,* or *gays.* In a society rife with homophobic fear and hatred, even the words *homosexual* and *lesbian* become used as hate-filled sexual slurs. Ryan reports that a recent study conducted by the National Mental Health Association found that gay teasing and bullying is the most common kind of harassment in schools today: "Almost 80% of teens say they have witnessed classmates being teased with gay slurs." She adds that, ironically, another study reveals that three fourths of those "who are targets of anti-gay bullying are actually straight"; and she notes that, "among many teens, labeling someone gay is, on its face, a deep insult, perhaps the deepest" (A-6). In Danville, California, a gay student stated that he has heard sexual slurs so often that he has become immune to them, and he added that if he were to challenge bullies, they would say that their words don't offend people or that he is taking their words the wrong way (Stephens). He is not alone. A National School Climate survey found that "four out of five LGBT (lesbian, gay, bisexual, transgender) students reported being verbally harassed at school; 31 percent had skipped school at least one day out of the previous month out of fear for their personal safety; 21 percent had been physically assaulted with a weapon" (Stephens C8).

Girls also find their sexuality specifically targeted by bullies as they denounce even very young girls as *whores* and *sluts* and spread false rumors about girls' promiscuity. Simmons tells the story of Jenny. Confident, successful, and happy in her former San Diego school, dressing in styles different from those of the girls in her new, small town middle school, she found herself a victim of a group of girls whose status she apparently threatened, and who decided to make her life miserable. They covertly renamed her Harriet the Hairy Hore and started a Hate Harriet the Hairy Hore Incorporated club (HHHI). In the halls, they would greet her with an exaggerated and drawn out breathy hhhiii (HHHI) then laugh. Their sexual verbal violence turned physical, and they began to body slam Jenny in the halls. They passed a petition to the other girls in seventh grade which said "I promise to hate Harriet the Whore forever," which all the girls, likely afraid of the wrath and ostracism of the instigators, signed and listed reasons why they "hated" Harriet. Finally, Jenny went to the principal with the petition, and the actions of HHHI ceased, though its instigators continued to glare at her. Throughout her ordeal, no teachers noticed or intervened (*Odd Girl Out* 25–30). Jenny recovered and eventually became captain of the softball team and pep club president. Yet one can not help but wonder, how many girls and boys, taunted aggressively and slurred sexually are not so lucky as Jenny.

We should not be surprised that teachers did not notice or intervene in Jenny's bullying. Until the late 1990s, girl-on-girl bullying was seldom recognized as a frequent and serious phenomenon, even though girls were routinely humiliated and ostracized. Mothers watched the harassment or exclusion of their daughters, and authors Judy Blume (*Blubber*) and Margaret Atwood (*Cat's Eye*) wrote about it. The 1963 *Webster's Seventh New Collegiate Dictionary* defines "bully" as a male: "a blustering, browbeating fellow … one habitually cruel to others weaker than himself" (110–111). While researchers recently have come to document girl- on-girl bullying, they agree that because boy-on-boy bullying relies on overt, public, in-your-face, and direct verbal put-downs and harassment, which may escalate into public violence on the part of the bully or the target, it is often easier to see than the bullying typical of girls, which occurs by way of a number of less readily observable discourse modes and patterns. At a recent National Council of Teachers of English Conference, Harmon listed several of these predictable discourse modes. The * following an item on her list designates a discourse mode often used in *relational aggression*, defined below.

- Name-calling, laughter, mockery, teasing, sometimes with sexual slurs and accusations.
- In-group talking negatively behind the target's back, perhaps visibly so that the target knows she is being talked about.*
- Silence—the cold shoulder in the halls or at the lunch table.*
- Exclusion—not including the target in group activities—parties, sleep-overs, and making sure the target knows she's not included.*
- Notes—sometimes anonymous, sometimes delivered publically so that the bullies can see the hurt caused by the note.
- E-mails and instant messaging—no need to face the target, so often are more savage than public teasing and name-calling.
- Phone calls—sometimes anonymous, sometimes with laughter in the background.
- Gossip and lies to create mass exclusion.*
- On in private/off in public—friends in private one-on-one situations; bully and bullied in public.*
- Denial that anything is wrong or refusal to tell the target why she is being targeted—what she has "done wrong."*
- Secrets—telling secrets, but excluding the target from them; and secrecy—the target keeping the bullying secret for fear it will get worse or because she has come to think it is her role to be bullied.*
- Threats not to be friends or bribes to get the target to act in particular ways if she desires friendship.*

FOR THOUGHT 4.7: Not all teasing is bullying. To be pushed once or to be called a name once or twice, although unpleasant and offensive, probably is not as well. How do you differentiate between verbal bullying and teasing? How do intent, intensity, repetition, and duration affect your definition? Have you ever bullied? What forms did the bullying take? How did your target respond? Have you ever been bullied? What forms did the bullying take? How did you respond? What roles did language and discourse practices play in the events you recount?

Mary saw several of the above discourse modes enacted when a seventh grade group of girls decided to exclude her daughter, Amy, from the lunch table and from their group. Her exclusion was announced by one of the girls passing out invitations to her overnight birthday party at the lunch table and very publically not giving one to Amy. The following Monday and Tuesday, no one spoke to Amy at the lunch table. By Wednesday, Amy's "friend" Halley (name changed), a girl whom Amy had convinced the group not to exclude only two weeks before, told her that the group did not want Amy sitting with them at lunch or hanging out with them any more. Amy had a miserable semester, feeling isolated and staying in the library to read instead of going to lunch because she could not face seeing her former friends together, many of whom she had "partied" with and shared fun with for several years. None of her teachers noticed; all of the girls involved were good students and "good" citizens of their middle school. Although she spent a painful several months, Amy survived. She gradually made new friends, all of them older than the girls who had bullied her, and she became active in band, forensics, and drama. Nonetheless, she never trusted the girls involved again and has had no desire to go to her class reunions. The experience still is a bitter memory to her, 18 years later.

All that occurred in 1987. Had it happened more recently a number of resources might have sensitized Amy's teachers and might have helped her mother help her. Rosalind Wiseman's *Queen Bees and Wannabes: Helping Your Daughter Survive Cliques, Gossip, Boyfriends, & Other Realities of Adolescence*, defines the roles played in girls' cliques and provides parents with ways to help their daughters in the face of exclusion and bullying. Rachel Simmons' *Odd Girl Out: The Hidden Culture of Aggression in Girls* includes valuable discussion of the reality of girl-on-girl aggression, theories as to its causes, and suggestions for confronting and dealing with it; her more recent *Odd Girl Speaks Out* offers stories from targets and bullies that could prompt classroom discussion of bullying. James Garbarino and Ellen deLara's excellent *And Words Can Hurt Forever* details issues of the power involved in and the potential damage that results from verbal and sexual harassment and bullying, whether the aggressors and targets are male or female. Garbarino and deLara end each chapter with a list of suggestions titled "What can you do?" which may be helpful to teachers, parents, and administrators. Cheryle Dellasega and Charisse Nixon's *Girl Wars: Twelve Strategies That Will End Female Bullying* defines *relational aggression*, that is, female bullying in which girl–girl relationships are used as a means to hurt or dominate others, and details 12 strategies to prevent or combat it. C.J. Bott's *The Bully in the Book and in the Classroom*, after chapters which discuss boy and girl bullying techniques and suggestions for what can be done about bullying, reviews 44 trade books whose audiences range from kindergarten to 12th grade readers and offers "Activities/Topics for Discussion" and "Quotes for Reader Response" for each book reviewed. In addition, she annotates hundreds more books which open classroom discussion of both male and female bullying. A goldmine for parents and teachers, Bott's book concludes by listing books and Web sites for further research. Two films, *Mean Girls* and *Odd Girl Out*, could be useful conversation starters about bullying in middle school classrooms and high school classrooms. The first is currently available on DVD; the second will be soon.

So far in these discussions of DELs, DLs, and bullies, we have referred to targets and users or aggressors, that is, users of derogatory labels, bullies, and their victims. In doing so, we have left out a small group of people, those who defend the target, and, unfortunately, a much larger group—those referred to earlier in this chapter as spectators and sympathizers—both of whom make up the category Bott refers to as witnesses. As teachers, though we may strive to do so, we may never convert all bullies, haters, and their sympathizers to compassionate behavior, but we must strive to assist targets to defend themselves and, thus, take some of the sting out of the hater's and the bully's words and actions. And we must strive to move the spectator from the position of fear, toleration, or silence to one of action, defense, and support for the rights of and respectful treatment of all. As C.J. Bott states, in each bullying situation, "There are many more witnesses of bullying and harassment than there are bullies and targets" (5). And there are far more spectators than there are haters. As teachers, we must have the courage to move from the spectator role, ourselves—if that has been the role we have played—and we must, through example and active teaching let haters know that hate will not be tolerated in our schools and inspire our student witnesses to move into the role of defender. At the very least, we can insure that haters, bullies, and users of DLs will never be able to say, "I was just fooling: I didn't mean anything by it." And teachers can insure that spectators and witnesses understand that by sitting by quietly, by failing to act to defend the target or quiet the hate, they tacitly give approval to the words and acts of bullies and haters. In short, by not acting they must share responsibility for the effects and the consequences of those words and actions.

FOR THOUGHT 4.8: Have you ever occupied the witness role as someone was bullied? Looking back, what might you have done to intervene or to support the person being bullied? Sometimes the legitimate fear of physical harm may prevent witnesses from intervening. In such cases what can they do?

APPLICATIONS FOR THE CLASSROOM

What Teachers Can Do

Fortunately teachers do not have to operate in a vacuum. All of the resources discussed above provide teachers with methods of responding to and countering hate language and bullying. In addition, most list additional resources, including Web sites, and some offer teaching activities. We are indebted to C.J. Bott and James Garbarino and Ellen deLara for their references to many of these helpful Web sites:

> www.glsen.org
> www.stopbullyingnow.hrsa.gov
> www.aauw.org
> www.aclu-sc.org/school.html
> www.opheliaproject.org/

We will add five more to the list.

1. Tolerance.org: Teaching Tolerance (www.tolerance.org), a user-friendly web project of the Southern Poverty Law Center, gives much valuable specific advice to teachers and administrators on how to "fight hate and promote tolerance" when faced with hate speech, hate symbols, hate literature, music, e-mail, and/or Web sites; hate graffiti; colleagues' bigotry; and hate incidents at school or in the wider community. It provides maps that show viewers where hate-groups are located in each state. One of its links, Deconstruct Biased Language, features 50 downloadable activities that teachers can use in their classrooms.

2. The Media Awareness Network (www.media-awareness.ca/english/issues/online_hate/tactic) provides viewers information on "what is hate?, online hate and free speech, online hate and the law, deconstructing hate sites, haters' tactics for recruiting young people … and responding to online hate."

3. Stop the Hate at http://stop-the-hate.org/ offers easy access to information about hate groups and a wealth of sites that offer assistance and lesson plans.

4. The Prejudice Institute, www.prejudiceinstitute.org, presents information on current issues, institutes, speakers, and fact sheets, among them an "Action Sheet: What Teenagers Can Do About Prejudice."

5. The Anti-Defamation League Web site, www.adl.org, contains up-to-date information on the activities of hate-groups, hate crimes, and hate crime laws; news articles and press releases; background information on free speech, civil rights, and extremism; and a section on combating hate.

In light of the ideas, resources, and activities presented in this chapter, teachers can take a number of actions:

1. Serve as a role model for acceptance and tolerance. Teachers must never laugh at name-calling or hate language or at a bullied or

teased student. Nor can they afford to sit silently as any of these occur, without appearing to condone and agree with it. C.J. Bott promotes a formula she found on the GLSEN web site (Gay, Lesbian, Straight Education Network—see above for web address): Name It, Claim It, Stop It. For example if a teacher were to hear a student in the hall denounce another as a "fuckin' faggot," she should approach the student confidently and say something like : "I heard you call him a 'fuckin faggot' (name it). I find that kind of language to be disrespectful and inappropriate (claim it). That kind of language may not be used on school grounds (stop it)" (11). Bott attests from her own personal experience of using the strategy over the years that it usually works to defuse situations and demonstrates that she will not stand passively by as students defame each other. Tolerance.org agrees and states "denounce hate speech immediately" and consistently with something like, "That word hurts people, so you may not use it in this classroom" or "Disrespectful words are never acceptable at this school."

2. Make it clear that hate language, slurs, and bullying are not allowed in your classroom. Many teachers, after discussion of these topics with their students, collaboratively establish classroom ground rules. These rules must include consequences for violators, and the consequences must be enforced.

3. If a policy on harassment and hate speech does not exist in your school, formulate one collaboratively that sets clear prohibitions on and consequences for hate speech and harassment. Bott suggests that anger management classes, empathy training, community service, communications skills training, and/or appropriate counseling be among the consequences. The policy should be placed in the student handbook and brought to the attention of students and their parents. It should include a means for reporting and investigating incidents of bullying and verbal and sexual harassment. Bott adds that persons of both genders—and not just administrators, as the thought of going to the administrator may be intimidating many students—should receive reports (13).

4. Hold ongoing discussions of language issues, including hate language and the language of bullying. Ask students to share which words they find most hate-filled and to tell why they do; students who claim that these words "don't mean anything" will not have much of an argument in the light of such student commentary. Discuss the meanings of DLs as well as their effects on targets and users. Take a stand against hate lyrics that use DELs and DLs or promote violence.

5. Educate yourself on the reality and effects of hate language and bullying. The resources above are an excellent start.

6. As hate events—language, symbols, acts—and bullying occur locally, re-gionally and nationally, discuss them with your students—bring in and ask them to find and bring in news accounts of these for class discussion. Share the summary list above of the effects of and motives for use of DELs and DLs with your students. Ask them to write about their own use of DELs and DLs and/or about being the target of derogatory labels.

7. Use literature—trade books, poems, plays, and short stories—as a means to discuss hate language and bullying. Don't overlook car-toons, if your local or regional newspaper carries a regular comics page. In December 2004, the comic strip "For Better or For Worse" ran a several-day series of frames on hate language and behavior di-rected toward a special education student.

8. Post reminders about respectful speech around the school; ask your students to create such posters.

9. Discourage the use of caricatures, especially Native American mas-cots. Insist that hate symbols—swastikas—for example, be removed from school grounds.

10. Report hate graffiti to the police or to the appropriate authorities if it occurs at school.

11. Educate your students about bullying, relational aggression, and the implications of the spectator/witness role. Foster role-playing to teach empathy for targets. Role play ways spectators can actively defend tar-gets: they can stand physically by a victim, challenge an aggressor, or ask an adult to intervene. Spectators, now defenders, can show empa-thy for the target by walking to class with him/her, sitting by her/him at lunch, sitting next to her/him in class (Dellasega and Nixon 83). Help targets of bullying and hate practice and role play responses to teasing and name calling, remembering that ignoring a bully and walking away is also a response, sometimes a powerful one.

12. Listen to and support targets of hate language and/or bullying. Urge them to report it and accompany them to do so. Encourage them to expand their circle of friends with whom they may share their special skills and talents. Praise acts of kindness.

13. Remember that teachers and coaches can be bullies, too. Try to elimi-nate bully behavior and/or hate language use (words, jokes, symbols, stereotypes, etc.) among your colleagues. Do not sit silently by as hate language occurs; rather, say something like "I don't like to talk that way." "I don't like to listen to that kind of talk," or "I guess I just don't find that funny"—or leave and say something later in private to the speaker.

This list is just a start; enacting it will not suddenly eliminate hate lan-guage and bullying, but enacting its items gradually, if not all at once, can cut down on these negative and damaging behaviors. And enacting these will make it clear to our students that we can, with integrity, act as role models of respect for others. Only then can we expect our students to follow our lead.

In this chapter we have addressed the power-fraught nature of hate language and its widespread use in bullying, demeaning, humiliating, and silencing its targets, or in enraging them and inciting them to violence. Bolstered by the media, the government, the Internet, religion, and, sometimes schools, hate language permeates schools even among children as young as preschool. Language is never neutral: language can create, reinforce, and reinscribe patterns of thought. When terms of derision and hate become entwined in our language, they become entwined in our thought and in our construction of both reality and ourselves. In the following chapter, we will address another issue related to the power of words, buttressed by a number of social institutions and discourse practices. Like the issue of hate language, it has major implications for our students and our classrooms: the issue of language and gender.

PERSONAL EXPLORATIONS

1. Visit the Web sites listed above. What do you find on each that can help you or others educate themselves about hate language and bullying?

2. Read *The Girls* (a quick and interesting read, which demonstrates relational aggression) by Diana McLellen. Which of the discourse modes listed above on p. 87 do you find at work in the novel?

3. Check to see if your university and your local schools have policies on hate speech and harassment. Are they adequate? Who do they protect? Do they include consequences? What sorts of consequences for harassment and bullying have been applied recently? Have any of Bott's suggested consequences been applied? Do the policies include a procedure to follow to report hate language and harassment? How easy is it to follow? To whom are instances of hate language, harassment, and/or bullying reported?

4. Check to see what your local school system has done to sensitize teachers to the problems of hate language and bullying. In your local schools, do you find an ongoing, systemwide effort to confront bullying and hate language? What can you find in the books and Web sites listed above that might be of benefit to teachers and administrators in your local schools? Bott strongly makes the point that unless administrators are committed to an ongoing effort to eliminate, or at least reduce, bullying in their schools, little will be accomplished by bringing in experts on bullying for teacher in-services or student assemblies.

TEACHING EXPLORATIONS

1. Using the ideas from this chapter, your own ideas, and the material and suggestions found on the Web sites above, develop outlines for a series of five interactive lessons on hate language. Find pieces of literature that you can use a focus for at least three of them.

2. What examples of hate lyrics can you add those we have included? Who is targeted in each of your examples? How can you use hate lyrics in your classroom to teach about hate? Are there lyrics to mainstream hate pieces you would not take into the classroom? Which ones? Why?

3. In January 2005 England's Prince Harry created controversy by wearing a Nazi uniform, complete with a swastika arm band, to a costume party. Given all England and the world had suffered at the hands of Nazis during World War II, the English public was outraged. What are possible explanations for his actions? What, if anything, should he have done once public outrage became evident? How would you respond if someone you know wore such a costume or KKK garb to a costume party you attended? If a student came to class or to a school event wearing hate symbols? How might you incorporate this episode or others like it into your classroom to discuss hate language and symbols?

4. Even though the book was written for a younger audience, Mary found her middle school students touched by Patricia Polacco's *Thank you, Mr. Falkner* as they saw a young girl bullied and verbally abused because she had difficulty reading. Following a look at the book, they became willing to share their own stories of hate language and verbal harassment. Find at least four examples, then collaboratively compile a class list of stories, poems, children's picture books, adolescent literature, and adult literature that might be used to open discussion on hate language and verbal harassment in classrooms.

5. An Associated Press article reports on "No Name Calling Week," a national project of the Gay, Lesbian & Straight Education Network. The project, geared to middle school students, although it takes aim at all sorts of labels and derogatory language, has drawn fire from some groups who say it overemphasizes the harassment of gay youth. The project has the endorsement of the National Education Association, the Girl Scouts, Amnesty International, and the national associations of elementary and secondary principals. As a part of the project, students read *The Misfits*, a novel by James Howe that presents a run for the student senate by four often taunted middle schoolers, one of whom is gay (Crary). Read *The Misfits*; then visit www.nonamecallingweek.org. Would you urge a school in which you teach to participate in the project? Why? Why not? If you would, how might you keep the lessons and ideas behind such a project ongoing, rather than for

just one week? If not, what sort of "no name-calling week" might you institute and promote? How would you keep the ideas and lessons in your project alive on an ongoing basis?

WORKS CITED

Bott, C. J. *The Bully in the Book and in the Classroom*. Lanham, MD: Scarecrow, 2004.

Brody, Jane. "A Bully's Future, From Hard Life to Hard Time." *New York Times* 13 Jan. 2004: C7.

"Bully." *Webster's Seventh New Collegiate Dictionary*. Springfield, MA: Merriam,1963.

Childress, Sarah and Dirk Johnson. "The Hot Sound of Hate. *Newsweek* 28 Nov. 2004: 7.

Crary, David. "'No Name-Calling Week' begins in schools." AP. 24 Jan. 2005. <www.boston.com/news/education/k_12/articles/2005/01/24/no_namecalling_week>

"Cross burnings." *U.S. News and World Report* 21 Apr. 2003: 48–49.

Dellasega, Cheryle and Charisse Nixon. *Girl Wars: Twelve Strategies That Will End Female Bullying*. New York: Simon, 2003.

Fineman, Howard. "Having a Gay Old Time." *Newsweek* 5 May 2003: 47.

Garbarino, James and Ellen deLara. *And Words Can Hurt Forever*. New York: Free Press, 2003.

Gates, Anita. "Hatred and Love for Somali Neighbors." *New York Times* 9 Feb. 2005: B5.

Gershman, Dave and Patty Maher. "Klan robe sold amid protests." *Ann Arbor News* 30 Jan. 2005: A1+.

Greenberg, Jeff, S.L. Kirkland, and Tom Pyszczynsky. "Some Theoretical Notions and Preliminary Research Concerning Derogatory Ethnic Labels." *Discrimination and Discourse*. Eds. Geneva Smitherman-Donaldson and Teun A. Van Dijk. Detroit: Wayne SU, 1988: 74–92.

Gross, Jane. "Fans' Anti-Semitic Slurs Incite a Flurry of Reaction at Schools." *New York Times*. <www.nytimes.com/2004/02/07/nyregion/07bias.html>.

Grotelueschen, Bethany. "Team Mascots." *Bay City Times* 26 Aug. 2003: 5A. [Bay City, MI]

Harmon, Mary Rose. "Discourse Patterns in Girl-on-Girl Bullying." Unpublished paper presented at the National Council of Teachers of English. Indianapolis, Indiana. 20 November 2004.

Herbert, Bob. "Gooks to Hajis." *New York Times*. <www.nytimes.com/2004/05/21/opinion/21HERB.html>.

Indigenous Language Institute. "He just used the proper Apache word for 'hello.' Should we wash his mouth out with soap?" *Men's Health* Dec. 2002: 45.

Judson, Janis L. and Donna M. Bertazzoni. *Law, Media, and Culture: The Landscape of Hate*. New York: Lang, 2002.

Kark, James. "The Racist Next Door." *Bay City Times* 1 June 2003: 1A+.

Kennedy, Randall. *Nigger: The Strange Career of a Troublesome Word*. New York: Pantheon, 2002.

Kristof, Nicholas. "Giving God a Break." *New York Times* 10 June 2003: A27.

Lemonick, Michael D. "The Bully Blight." *Time* 18 Apr. 2005: 144–145.

"Military Has Discharged 26 Gay Linguists." AP. 31 Jan. 2005: <www.foxnews.com/story/0,2933,144375,00.html>.

Moody, Nekesa Mumbi. "Gays outraged over John-Eminem duet." *Saginaw News*. 19 Feb. 2001, A8.

National Alliance. "Love Your Race." Leaflet. Feb. 2004.

"National Vanguard: Our Cause Reborn." <www.nationalvanguard.org/story.php?id =4977>.

"North Carolina: Cross Burning in Durham." *New York Times* 27 May 2005: A15.

O' Keefe, Mark. "Judeo-Christian-Islamic." *Ann Arbor News* 26 May 2003: E1–E2.

Page, Clarence. "How to clean up rap's bad boy culture." *Detroit News*. 19 Jan. 2005: 11A.

_____. "Shaq vs. YAO: New World Diss-order." *Saginaw News* 29 Jan. 2003: A5.

"Panzerfaust Apparently Out of Business." 1 Mar. 2005: <www.adl.org/extremism/panzerfuast–update.asp>.

Petry, Ann. "Like a Winding Sheet." *The Norton Anthology of African American Literature*. Eds. Henry Louis Gates, Jr. and Nellie Y. McKay. New York: Norton, 1997: 1178–1184.

Raspberry, William. "Trent Lott Not Alone in Actions." *Saginaw News* 25 Dec. 2002: A7.

Rivlin, Gary. "Hate Messages on Google Site Draw Concern." *New York Times*. 7 Feb. 2005: <www.nytimes.com>.

Rook, Christine. "No Offense, But Some Words Do Offend Others." *Lansing State Journal* [Michigan]. 11 June 2004: 1D+.

Ryan, Joan. "Bullies Mirror Our Own Fears." *Saginaw News*. 25 Dec. 2002: A6.

Sanneh, Kelefa. "Dancehall's Vicious Side: Antigay Attitudes." *New York Times*. 6 Sep. 2004: B1+.

Simmons, Rachel. *Odd Girl Out: The Hidden Culture of Aggression in Girls*. New York: Harcourt, 2002.

_____. *Odd Girl Speaks Out: Girls Write About Bullies, Cliques, Popularity, and Jealousy*. New York: Harcourt, 2004.

Stephens, Sara. "Words Wound." *Saginaw News*. 23 Apr. 2003: C8.

"The Rights of Gay Americans." *New York Times*. Editorial. 27 Mar. 2003: A24.

The Media Awareness Network. <www.media-awareness.ca/english/issues/online_hate/tactic>.

Thompson, Mark. "A Long Career of Marching With the Cross." *Time* 3 Nov. 2003: 30.

Tolerance.org: Teaching Tolerance. <www.tolerance.org>.

Watterson, Bill. "Calvin and Hobbes." Cartoon. Universal Press Syndicate. 13 Nov. 1993.

Weiss, Rick. "Agency stirs ire by obfuscating title of talk on gays." *Washington Post* rpt. *Saginaw News* 16 Feb. 2005: B2.

Wikipedia. "David Allan Coe." <http://en.wikipedia.org/wiki/David_Allan_Coe>.

Wiseman, Rosalind. *Queen Bees and Wannabes: Helping Your Daughter Survive Cliques, Gossip, Boyfriends, & Other Realities of Adolescence*. New York: Crown, 2002.

Zakaria, Fareed. "Time to Take On America's Haters." *Newsweek* 21 Oct. 2002: 40.

Chapter 5

Language and Gender:
The Cart Before the Horse?

Before you read this chapter, take the following True/False quiz. Save your answers; you will be referring to them as you finish reading this chapter.

1. Women tend to choose language constructions and patterns closer to Standard English more often than men do.
2. Women talk more than men.
3. In English, there are more derogatory terms for men than for women.
4. When a woman and a man make exactly the same speech, listeners tend to evaluate both speakers about equally and to listen equally closely to both.
5. Parents tend to interrupt their daughters more often than their sons.
6. Women tend to speak more indirectly than men when making requests or giving commands.
7. In mixed gender conversations, women interrupt conversations in ways that alter the course of the conversations more often than men.
8. When people hear or read "he," "mankind'" and "man" used generically, they regard those terms as inclusive of both men and women.
9. In classrooms, teachers call on and praise girls more frequently than boys.
10. The textual selections read, studied, and discussed in most U.S. classrooms reflect gender balance, gender-fairness and gender equity.

CARTOON 5.1   DOONESBURY © 1992 G.B. Trudeau. Reprinted with permission of UNIVERSAL PRESS SYNDICATE. All rights reserved.

The situation pictured in the above cartoon strikes us as far from funny, and as research demonstrates (Sadker and Sadker; Romaine 1994, 1999; Spender; Coates) occurs too frequently in classrooms that reflect and reinforce the gender inequities of the larger culture, many of which are reinscribed and maintained by language choices and discourse practices in classrooms. In previous chapters, we have discussed the power of words as weapons, and we have argued that the thrust of words' power comes primarily from users who have the social, political, and economic means to create and enforce categorizations and definitions. In doing so, they gain cultural capital and power over others. Power also derives, in part, from persons' non-interrogated use of and/or acquiescence to the categories and definitions others have determined as well as to the hierarchal attitudes these convey.

Notions of superiority and inferiority embedded in the lexicon of gender, particularly in the terms *sex* and *sexist*, are not recent phenomena. In *Keywords* (1983), Raymond Williams states that 17th century writers used the terms the "gentle sex," "weaker sex," and "fairer sex" to describe women. By the early 19th century, "the second sex" was a commonly used reference (283). Dennis Baron (*Grammar*) adds that as early as 1781, an influential English grammar boldly stated that the Supreme Being is masculine in all languages because the masculine sex is the superior and the more excellent (*Grammar* 3). *Sexist*, as a counterpart to *racist*, gained currency in the 1960s as critical of discriminatory attitudes toward women (Williams 283). In recent years, because, historically, it has not been associated with notions of hierarchy, the more inclusive term *gender* has replaced *sex* in most theoretical and pedagogical discussions of women's and men's differing language practices in an attempt "to describe socially constructed categories based on sex," that is, to make cultural rather than biological distinctions (Coates 3). We follow this practice. In addition we refer to what is sometimes called *sexist language*, "language that denigrates or is believed to denigrate" (Coates 3) women or men, as *gendered language*, and we contend that such language not only denigrates, it plays an important role in the cultural constructions of what it means to be female and male. Another contested phrase we use is *gender equity*. But, we wish to make it clear that in using this phrase we do not imply that women should aspire to or adopt so-called male standards of success based on competition and aggression or male modes of communication and language use, thus marking deviations from them as substandard and deficient. Rather, we use the phrase to envision a world where the attributes and contributions of all, regardless of gender, are honored and valued and where language choices and discourse practices open rather than close possibilities for all. Finally in our discussions of gender and language, we realize that the term *gender* does not neatly divide into two categories, male and female, each delineated by dichotomous characteristics and language use patterns. Like Coates and so many others, we see gender on a continuum and recognize that language use and communication style differences within the categories "male" and "female" often surpass those between females and males.

However, we argue that language differences between genders serve to maintain their inequitable power. In what follows, we will investigate the differing ways in which males and females tend to use language and the differing ways they often find their language use and communication styles to be received by listeners. After acknowledging the *resistance to language and gender issues* we often find in our classes and suggesting ways of *countering resistance*, we will extend our discussion by focusing on:

1. *Words*. The English vocabulary abounds with words and labels that reinforce and perpetuate gender stereotypes, demean one or both genders, and work to assure that women's and men's power will be regarded differently, with women too often seen as subordinate to men. Investigating gendered words can promote changes that, in part, can lead to greater gender equity.

2. *Syntax and discourse practices*. Achieving the gender-fair language use essential to gender-equitable classrooms and to a gender-equitable culture at large requires more than careful word choice. Doing so also necessitates examination and alteration of gender-laden English *syntax* and *discourse practices*.

3. *Media*. A review of media as culturally constructed artifacts that embed gender- biased messages extends and deepens our discussion, as we assert that such artifacts too often depict, reinforce, sustain, and promote gender inequity.

4. *Classroom media and practices*. Careful observation of classroom media and classroom practices reveals that many communicate culturally embedded gender inequity, sometimes subtly, sometimes blatantly.

Gender inequity being so deeply ingrained in contemporary U.S. culture, any examination of language and its role in perpetuating gender inequity must move beyond the words and semantic level to examine the syntactic, discourse, and cultural levels and apply each to classroom practice. It is our hope that such examination will lead to more equitable language practices and media choices on the part of teachers, who will, in turn, actively incorporate such investigation in their own classrooms to help their students understand, resist, and counter gender inequity.

RESISTANCE TO LANGUAGE AND GENDER STUDY

Before we examine the gender-laden nature of English and its effects, we need to alert teachers that gender study is often accompanied by strong resistance by some of the women and men in classrooms and by some teachers and professors in schools and universities. At Mary's university, the construction of a minor in Gender Studies was met by strenuous opposition from about one third of the faculty who stated that such a program catered to special interests and did not demand academic rigor. In our Introduction to Language and Language and Education courses, we often encounter resistance to gender and language issues, as evidenced in both written responses and early class discussions, despite students' previous acknowledgment of words' power to undermine self-worth and reinforce racist and classist power structures. The resistance that occurs often takes the form of outright denial that issues exist or of dismissal of those issues' importance. Resistant students may minimize the gender and language issues under discussion or state they are relevant only to previous times: "That was in your generation; men and women are equal now and have equal opportunities" or "It doesn't bother me; I hear it but it just doesn't affect me" or "Yeah, so what's the big deal?" A few students—both women and men—dismiss gender issues as only the concerns of angry feminists, using *feminist* much as one might use another well-known "F-word." During a recent discussion of the National Council of Teachers of English *Guidelines for Gender-Fair Use of Language* (Prosenjak, Harmon, Johnson, et al), several students stated that the document was unnecessary and added that "those women (the document's authors) need to get a life." Students, most often women, sometimes state they feel sorry for men now that so many women are feminists; they add that women should stop whining about inequity and just get busy. For many, the word *feminist* has become so marked, that in class discussions, women often preface their remarks by stating, "I am not a feminist, but..." or "I don't want to be called a feminist, but ...."

COUNTERING RESISTANCE

How to proceed in the face of such resistance? First, we must remember that even though the resisters often include a very vocal minority, many students are willing to be open-minded as the study of gender and language begins. Knowing that, we must ensure that these open-minded students take active roles in class projects and discussions and that they speak with and work with students who, at least at first, may not think as they do. Both Mary and Marilyn find that as students work with and relate to other students, resistance lessens—and so does potential tension; no longer does the teacher appear to be the sole advocate of a particular stance. We have found a number of strategies effective in encouraging these student-to-student conversations. What follows will detail six of them: Direct classroom discussion of resistance and its roots; student-written responses to classroom reading; analysis of recorded conversations; the use of media resources; student research projects; defining and claiming *feminist/feminism*.

    1. Direct Discussion of Resistance and Its Roots. Judith Anderson and Stephen Grubman provide background for this discussion. They list reasons for hostile reactions to gender study, including fear of change, shame, loyalty to loved ones and friends who make gender-biased language choices and who demonstrate gender-biased attitudes, ignorance, and personal prejudice. They add that heightened confidence, security, and self-sufficiency will increase resistant students' willingness to self-disclose and self-examine, and thus, likely lessen resistance. Teachers can foster this growth and counter resistance as gender is discussed in their classrooms by engaging in all or several of the practices suggested below.

    a. Modeling gender-fair language and discourse practices. Teachers must model and instruct students in the sorts of communication practices that lead to the open-minded discussion of issues: eye contact, genuine and active listening, and the avoidance of interruptions and defensive retorts (230). In addition, teachers must be sure to always use gender-fair language themselves and to encourage such language both in and out of classrooms. Too often teachers and coaches tell gender-laden jokes, refer to women as *girls* or *chicks*, or make stereotyping and gender-disparaging remarks like "What's the matter with you? Are you all a bunch of women?" (shouted at the male football team) or "Isn't that just like a man (or girl, boy, or woman)." A 4th-grade math teacher we have observed, as he hands back assignments or tests, often states "You let a *girl* beat you?" to the boys when girls receive higher scores than boys.

    b. Facilitating discussion so that the teacher does not dominate the conversation and so that both teachers and students listen critically and differentiate between facts and opinions. Teachers must strive to be open to and to encourage commentary on all sides of issues. To shut someone down will only create an adamant resister.

    c. Noting, questioning, probing, and challenging gender-biased assertions and assumptions both in and out of classrooms and encouraging students to do so.

    d. Carefully structuring classrooms in which neither males nor females dominate classroom discourse and in which students work together collaboratively and talk to one another about language, gender, and power issues.

Obviously, if they are to be used successfully, these practices must be in play throughout the term or year; they can not suddenly spring into life only when gender issues are under consideration.

    2.   Written student responses to research-based but accessible readings which raise issues and foster discussion. Widely anthologized essays we find particularly successful include:

Eugene R. August	"Real Men Don't: Anti-male Bias in English"
Karen De Witt	"Stand by Your Man 'Mrs.' Makes a Comeback"
Bernard R. Goldberg	"Television Insults Men Too"
Casey Miller and Kate Swift	"One Small Step for Genkind" and "Women and Names"
Alleen Pace Nilsen	"Sexism and Language: A 1990's Update" and "Sexism in English: Embodiment and Language"
Anna Quindlen	"The Name is Mine"
Deborah Tannen	"'Put Down That Newspaper and Talk to Me!' Rapport-Talk and Report Talk" and "'I'll Explain it to You': Listening and Lecturing"

We follow these with The National Council of Teachers of English *Guidelines for Gender-Fair Use of Language.* As students read, we ask them to write responses which react to, apply, and reflect on the readings and to share their responses in small groups. Often, they write personal stories of related incidents in their own lives. We find some students—both male and female—who are generally unsympathetic to gender and language issues as they affect women to respond more sympathetically to essays that consider men's gender issues. We ask them to think about why their resistance seems lower to these male-centered essays than to the others. When students state that a woman's changing her name in marriage promotes family unity, we ask them questions like, "If that's true, why doesn't the man just as readily adopt the woman's surname in marriage as the family's name?" More often than not, we do not need to pose these questions ourselves; students in the class take the lead. What follows are excerpts from recent student responses which, when shared, provoked much student commentary in Mary's Language and Education class. Shared stories like these with ample time for student commentary may do more than anything else we do in class to counter resistance.

a. I have a friend who kept her last name after she was married. This was a big issue for her husband; he felt inferior as a man; his entire family referred to him as "the little woman .... She was seen as a selfish feminist for not honoring her husband's name.
[From a student who early on wrote, "My first reaction is that sexism in language is not an issue and not as deep rooted as the articles we read portray it to be."]

b. Just recently, in my American history class covering the period of 1815–1850, one of the men in class said, "How do we know what Rachel (Jackson—note the use of only her first name) was really like with men anyway? How do we know she wasn't just a slut?" The professor 'corrected' him by calling Rachel a "flirt" instead. I could not believe my ears when the guy said that and then was amazed at how the professor behaved when he used the term *flirt*.

c. As a new female instructor in the Marines and the only female among 50 males, I tried to get the inside scoop on how to handle male-dominated classrooms in the military. I went to three classrooms and got discouraged. I found their [male instructors] ice-breakers were gender jokes geared to sexual content. Others referred to males they considered weak as 'women.' [She recounts how she became determined to be the best Marine in the company to gain the respect of her colleagues and students. She succeeded by scoring the highest in physical fitness and by leading hikes and runs. Only then did she win the respect from the company which allowed her to be listened to in class.] I didn't have to use swearing, harassment, or belittling to make myself heard.

d. Recently I was in a discussion with a group of friends about the concept of "ho" and why women are the only ones labeled with the infelicitous title. As the conversation continued, we realized that the same behavior of a "ho" that is considered dishonorable, shameful, and scandalous is the exact same as the behavior of a male who is labeled with the positive "player," an almost respectful term.

e. Marriage brings out a lot of sexist language. I was determined not to say "honor and obey." My husband and his family were at a loss for words at the rehearsal when I stopped the minister and told him that we had to re-work the words. After a heated argument, I suggested that if I had to say those words, so did my husband. He was horrified, and I made my point.

f. As my wedding day approached, I informed my future husband that I planned to keep my maiden name. He was appalled. In fact he went so far as to demand that I take his name or we would call the wedding off .... I eventually gave in .... I recall feeling a sense of loss when the minister announced us as Mr. and Mrs. Darren____. Couldn't he at least have presented us as Darren and Genelle____?

g. After an especially hard day as I gave my husband a very long answer to his question about how my day was at work, he said, "Honey, are you sure it is not that time of the month, because you sure are overreacting and acting all emotional. Suck it up."

h. My boyfriend's father must always have control of the conversation. Every time I say something to him, he always finds a way to change the conversation to something that he knows and understands well. He will then talk the topic to death .... I do not believe that I will ever understand why my boyfriend's father believes that he can just disregard whatever it is that I am saying and begin his own discussion and expect me to listen politely when he pretends to be all knowing. I believe that he is indirectly trying to prove that he is superior.

FOR THOUGHT 5.1: Which issues of gender and/or gender and language can be found in the stories above?

When shared in small and large group discussion, powerful stories like these, only a few of the many we have received over the years, work well to convince many of our resistant pre-service teachers of the reality of gender bias and of the work needed in classrooms to promote gender-fair language choices and discourse practices as contributors to achieving gender equity. Such stories also bring to the personal level many of the points presented below about the roles of words and syntax; discourse practices; and culturally embedded attitudes, language conventions, and artifacts in reinforcing gender stereotypes and gender inequity.

3. *Analysis of Recorded Conversations.* Early in our language courses, we assign our students to eavesdrop on conversations and to record (in writing) a minimum of four exchanges to bring to class for small group analysis of the conversation's purpose, opening sequence, closing sequence, patterns (question/answer, apology/acceptance, command/acquiescence, assertion/agreement or counter, etc.) setting, communication means (face-to-face, telephone), direct and inferential aspects, and the nature of the relationship between the two speakers. This exercise in pragmatics asks them to note any power plays or power shifts that occur and to speculate as to the cultural assumptions that may be embedded in the conversation. We make this assignment early in the term, before we have discussed gender, so that the issues raised in these conversations can serve as introductions to many of the language issues we will cover in class. Often, some of the conversations address gender. Two will serve as examples, one recorded by Mary and another by one of our students.

Fed. Ex. Deliverer: (man of about 25 years of age)	Hello.
Mary (53 years of age):	Hello.
Fed. Ex.:	203 Osburn? Harmon?
Mary:	Yes.
Fed. Ex.:	I have a package for a Doctor Harmon. He's supposed to sign.
Mary: (smiling and reaching for the package)	That's me. Thanks.
Fed. Ex. (sounding surprised):	*You* are Dr. Harmon?
Mary:	Yes. That's me.
Fed. Ex.:	Oh. O.K. Sign here, sweetie.

To model and demonstrate, Mary uses the sample above, as well as several which address issues other than gender. Students readily see that the speakers are strangers, of gender and significant age difference, and that the Fed. Ex. delivery person is surprised that a woman is a doctor. A few suggest that his final comment may be an attempt to regain a sense of power in this conversational situation more in line with his views of gender roles. Many notice that Mary remains silent; there is no closing sequence, and the delivery person seems to have the last word. As gender and power issues resurface later in the semester, reference can be made back to the above conversation or to the one below contributed by Gerilyn Szotack.

Me:	Thank you for calling Major Lumber, how may I help you?
Male Caller:	Service Desk, please.
Me:	Can I help you with something?
Male Caller (laughing):	You? Oh, I don't think so; you probably don't know anyway.
Me:	Are you sure I can't help you?
Male Caller:	Let me talk to one of the guys.
Me:	In which department?
Male Caller:	Electrical.
Me:	Hold on a second.
Male Caller:	I knew you couldn't help me!
Me: (Cutting him off as he is speaking):	Hold please!

Gerilyn stated in class that conversations like this one occur frequently when men call the lumber company where she works as a receptionist. In class, we analyze the conversation for the assumptions made about gender and for assertions of power. Among the questions we pose are: What is the relationship between speakers? How does that relationship affect the conversation's content? What implied/indirect messages do the caller's words reveal? Where does the caller assert power, if he does? Where does Gerilyn assert power, if she does? How? How do Mary's and Gerilyn's responses to the male speaker's final comment differ? Why do you think they do? What cultural assumptions appear to be embedded in both conversations? One of our male students pointed that the cultural assumptions at work in Gerilyn's conversation limit men as well as women. He added that too many people expect men to be handy with and know all about machines, lumber, and tools; he is not; nor does he desire to be. A musician, he knows a great deal about and loves music. Thus some folks look at him askance.

4.   *Use of Media.* We will have more to say about various media and their roles in representing and reinforcing stereotypes and hierarchical power positions later in this chapter; here we simply list the kinds of media we find useful in promoting discussion of gender and language.

a. Comic Strips and Cartoons. We have made an extensive collection of comic strips and cartoons that appear in local daily newspapers and which depict gender and language issues both directly and indirectly. Among the issues they highlight are women "swearing," girls not being called on in classrooms, the use of demeaning words (*baby, chick,* and even *chickorama*, a highly sexualized game of fantasy football imagined by two teen-aged boys where bikini-wearing female stars are the team members), and women's and men's differing modes of communication. Once we analyze some of these with our students, many begin to bring in those they find, which they, in turn, share with us and the class.

b. Advertisements which depict gender stereotypes reinforced by gendered language. When students tell us about or bring in taped samples of advertisements in which women are engaged in stereotypical "male" behavior, e.g., assessing body parts, we suggest that instead of creating equity, such ads reinforce and solidify male standards of objectification of the body as desirable and covertly urge women to adopt these standards rather than challenge them.

c. Television and film content and language. We ask our students to consider:

Who stars in which roles? What are characters' occupations and interests? Who engages in which behaviors and in what sorts of conversations? What kinds of labels are given to men by male and female characters? To women? Who speaks most often? About what and to whom? Who name-calls? How?

Who is in leadership roles? How do they speak to subordinates?

Who swears, curses, uses obscene language? To or about whom?

Why does any of the above matter? To persons of their age? Of their students' ages?

d. News articles which directly treat gender and language issues. Again, we have amassed an extensive collection over the past 10 years, and as we share and discuss a few with our students, we soon find them bringing in articles to discuss with their classmates. In small groups as students share, read, and respond to articles, engaged discussion about gender and language issues results. To illustrate, we have used *Time*'s "It's Mrs.; Not Ms.," which documents that fewer women keep their surnames when marrying than was the case in the 1980s and theorizes as to why, (Bower W4) in conjunction with student story "f" above and with a series of strips from the comic *Cathy* in which newly married Cathy weighs the implications of keeping her surname or taking her husband's (Guisewite) to promote discussion of naming issues for women.

e. Videos and DVDs. Many are available. Some of those we have found useful are Deborah Tannen's *He Said, She Said* (2001) which examines and exemplifies tendencies toward difference in female and male conversational styles, The University of California at Berkeley's *Gender and Communication: Male–Female Differences in Language and Nonverbal Behavior* (2001), which offers a presentation of more breadth if somewhat drier in style than Tannen's, and Jean Kilbourne's *Killing Us*

Softly: Advertising's Image of Women (2002), which documents the reality of the stereotypical, sex-laden, and/or violent nature of the words and images in advertisements that depict women and links such ads with violence toward women. After viewing these, students share their reactions to them as well as their own stories of situations much like those they have just seen.

f. Student-made videos of high school classrooms. Students carefully analyze who gets called on and who does not; who talks and about what and for how long, who sits where and in which arrangements, and to whom the teacher directs attention. In one video, taped in a 10th grade high school English class, the classroom was arranged with a major divide down the middle; boys, by choice, sat on one side, girls on the other. The teacher made a presentation of about 12 minutes. In that time, she called only on boys to answer her questions, and she looked more frequently at the boys' section of the classroom as she delivered her presentation.

g. Literature. As record, repository, and reservoir of language, literary pieces lend themselves well to discussions of gender and language (as well as many other language issues), either by direct comment (*Fried Green Tomatoes*) or by a display of derogatory gendered language use (*The Color Purple*). Harmon (1993, 2000) demonstrates that often high school literature anthologies contain images and works where gendered language and stereotypes occur without including any directed discussion to bring them to light and undermine them. Sometimes, the literature texts themselves, in the non-literature portions—the inner and inter-chapter commentary, the questions and introductions which accompany selections, and the introductions to authors—carry overt and covert messages of gender bias. And, many anthologies and classrooms underrepresent women authors, so that women's voices aren't as often heard as men's. Too often, when women's works are read, they feature a male hero or a woman who is male-centered, powerless, or dying. The current *Harry Potter* series, which enjoys almost phenomenal popularity, can serve as an illustration. So can stories like "The Jilting of Granny Weatherall," "A Wagner Matinee," or "The Sculptor's Funeral," which are included all too often in anthologies.

FOR THOUGHT 5.2: Would J. K. Rowling's series have been as popular with both children and young adult readers if its hero were female? Why or why not? Which other works by female writers can you list that feature male protagonists? Theorize as to why Rowling might have chosen to abbreviate her name. Why do you think that 19th century writers like Mary Ann Evans (George Eliot) and Emily Bronte (Ellis Bell), who wrote *Silas Marner* and *Wuthering Heights* respectively, initially masked their names?

---

5. *Student Research*. Our students frequently pick gender and language topics for individual or group research and share their projects with the class. Among those recently chosen by our students are:

An examination of newspaper pictures and headlines

An examination of popular cartoon features on television

A collection and analysis of wedding-related words and phrases

An examination of children's books in three local elementary schools

A survey of which labels and taboo language men and women find most offensive

An examination of discourse practices in three high school English classes

An examination and an analysis of words that refer to older women and men.

6. *Defining and Claiming the word* Feminist. After hearing the word *feminist* spoken disparagingly or hesitantly by our students, we ask them to write their definitions for the word. Definitions range from "women who want opportunities equal to men's" to "women who want men's power or to be more powerful than men" and "women who wish they were men." We offer Liz Whaley and Liz Dodge's definition of *feminists*: "Feminists believe that social, economic, and cultural barriers exist for women. Further, feminists work in both the public and the private sphere to break down those barriers. Finally, feminists look back over their shoulders to see what they can do for the young people, especially the young women, coming after them" (2). We query the negativism that surrounds the word and students' hesitation to claim it for themselves, noting the power of negative media images and talk radio (feminazi). We remind them of the power of naming and definition, and of Creel Froman's strong statement, quoted by Catherine MacKinnon in *Only Words*, "subordination 'is doing someone else's language'" (25). If feminism can be construed negatively and if people, especially women, become reluctant to identify themselves as feminists, whose interests are served? Most students readily acknowledge that those who wish to maintain the status quo profit from these negative associations.

While the above strategies may not dispel all resistance to the study of gender issues, they help create a climate of open conversation and debate, which in themselves work to increase students' willingness to examine the gendered nature of language use in the culture at large and in classrooms. Students more readily query the role of gendered language in the maintenance and reinforcement of hierarchal positions of social and economic power and the inequity of such positioning. And most acknowledge the necessity of challenging these unequal distributions of power both as classroom teachers and as inhabitants of a culture in which gender inequity still resides.

FOR THOUGHT 5.3: Which of the above strategies in the Countering Resistence section of this chapter do you think will be most helpful to you as you incorporate discussions of gender and language in your own classrooms? Which do you think will not work? Why?

THE ENGLISH LANGUAGE
AND ITS COMMUNICATION OF GENDER

Contemporary sociolinguists generally agree that in English, more differences in language use and discourse practices exist within genders than between genders, that differences must be stated as "on average" or as tendencies, and that differences must be looked at in social, economic, or political contexts. Yet, most also agree that women and men do often make different language choices, do have very different gender-based names and labels attached to them, and do communicate differently. These differences will be the focus of the next section of this chapter because they work to perpetuate inequitable stereotypes and power positions for women and men if left unexamined and deconstructed. Suzanne Romaine sums up the necessity of examining the gender-laden nature of the English language and its discourse practices:

> Language is the primary means through which we understand the world and our place in it. "In the beginning was the word" (Genesis 1:1). It is the world of words that creates the world of things and ideas. We do things with words. The Bible relates that even before God created Eve, he brought all the animals to Adam to see "what he would call them: and whatsoever Adam called every living creature, that was the name thereof" (Genesis 2:19). If the world is brought into being through acts of naming, then naming a thing is the first stage in appropriating it and assuming power over it. Language can alter reality rather than simply describe it. When a minister or judge says "I now pronounce you man and wife" to a man and a woman legally entitled to be married, they do indeed become for legal purposes husband and wife .... Saying so makes it so. (*Communicating* 15–16).

If the names and labels men and women are given, and if their language choices and discourse practices differ in significant ways and reveal positions of differing social and economic power, these must be examined and undermined to achieve gender equity. The world of words must be in sync with our goals, or it will ultimately defeat them.

Semantics: Only Words?

Slut, cunt, whore (or ho), and bitch; Mrs. Darren Wolfe or Miss Juanita Alavarez; Lady Cardinals; waitress or actress; mistress or madam; spinster, hag, old maid, or crone; Marilyn rather than Dr. Wilson; baby, chick, or kitten; cutie or sweetie; peach or tomato; lady or girl. This list is but a partial demonstration of the range of labels given to women which mark them as different from men and which often stigmatize or demean them. Of course, we acknowledge that such a list exists for men as well: stud, dick, prick, bastard; Mr., master; waiter or author; son of a bitch; bachelor; boy toy, etc.; yet, we, as have so many linguists (Romaine 1994, 1999; Coates; Penelope; Trudgill; Nilsen 1991, 1999; Baron 1986, 1989), will argue that gender-biased asymmetry underlies gendered vocabulary in the English lexicon, that this asymmetry most often disadvantages women and contributes to unequal distributions of power, and that conscious language choices such as those suggested in the *Guidelines for Gender Fair Use of Language* can help undermine asymmetry and promote gender-equity. What follows will demonstrate the imbalances of social power afforded men and women by various names and labels commonly given to each.

Titles of Address, Respect, and Kinship. The titles given to women and men display an asymmetry and an imbalance of acknowledged power. Examine the differences in:

Mr.	Mrs., Miss, Ms.
Lord	Lady
Gentleman	Lady
Master	Mistress
Sir	Madam
Man	Woman
Father	Mother

English speakers do not give men titles that reveal their marital status or a man's relationship to a woman, but they commonly do give them to women. Or they render the woman's individual identity invisible by referring to her by her husband's name: Mrs. Stephen Wilson. The term *Ms.*, originally proposed as a title for all women regardless of marital status, in common practice has become a form of business address or means of addressing a divorced woman. Speakers often give *lady* sexual connotations (She's my lady; ladies of the night) that *Lord* (also a title for divinity) and *gentleman* do not have. Even the euphemism *Gentleman's Club* describes a place where women, not men, are gazed on as sex objects. The men who attend are *gentlemen*; the women who are on display are *showgirls*. *Sir* is a term of respect; a *madam* may run a house of prostitution. English universalizes *man* as inclusive of all people, not *woman*, which often is linked to sexual innuendo. *Master* denotes respect and mastery (master craftsman); *mistress*, like *madam*, has sexual connotations. *Manly* and *womanly* are used very differently; the former always signifies strength; the latter sometimes signifies weakness: to tell a man his behavior is womanly equates *womanly* with timidity. One speaks of a professional man without sexual innuendo; however the term *professional woman* can refer to a prostitute, synonyms for which include *painted woman*, *scarlet woman*, and *woman of the streets*. In a *Newsweek* article, "A Crackdown on Call Girls," an indicted "madame" is pictured standing in front of her office. "PROFESSIONAL," reads the caption. The prostitutes are referred to as *ladies* and *girls* by the pictured madam and as *girls* by the article's author, Arian Campo-Flores. Interestingly, it is the madam who is under indictment, not the "men who descended hungrily on the brothels and sometimes unloaded thousands of dollars in one night" (59). *Father*, another male term associated with divinity, becomes an act of potency: to father children. *Mother*, as a part of insult games (your mother wears combat boots) and in slang, as short for *motherfucker*, is a common pejorative slur especially when altered to *Mutha*. Mothers, daughters, and sisters are left out of patriotic songs which speak of "land where my fathers died," and "crown thy good with Brotherhood." Fellowship (or a Fellowship) semantically excludes women as does fellow- feeling. And women are excluded from divinity as the following prayer, variations of which many Christians learn as children and repeat throughout their lives, makes clear: Glory be to the Father and to the Son and to the Holy Ghost. As it was in the beginning, is now and ever shall be. World without end.

Girl as a form of addressing adult women and *guys* used when addressing both women and men and girls and boys merit special attention. When teachers address their mixed gender classes with "Hey guys," "Listen up, guys!" "Alright, you guys, now let's …," or like phrases, they semantically exclude their female students from classroom discourse. It could be argued that *guys* has become a gender-neutral term; in fact a recent definition reads "used in plural to refer to the members of a group regardless of sex" ("Guys"). But because, when spotting a friend, a speaker would never say "Hi Guy", if the friend were a female; and because the expressions "guys and girls/guys and gals" which clearly differentiate gender are common ones, the claim of gender neutrality can be disputed. More gender-neutral terms and phrases include *people*, *students*, *girls and boys* (or *boys and girls*), and *folks*.

Despite currency of phrases like *good old boy* and *old boys' network*, adult men are rarely called *boys*; when they are, they are usually offended, especially if the word takes on racial as well as gender connotations. Just as many grown men find it insulting to be called *boy*, many grown women find it insulting to be called *girl*, unless those addressing them are close friends. Yet, grown women are frequently addressed as *girls* by servers, commentators, and general speakers and in literary pieces and news articles. Not only does *girl* reduce a grown woman to a child, the word, as shown above in the above *Newsweek* story, often takes on sexual connotations *boy* doesn't have unless used in the phrase *boy toy*, a recent addition to the English lexicon. Julia Penelope Stanley (1977, 1990), Casey Miller and Kate Swift (1991), and Robin Lakoff (1975, 1991) were among those who, as long as 30 years ago, found the practice of labeling women past adolescence *girls* to be trivializing, reductive, and patronizing and who asserted that such labeling along with that which classifies women with the immature—*kitty, baby, babe, doll*—contributes to the imbalance of social and economic power between men and women. "Girl" suggests a person "too immature and far from real life to be entrusted with … decisions of any serious nature," (1991, 296) states Lakoff. Miller and Swift illustrate their objections to the term as trivializing by recounting the ordination of the Reverend Barbara Anderson to the American Lutheran Church. Beneath her picture in the newspaper read the caption, "Happy Girl" ("One Small Step for Genkind" 254). More recently Peter Trudgill notes the use of *boy* for males over about twenty is "very unusual," but adds that "it is not unusual to hear of a group of people [all adults] that it consisted of, say, *five men* and *six girls*. It has been, in other words, more usual to use the more childlike word for women than for men" (82). Summer 2004 witnessed the derision of women as California Governor Arnold Schwarzenegger repeatedly referred to those who disagreed with him as "girlie men;" and bumper stickers read "Don't Be a Girlie Man Vote for Bush." And a 2005 *Newsweek* article on the political leadership of the state of Washington was titled, "Welcome to Girls' State" (Breslau 30). Haig Bosmajian, an early commentator on the oppressive nature of gender-biased language, succinctly sums up the argument: "As long as adult women are *chicks, girls, dolls, babes*, and *ladies* [with its stereotyped expectations of women: act like a lady], their status in society will remain inferior; they will go on being treated as subjects in the subject-master relationship" (9).

Occupational Titles.   The conversation quoted earlier in this chapter between Mary and the Fed. Ex. deliverer points out the gender-laden assumptions that accompany occupational titles. Students are much more likely to address their female rather than their male professors by first name or to call them Mrs., not Doctor. Former Secretary of State Henry Kissinger was commonly spoken to or of as Dr. Henry Kissinger or Dr. Kissinger. We can not recall ever having heard Former Secretary of State Madeline Albright, also a Ph.D, called Dr. Madeline Albright or Dr. Albright, and we seldom hear Secretary of State Condoleezza Rice referred to as Dr. Rice. *Salesman, spokesman, businessman, policeman, craftsman, fisherman, chairman, mailman,* etc., terms still in common usage despite the gradual shift to substituting *person* for *man* or to using alternative forms (mail deliverer, chair, fisher, law officer), all carry gender assumptions, as do the warning signs which read "men working" or "men at work." The more recent term *web master* similarly reveals underlying gender bias; *web expert* provides an inclusive alternative. The list below further illustrates the gendered nature of occupational titles.

doctor	lady (or woman) doctor
nurse	male nurse
waiter	waitress
actor	actress

Change in language is occurring; *waiter* is gradually being replaced with *server*; *actor* and *host* increasingly refer to both females and males as does *author*. But, the first three pairs demonstrate that some careers, despite their now being held both by women and men, are gender-aligned in many person's minds. Nurse, secretary, and elementary school teacher are still often seen as female occupations. Corporation CEO or CFO, engineer, and physician are among those high status occupations still commonly thought of and spoken of as male.

FOR THOUGHT 5.4: Fill in the blank in the following sentences:

A construction worker usually gets____pay check on Friday.

A nurse must expect to work nights if____wants to be promoted.

We find that, when given these sentences without any sort of introduction, most of our students fill "he" in the first and "she" in the second, demonstrating the entrenched nature of occupational titles and gender assumptions. After asking our students to place "she" in the first sentence and "he" in the second and noting their uneasiness at the pronoun shift in sentence two, we introduce the concept of the "pseudo-generic." *He* alone, despite what we all have been taught, does not represent both women and men in actual use.

Pseudo-Generics. Many linguists offer commentary on the non-generic nature of the so-called generics *he/his* and *man/men* when used to refer to both men and women in sentences like those which follow: *If the student reads increasingly complex stories, he will broaden his definition of "story"* and *With courage,* *man will prevail.* Among them are Trudgill, Romaine (1999), Spender, Penelope, Baron (1986, 1989) and Kosroshahi (1988). All find generic *he* and *man* in actual usage to be exclusionary of women, that is, to be *pseudo generics* (Penelope 116), as has been shown by any number of experiments in which people from the ages of kindergarten to first year college students have been asked to draw representations of the persons being spoken of in sex-neutral sentences where these so-called generics are used. Consistently, both women and men draw far more male than female figures; though men do so more often than women. Goldman argues that *man* usually refers to males when used generically, as a careful reading of the metaphors that accompany such use reveals. She demonstrates by examining the metaphorical passages in Thoreau's *Walden* that culminate in his famous "The mass of men lead lives of quiet desperation" (124–127). Thoreau's equally famous, "If a man does not keep pace with his companions, perhaps it is because he hears the beat of a different drummer. Let him march to the beat he hears..." (216), with its references to soldiers and drummers, all male in Thoreau's day, also serves as an example. Baron concludes:

> The common use of the generic masculine renders women linguistically invisible, a situation that subtly controls everyone's perceptions of what women can do .... The exclusion of any specific reference to women (Everyone loves his mother) has the psychological effect of limiting the reference of such language—and standard English in general—more or less exclusively to men. (1989, 190)

And the generic *he* just doesn't work in actual discourse. Consider the following sentence sequence: *The average person follows a number of small routines as he gets ready for the day. As he showers or blow-dries his hair or puts on his makeup, he eases himself into the demands of the morning.*

Despite all that has been written on the biased and gender-laden nature of the so-called generic *he*, it still enjoys widespread use. The *Saginaw News* stated in May 2003, "By law, Michigan's governor is a 'he'" in an article about revamping the language of Michigan's constitution to achieve gender-neutrality now that Jennifer Granholm is governor. Efforts to do so have been dismissed as "a nice gesture" with "absolutely no legal reason" by Stephen J. Safranek, Professor of Law at Ave Maria School of Law in Ann Arbor, Michigan (*Moses* A3). *The New York Times* notes that Utah, New York, and Rhode Island have made the switch to gender-neutral language, but that Wisconsin, in 1995, "narrowly rejected a proposed constitutional amendment to replace male pronouns with gender-neutral terms" ("State Constitutions" 21 May 2003).

Names, Labels, and Diminutives. The power to name, as has been stated above, often parallels hierarchical power structures in a society as do the kinds of names one is given. Miller and Swift (1991 272–287, 1977), Nilsen (1991, 259–270), and Romaine (1999) offer insightful commentary on English naming practices. In Western culture, most women's names change when they marry; they take their father's name at birth and they take their husband's when they wed. Thus, states Suzanne Romaine, only men have the right of permanency to their names. In traditional ceremonies, men and women in marriage are pronounced man and wife; the man remains named a person, but *wife* names a role. As Romaine points out, even when ceremonies change the wording to *husband and wife*, the traditional role of male before female is retained (*Communicating* 146–147). While some women insist on their right to retain their surname, or to re-name themselves, such naming practice often meets with personal or cultural resistance.

Just as, according to traditional biblical stories, woman was a derivative of man, women's names often are alterations or diminutives of men's names; the reverse isn't true in English.

Michael	Michelle
John	Joan, Joanne
Patrick	Patricia
Juan	Juanita (the "ita" suffix means little)

If men's names have more than one syllable, they more often have the primary accent on the first syllable when pronounced; women's names of more than one syllable more often than men's are accented on the second syllable. In addition to those above, Elizabeth and Amanda serve as examples, but Sarah and Jennifer are exceptions, as are names given to both men and women such as Brandon, Shannon, Morgan. More men's than women's names have only one syllable: Kurt, Craig, John, Brent. More often than men's, women's names end in *y*, *i*, or *ie*, a diminutive associated with smallness, children, or child's talk (birdie, chicky, kitty, puppy, sweetie): Lori, Jenni, Kitty, Carrie. Thus, men's names may strike the ear as "tougher," "stronger," and more authoritative than women's names, traits associated with male and female stereotypes (*Communicating* 140–146). To name a boy "girl" insults him; just as to sneeringly call young male military recruits "women" is intended to insult them. States Penelope, "Calling any male regardless of age 'a girl' is a standard insult …. Among men, *girl* is a 'fighting word'" (105). When a man's name becomes popular as a woman's name, it soon no longer seems as suitable for men: Marion, Francis, Beverly, and Shirley are examples from the past. Will Brandon, Ryan, and Morgan eventually subject men to the same ridicule felt by the protagonist of a one-time popular song, "The Man Called Sue," just as the boy who is called *sissy* is far more stigmatized than the girl who is labeled *tomboy*? If so, names and naming practices will continue to reflect and reinforce gender bias and asymmetries of power.

Penelope states that those objects that men control, desire, or desire to control are given women's names, are named for women or parts of women's bodies, or are referred to by female pronouns. Adds Romaine, "Because it is men who make the dictionaries and define meanings, they persistently reserve the positive semantic space for themselves and relegate women to a negative one" (*Communicating* 112–113). Cars, planes, ships, and guns, all, until recently, primarily owned and manipulated by men, are commonly seen as female and referred to as *she*. Language, until recently defined and categorized exclusively by men, is a woman, i.e. the mother tongue. The Greeks depicted Rhetorica and Grammatica as women at a time when only men made the rules for both and received formal education in both. Justice and liberty's female forms also come from times when only men had the political and economic power to define and enforce what those abstract terms meant. Some uncontrollable forces have been given women's names: luck, as in Lady Luck. Until recently, hurricanes received only women's names; nature is often called Mother Nature, and Earth is dubbed Mother Earth. Nilsen points out that women are more likely to be given the names of or addressed as food, flowers, and animals: Candy, peach, Lily, Rose, Kitty, chick, bitch. She lists just a few of the many geographical locations named after women's breasts: The Grand Tetons (French for Teats), Nipple Top, and Squaw Tit. And she argues that the names and labels given to men enjoy more status and positive associations than those given females. The disparity between *brave* and *squaw*, the latter an Algonquin slang term much like *cunt* in its negative sexual connotations, is one of many illustrations she provides (1991 262–266, 1999 173–189).

Derogatory Words, Slurs. The abundance of derogatory words and negative, sexual slurs directed at women found in the English lexicon gives added evidence of the accuracy of Nilsen's, Penelope's, and Romaine's contentions. In 1977, Stanley (Penelope) found ten times more sexual slurs for women than for men: 220 to 20 (in Romaine 1999, 98). Of those, several, *mother fucker, son of a bitch,* and *bastard,* when leveled at men, also denigrate women. She reports that Schultz listed 100 more pejoratives for women and argued that sex-specific terms for males primarily have positive associations with power while most words which refer exclusively to women came to be associated with prostitution or sexuality: *nun, courtesan, madam, mother, lady, woman, girl, mistress. Hussy,* originally an elided form of *housewife,* gradually took on meanings of slut or prostitute. Penelope concludes that "any word that refers to women eventually perjorates and becomes an insult or explicit sexual slur" (Penelope 121).

The use of sexual slurs abounds in schools, and as pointed out in the previous chapter, is a primary weapon used to demean targets and enhance the power of users. When we ask our students to list all the negative gendered words they've been called, we find that all of our female students report having been called a bitch by both women and men. Many report having been called a slut or a whore by both men and women and a cunt by men. While there are no words that all men report having been called, words that many list are *asshole, stud,* and *prick*. But they agree that *stud,* when said in praise of sexual or muscular prowess, and *player,* when used to label a man who *scores* sexually are seen as positive terms. While making exceptions for in-group name-calling by intimate friends, all of the women reported feeling insulted, demeaned and violated by *slut, whore, bitch,* and *cunt*; many felt angry. Many male and female students listed terms which demean homosexuals: *dyke, fag, faggot* and added that *that's so gay* and *you're so gay* are used pejoratively to taunt as early as elementary school.

Particularly potent, sexual slurs work as a means of control. Because until recently men had full legal, religious, and economic control of women's sexuality, it comes as no surprise that the English lexicon contains so many more negative labels for women than for men. For old women, no longer of sexual and/or economic value to men, Mary's class found far more negative terms than for old men and found more positive terms for a dog than for an old woman. *Fried Green Tomatoes*' Evelyn, already quoted in chapter 3, clearly recognizes the power of men's disapprobation as expressed through sexual slurs when she recalls that her sexuality and behavior have been controlled by male definitions. Fanny Flagg narrates:

> After the boy at the supermarket had called her those names, Evelyn Couch felt violated. Raped by words. Stripped of everything. She had always tried to keep this from happening to her, had been terrified of displeasing men, terrified of the names she would be called if she did …. She had stayed a virgin so she wouldn't be called a tramp or slut; had married so she wouldn't be called an old maid; faked orgasms so she wouldn't be called frigid; had not been a feminist because she didn't want to be called queer and a man hater, never nagged or raised her voice so that she wouldn't be called a bitch …. (236–237).

Both men and women use slurs to discredit women who challenge men's authority and the traditional male/female power hierarchy or who charge men with sexual harassment. Leona Tanenbaum's examination of what she calls "The Sleaze Factor," states that "women are characterized as 'slutty' or 'sleazy' simply because they don't conform to the traditional feminine gender role. As a result they lose all professional credibility." She concludes, "Many controversial or unpopular women, particularly those involved in sexual harassment and rape cases are routinely discredited by being portrayed in sexual terms" (E1). In *The Language Wars*, Robin Lakoff reviews the Senate Hearing in which Anita Hill accused Supreme Court nominee, Clarence Thomas, of sexual harassment, and delineates the many means through which Hill was discredited, one of them being the implication that she welcomed Thomas' advances (2000). Tanenbaum suggests that Hill's accusations were dismissed by the Senate because she was hyped by her detractors "'a bit nutty and a bit slutty'" (E1). Hillary Rodham Clinton, no quiet appendage to a famous husband, has frequently been described in derogatory sexual terms by her detractors as an indeterminate man/woman, as a bitch goddess, and as Hillary, the icy and bitchy Snowqueen (Lakoff 2000).

The Case of NO.   Although in itself not a gendered word, *no* can be defined quite differently by women and men. Since its use is of critical importance as to what constitutes both rape and sexual harassment, *no* must be explored in any discussion of gender-laden words. If that were not the case, there would be no need for "no means no" posters and stickers. Romaine offers an extended analysis (*Communicating* 221–249) of the differing ways men and women define rape and sexual harassment and the tendency of more men than women to dismiss all but egregious cases as "boys will be boys" behavior. Clearly "no" does not mean "no" to the 12% of female adolescents and the 39% of male adolescents polled in Los Angeles who state that *forced* sex (emphasis added) would be legitimate if a male spent a lot of money on a woman on a date and the nearly one third of the females and over half of the males who found forced sex to be O.K. if the woman had led the man on (229). In a study of college students, "led him on" included any of the following: "asking him out, letting him pay for a date, going to his apartment" (230).

Literature and film often reinforce men's and women's differing interpretations of *no* and of harassment and rape. Films like *Fatal Attraction* and *Disclosure* depict a woman as stalker and sexual harasser, despite the fact that far more women than men are the targets of stalking and sexual harassment. Romaine points to a Hemingway story in which after being told no and even while realizing that the woman in the story is afraid, the male protagonist doesn't listen or stop. Hemingway's "She was frightened but she wanted it" from his male character's perspective reinforces the idea that women's no's really mean yes (243). Nancy Mellin McCracken's "Re-Gendering the Reading of Literature" cites T. Coraghessan Boyle's "Greasy Lake" in which, on the shore of Greasy Lake, a spot where "toughs" hang out, an attempted gang rape remains attempted only because it is interrupted. One of the perpetrators, the male narrator looking back on his adolescent self, justifies raping the young woman after finding her "making out" in a parked car with her lover: already sexually active, she was "tainted." The narrator describes the attack:

> We were on her like Bergman's deranged brothers ... panting wheezing, tearing at her clothes, grabbing at her flesh .... There we were, dirty, bloody, guilty ... shreds of nylon panty and spandex brassier dangling from our fingers, our flies open, lips licked .... We were bad characters ... anything could have happened. It didn't. (Boyle in McCracken 63)

Assault and attempted rape are dismissed as "it didn't." Anything could have happened, but nothing did. Although McCracken does not suggest doing so, asking students to write about the incident from the woman's perspective might deconstruct the narrator's conclusion that nothing happened. A third literary example, Harry Mark Petrakis' "The Wooing of Ariadne" features a male protagonist in love with the beautiful and independent Ariadne. As he pursues her, she emphatically and consistently tells him no. He launches a loud campaign to defeat her opposition and harasses her at a dance, follows her, visits her father's store, repeatedly knocks on her door, shouts to her from the sidewalk, and creates a scene at her church. Eventually, she accedes and decides that he may call her, much to his triumph and joy. The story's dismissal of "no means no" and stalking laws is ignored by the publisher of the high school anthology that contains the story in its post-story discussion of the text. Rather than query the power issues in the text which teach that harassment will prevail, the post-text discussion praises the protagonist's final lengthy appeal as "eloquent" (Harmon 1993, 151). That "no" really means "yes," as presented in the story, is reinforced by the pedagogical apparatus of the anthology.

FOR THOUGHT 5.5: How do you define rape? In what sorts of situations is the phrase "askin' for it" used in discussions of rape? How does the phrase function to shift blame in discussions of rape? Why is this blame shift important? Does preceding the word *rape* with *date* or *spouse* alter your definition? If so, how? How does your definition of rape compare to those of your classmates? Do males and females define the word differently? What role do our definitions of a term play in our judgements—legal and otherwise—of those who act out the term and of those who are acted upon? What role does *no* play in your definitions?

English Grammar and Syntax: But Isn't Grammar Neutral?

Women's use of English grammar and their place in its literary production and syntactic framework historically has been subject to much male critique. Jennifer Coates, as she briefly recounts the commentary of folklinguists and early grammarians posits what she calls the Androcentric rule: "Men will be seen to behave linguistically in a way that fits the writer's view of what is desirable or admirable; women, on the other hand will be blamed for any linguistic state or development which is regarded by the writer as negative or reprehensible" (16). Early folklinguists trivialized women's lexical innovations as a "vocabulary of words which perish and are forgot within the compass of a year," (Cambridge 1754 in Coates 17) yet saw men's neologisms as "the chief renovators of the language" (Jesperen 1922 in Coates 18). A woman's vocabulary was generalized to be "as a rule, much less extensive than that of a man" (Jespersen in Coates 19). *Women's language*—its syntax, grammar, and lexicon—was often mocked: in 1754, Lord Chesterfield patronizingly satirized his "fair countrywomen" for their over use of adverbs and intensifiers (so sorry, so pretty); in 1741, he had carlier observed that "most women and all the ordinary people in general speak in open defiance of all grammar" (in Coates 25). Bishop Thomas Wilson shared the frequent contempt for women's speech: "for many a pretty lady by the Silliness of her Words hath lost the Admiration which her Face had gained" (1724 in Coates 28). And as late as 1922, Jespersen contended that women speak in unfinished sentences because they do not think before they speak (in Coates 25).

In light of the above commentary and to fully understand the gender-laden nature of English and the female/male power asymmetries English usage reflects and reinscribes, we must look beyond semantics and examine English syntactic patterns. Because Penelope and Romaine (1999) offer extensive analyses of the ways in which English syntax reflects and promotes gender inequity, we will exemplify only the three we find the most pervasive. Then, we will comment on a frequently noted grammatical practice, the tendency of female speakers to choose grammatical forms closer to standard forms than those men choose.

Ordering: The Cart Before the Horse. Men and women, boys and girls, his and hers, Mr. And Mrs., husband and wife, man and wife, he and/or she. All these traditional constructions place the male before the female, and in doing so, sustain gender inequity. That notions of male superiority affected prescriptive placement practices is hard to dispute after reading 16th—18th century grammarians' contentions that "the Masculine gender is more worthy than the feminine" (Poole in Coates 24), that "The Masculine person answers to the general Name, which comprehends both Male and Female" (Kirby in Coates 24), and that "Some will set the Carte before the horse, as thus, My mother and my father are both at home, even as thoughe the good man of the house ware no breaches, or that the graye Mare were the better horse .... let us keep a natural order and set the mane before the woman for manners Sake" (Wilson in Coates 24). Since *man and wife* names a person and a role rather than two people, reversing their ordering will not promote equity. Thus, we suggest replacing *man and wife* with *husband and wife*. Reversing the order of this phrase and the rest of those above and alternating the reversed form with the traditional one provides for more gender-fair language use in both speaking and writing.

Third Person Singular Pronouns: Nominative, Possessive, Objective.

He, she, it	They
His, hers, its	Their
Him, her, it	Them

Third person singular pronouns encode gender and sometimes create gender asymmetries; their use poses no problem when speakers or writers and their audiences know the gender of the person under discussion. Difficulties arise when pronouns refer to a mixed group of people or to an antecedent of indeterminate sex: everybody, anybody, everyone, the student, the child, the adult reader, the pianist.

Does everybody have_____book?

The student needs a tablet; be sure to supply_____with it.

If_____practices consistently, the pianist will increase the agility of_____fingers.

Everyone should raise_____hand when_____knows the answer.

Everybody gets a cookie; Shannon, please give_____one.

To simply supply the singular male third person pronoun in each of these sentence as has been the practice in the past, reinscribes women's invisibility. Rather than produce gender-biased sentences, Prosenjak, Harmon, Johnson et al. suggest:

1. Recasting sentences like those above in the plural: *If they practice, pianists will increase the agility of their fingers.*
2. Occasionally choosing passive voice: *The student should be supplied with a tablet.* (However, see the section below on the agentless passive.)
3. Substituting the second person for the third: *You should raise your hand when you know the answer. Do you have your books?*
4. Using and alternating *she or he, his and hers, her and him,* and in written discourse, the solidus *s/he.*
5. Recasting the sentence to eliminate the troublesome pronoun problem altogether: *Consistent practice will increase the agility of the pianist's fingers.*
6. Using the singular they/their/them: *Does everybody have their book? Everyone should raise their hand when they know the answer. Everyone gets a*

cookie; Shannon, please give one to them. Informal speakers have long used the singular they/their/them; Newman reports that in a study of television interviews and talk shows, speakers used they/their/them 60% of the time to refer to singular antecedents (in Romaine 1999, 105). However, because this construction often is judged incorrect in formal and academic discourse, we suggest that users choose alternatives 1-5 in those contexts.

The Passive Voice: The Absent Agent.   Most sentences in English follow the pattern subject/verb/object when the sentence contains action; listeners and readers know the subject (the agent who acts), the action performed by the agent, and the person or object which received the action or was acted upon. In Marilyn hit the ball, Marilyn is the agent; the ball is the receiver of action; and the action is hit. Listeners and readers have no doubt as to who did what to whom as Marilyn is specifically named. But if we state the sentence simply as "the ball was hit," this use of passive voice exemplifies what Penelope, Romaine, and others refer to as the agentless sentence, one in which no one is named as responsible for the action the sentence depicts. In other words, no agency is assigned.

The agentless sentence should be avoided when it tends to displace the listener/reader's focus from the agent to the person or object acted upon or when used to deflect blame. Then-President Reagan's famous admission in regard to the deception and illegal acts that surrounded the Iran-Contra affair, "Mistakes were made," deliberately leaves out agency and responsibility; it is a far different statement from "Key persons in my administration made mistakes." Researchers find discourse about rape, battering, and sexual harassment routinely couched in the agentless passive, thus focusing attention on the receiver of action, usually female, rather than on the subject/agent, usually male, subtly echoing "blame the victim" discourse that all too often surrounds such crimes. Recent news broadcasts on two local television channels headlined with "A teen-aged girl was sexually assaulted in a local park" and "A teen-aged girl says she was grabbed, beaten, and raped in an area park." Both sentences focus on the person raped rather than the rapist. In the second headline, the word *says* may lead viewers to wonder, "Was she or wasn't she; is she just making this all up?" What followed almost immediately were comments by two older women to the effect that a woman should never run in the park alone and that one should always have a companion or a dog with her if she walks in the park. From both the headline which fails to directly state that a man grabbed, beat, and raped a woman and the older women's comments implying that "she should have been more careful," blame the victim and "she was asking for it" emerge as strong subtexts. Responsibility has shifted from the man who raped the woman to the woman herself.

The Use of Standard Pronunciation and Grammar: Ain't it fine? Our final point regarding gender-laden aspects of English grammar and syntax serves as a bridge to the next major section of this chapter, the differences between genders' discourse practices. Widespread research with groups of adults of varied ages, ethnic groups, nationalities, and social classes and with groups of children as young as six years old consistently reveals that women more often than men tend to chose the pronunciations and grammatical structures of the prestige variant of their spoken language. Men more often than women tend to choose non-standard (vernacular) or stigmatized variants, such as the double negative or the word *ain't* (*I ain't got no shoes* or *Don't give none to him*). Trudgill (1995), Coates (1993), and Romaine (1999) all review and advance theories as to why this difference occurs. Among those they suggest are:

1. Women are more socially insecure and status conscious than men and, therefore, chose prestige forms.
2. Women, until recently denied men's "marketplace capital," seek "symbolic capital" via language use; the use of standard forms gains them respect and influence.
3. Women, the primary caretakers of children, choose standard forms to insure their children improved social status.
4. Since "proper" language is associated with propriety and since there are greater social pressures on women to be "proper ladies," women's fear of stigmatization causes them to adopt standard forms.
5. Non-standard forms carry with them connotations of toughness and masculinity; boys and men choose them so they will not be derided as feminine.
6. Because they are raised according to differing cultural expectations, women and men comprise different cultures; differing language choices give each a heightened sense of group identity and solidarity.
7. Biological differences in the areas of women's and men's brains responsible for language learning and sensitivity account for these observed differences.
8. Person's network structures affect and reinforce language choices. Traditionally, men more often than women form social networks (work groups and labor unions, fishing buddies, card groups, sports teams, the local pub group) that are more tightly interwoven than those of women. Group solidarity within networks of vernacular speakers reinforces their choice of vernacular forms, even when they know standard forms. As Coates explains, "less tight networks to which women belong are less efficient at enforcing vernacular forms. Women may use forms closer to Standard English for the negative reason that they are less exposed to vernacular speech and more exposed to Standard English" (100).

FOR THOUGHT 5.6: Which of those above most likely explain women's more often choosing standard forms and men's more often choosing vernacular forms?

Discourse Practices and Styles

To achieve gender fairness, simply reversing the order of *he and she* to *she and he* and choosing *chair* instead of *chairman* or *firefighter* instead of *fireman* will have limited effect if the discourse practices and the media messages which bombard us daily counter our efforts. Examining and changing word choices and syntactic arrangements are relatively simple matters when contrasted with examining and changing discourse patterns which may be deeply embedded in persons' culturally constructed views of the world. Yet to do so is essential if we wish to deconstruct and undermine practices and stereotypes that serve to limit and constrain both women and men and to maintain traditional power hierarchies.

Sociolinguists differ on the causes, importance, and extent of differences in male and female communication, and they caution that one can never make blanket statements. One must take cultural and specific communication contexts into consideration and regard statements of difference as tendencies rather than universals. Yet, most acknowledge that some degree of difference exists in men's and women's communication styles and in the way women's and men's communication is received by listeners, viewers, and readers. We contend that differences in men's and women's language use and communication patterns are real; that they are culturally constructed rather than innate and biological; that they are not universal, essential, or immutable; and that their origins lie in what Wood (1998) details as standpoint theory.

> Standpoint theory claims that the material, social, and symbolic circumstances of women's and men's lives differ in ways that are epistemologically significant. The disparate circumstances typical of most women's and men's lives promote distinctive identities, perspectives, priorities, views of social life, and ways of interacting. Standpoint theory draws on research with speech communities or communications cultures .... Findings indicate that masculine communication cultures accentuate instrumental goals, linear organization, individualistic orientations, and monologic, competitive forms of speech. Feminine communication cultures generally accord greater priority to expressive goals, fluid organization, collective or communal orientations, and interactive, cooperative forms of speech. (Wood and Dindia, 29)

In addition, we contend that examining the differences in women's and men's communication detailed by researchers is vitally important, even if, as some researchers contend, they are statistically small and even if, as is true, there is more dissimilarity in language choices and communication styles among female speakers and among male speakers than between female and male speakers. As chapter 6 will show, relatively small dialectal differences in diction, usage, communication style, syntax, or pronunciation affect the ways large numbers of speakers are perceived and received by listeners, who often judge speakers in biased and prejudicial ways. Variants are either stigmatized or given prestige and become interpreted as markers of competence, intelligence, educational level, race, and/or class. These differences affect how seriously speakers are listened to and influence critical decisions such as those of employment and promotion; thus, they serve to advance some speakers and constrain others. Similarly, if differences in men's and women's communication patterns and language choices are interpreted to the disadvantage of either gender, and a wealth of evidence reveals that differences are most often interpreted to the disadvantage of female communicators, these differences must be examined, and whenever possible, their negative interpretations must be deconstructed. Mulac and Wood (1998) agree. Although wary that differences in male and female communication styles will be misinterpreted to the detriment of women as they have been historically, Wood states, "it would be a mistake to ignore or give scant attention to differences ... differences have been a lynchpin of persistent and painful inequities in the lives of men and women" (33). Says Mulac, despite

> overwhelming similarities in their use of language, men and women produce subtle differences in a wide variety of communication contexts .... observers are responsive to these subtle differences as they make judgements about men and women .... No matter who makes the appraisals, these subtle language differences have substantial consequences in how communications are evaluated. The inescapable conclusion is this: The language differences *really do* make a difference. (148)

Myths

Before examining some of the differences referred to above, some myths about men's and women's language use must be laid to rest, as their mythic power prompts listeners to dismiss women's speech. The first of these is the old notion that women talk more than men. Women's alleged talkative nature and admonitions to them to be silent have been promoted in art and adage. In Hardy's *The Return of the Native*, the village tavern, a gathering place for men, is called the Silent Woman. An English proverb reads, "Many women, many words; many geese, many turds"(in Coates 33). The Prophet Muhammed has said that a woman's tongue prevents her from entering heaven. A 1660 French print pictures a shop with an insignia that reads "Everything about her is good" and whose symbol is a headless woman. The anvil on which women's heads are hammered or severed is inscribed with "Strike hard on the mouth; she has a wicked tongue" (in Romaine 1999 152). Despite these mythic, misogynist renderings of women's volubility, research fails to back them up. Spender, Sadker and Sadker, Romaine (1999 157–165), and Coates all detail studies which show that men talk more than women in a variety of situations—in collegial conversations; in most classrooms where teachers routinely call on males more often than females or males interrupt or interject more frequently than females; at work; on the Internet; and in mixed gender professional discussions. In mixed gender conversations, men tend to dominate by more often interrupting women in ways that alter rather than facilitate the conversation and by controlling the topics of conversation (Coates 139). Spender found that in all the many mixed gender collegial conversation she recorded, women—even self-avowed academic feminists—never spoke 50% of the time and that both women and men perceived a woman as talking too much when she spoke for more than about 1/3 of the conversational time. Part of that 1/3 of the conversational time used by women was taken up by their being the primary performers of conversational "maintenance work": facilitating the conversation and keeping it going by asking questions and/or making supportive statements such as *Oh, really?* and *mmm-hmm* (8–11). Tannen suggests that men talk more in the public sphere; whereas women talk more in the private sphere (*He Said*). Women may talk more in the home, but there, males often dominate discourse through silence or inattention as their female conversational partners search for topics and questions that will maintain their participation (Coates 113–114).

A second myth we must query states that women's speech is more tentative and, thus, weaker and more uncertain than men's due to women's more frequent use of indirectness, qualifying statements (I may not be an expert, but my sense is that …), hedges (I mean, you know, I think, sort of) and tag questions. Wood (2003) and Coates note that, indeed, women do use more hedges than men, but add that hedges can show certainty, not uncertainty in many conversational contexts. Additionally, Coates finds that in all women conversations, hedges are often used to mitigate face-threatening conversational situations to avoid one speaker's feeling "put down." Both Coates and Wood suggest that hedges and a tentative tone serve as strengths rather than weaknesses in facilitating conversations and keeping them open and ongoing (Coates 116–119; Wood 122). Women do tend to make requests or issue commands in a more indirect manner than men. For example, rather than saying "Let's stop to eat; I'm hungry," women might ask their companions "Are you hungry yet?" or "Would you like to stop to eat?" Studies have also revealed that women are more likely to use tag questions or other interrogative forms following assertions: "It's a nice day, isn't it?" (Coates). Rather than signs of weakness and uncertainty, forms such as these may be better interpreted as collaborative approaches and as efforts to actively engage both listener and speaker in conversational exchange. It is only when judged against male patterns of communication that women's are deemed weak. To judge women's discourse styles as weak or uncertain is as incorrect as to pronounce men's communication styles as overly aggressive when men issue direct requests and commands or as weak when they show more indirectness than women in making apologies or in stating that they have been upset or hurt (Tannen 2001, *He Said*).

Differences

In addition to the discourse-style differences above, others have been documented and reviewed: Renzetti and Curren; Wood 1998, 2003; Tannen 2001, 1990; Sadker and Sadker; Romaine 1999, 1994; Mulac, and Coates are among those who have done so. What follows lists those differences most frequently presented in discussions of gender and communication research.

1. As they speak during play, groups of boys compete for the floor, tease, joke, threaten, give commands, try to take and maintain center stage, interrupt, engage in conversational contests to determine status. Girls tell secrets and stories in smaller groups, engage in building relationships and community. Even when engaged in simultaneous speech, girls collaboratively weave together conversations by listening actively, adding to others' contributions, supporting speakers with minimal responses, acknowledging what others have said, and sharing the floor to give others opportunities to speak.
2. Men socialize less intimately with each other than women do and are less likely to disclose personal information. Their most frequent conversational topics are less personal—leisure activities and sports. Women self-disclose more often; their most frequent conversational topics are their relationships and experiences with or feelings about other people.
3. When women tell stories, the stories tend to feature joint action by groups of people, relationships and feelings, and tales of adherence to or violation of community norms and the results of such behavior. Men's stories most often feature male protagonists acting alone successfully in physical and/or social contests.
4. Girls and women directly face each other as they communicate. Boys and men are less likely to do so.
5. Women's and men's interruptions differ. Men interrupt more frequently than women, and men's interruptions often assert control of

the conversation; women's interruptions more often support or encourage the speaker through minimal responses and cues (*Wow, that's
interesting, yeah, yes, uh-huh*). When men make affirmative minimal responses, their responses usually indicate agreement. Both mothers
and fathers interrupt their children; fathers interrupt more often
than mothers; both parents interrupt their daughters more often than
their sons. Thus girls learn early that their speech may not be valued
or taken seriously. That knowledge is often reinforced in schools
where teachers call on boys or allow boys to "call out" interruptions
without reprimand more often than girls or where teachers call on
girls for short, one-word or one-phrase answers but call on boys for
more abstract, drawn-out, complex answers.

6. Women use speech as a primary means to foster connections, to enhance relationships; men use speech primarily as a means to negotiate
   or maintain status and for transactional purposes: to problem solve, to
   exhibit knowledge and skill, to prove themselves, and to discover
   facts, get information, give advice, and suggest solutions.

7. Men's communication tends to be more direct and assertive with fewer
   hedges, qualifiers, or disclaimers, except for when making apologies
   or when telling about something that has upset or hurt them, both of
   which involve a loss of face and/or status.

8. Women work harder at conversational maintenance than men
   through giving response cues, probing and questioning, initiating
   topics, and prompting.

9. Men's conversation tends to be less personal and more abstract with
   fewer details and more generalizations, as well as less emotionally re-
   sponsive than women's. Women, more often than men, flesh out their
   conversations with details and use specific, personal anecdotes for
   support. Men's stories and statements contain more "I" phrases—first
   person phrases—than women's.

10. Men control more physical space than women, and they dominate the
    floor in mixed-gender interaction, even when they are in subordinate
    occupational positions to women, by taking the floor more often, by
    holding the floor longer, and/or by interrupting, ending, or rerouting
    conversations.

11. Women tend to smile more than men and to give and receive more
    compliments and apologies than men. More than one half of the com-
    pliments given to women by both women and men relate to their ap-
    pearance. Men compliment women more often than they compliment
    other men; when men compliment men, they more often remark oth-
    ers' possessions rather than their appearance.

12. When women discuss problems, they often seek empathy and sup-
    port, not solutions to problems; men tend to offer solutions.

Male discourse styles often provide the standard against which speakers' and writers' success is measured. When men speak, both women and men "more actively attend" to them than to women speakers (Renzetti and Curren 142). Wood reminds us that "in western society, the public sphere traditionally has been considered men's domain" and until relatively recently women did not act as public speakers. Men's public speaking style—linear, direct, confident, assertive—is more highly regarded than women's somewhat less linear and more collaborative, personal, and inclusive style, which tends to place women speakers at a disadvantage in public life. Women's style of speaking "is judged by a standard that neither reflects nor respects their communication goals and values." Wood's suggestion that "appreciating and respecting the distinctive validity (and value) of each style of communication" to create " a better foundation for better understanding between people" coupled with both women and men's greater flexibility in both using and granting credence to varied discourse practices is an important means to eliminating disadvantage and linguistic inequity (*Gendered Lives* 128). Men can learn to both speak and listen more collaboratively, sensitively, and inclusively and in a less self-directed manner; women can learn to speak more directly, confidently, and assertively.

As teachers construct the means for and facilitate classroom discussion, they will want to take the above discourse style differences into account to ensure both their female and male students the opportunity to express themselves openly and to grow as speakers. Prosenjak, Harmon, and Johnson et al. suggest the following ways to do so.

- Praise, encourage, and respond to the contributions of females and males equally.
- Call on females as often as males to answer both factual and complex questions.
- Create a classroom atmosphere where females are not interrupted by others more often than males.
- Establish collaborative groups composed of both males and females to provide opportunities for all voices to be heard. We add that collaborative groups must be structured so that leadership, reportorial, and secretarial roles shift to all group members and so that one or two members of the group cannot dominate the group's conversation. Literature circles, with their emphases on participatory tasks for each group member and on each member assuming different roles as groups meet on an ongoing basis, work well to facilitate all students' contributions.
- Avoid praising students' appearance and physical attributes; instead value intellect.
- Choose females for leadership roles as often as males.

• Avoid comments or humor that demean or stereotype males or females.

In addition, teachers must make gender equity and respect an active part of all classrooms through directly discussing them *before* inequitable discourse and discourse practices occur; collaboratively setting class ground rules for inclusive and respectful class discussions and behaviors; modeling gender-fair and inclusive practices, ensuring gender-balanced and gender-fair text selection, and constructing seating arrangements that encourage class work and conversation across genders. Teachers should consider having their classrooms videotaped over a period of a week or two to carefully observe themselves in action in their classes to determine if their classroom discourse practices are gender-fair.

FOR THOUGHT 5.7: Which, if either, of the above myths above have you subscribed to? Has the discussion above altered your mythic framework regarding women's and men's discourse styles? How many of the discourse differences noted above have you observed or experienced? Which of the above might create problems or misunderstandings for women and men as they converse with each other? Which have implications for the classroom as you work with male and female students?

CULTURALLY EMBEDDED GENDER: MEDIA, SCHOOLS, CLASSROOM DISCOURSE

Print and non-print media permeate our lives. Every day, messages from books, television, videos, newspapers, the Internet, billboards, magazines, films, radio, CDs surround and shape our daily routine. Media play an ever increasingly important role in schools as films, CDs, software packages, newspapers, packaged bulletin board displays, videos, magazines, and the Internet supplement classroom textbooks. Long before entering our classrooms, our students have been active consumers and are, in part, the products of the swirl of media that surrounds them. Wood reports that the average 18 year old has consumed more than 19,000 hours of television; 4/5 of all households have VCRs; 2/3 have cable; and MTV is the #1 cable network for persons 12–24 years of age (*Gendered Lives* 263). Not only do media reflect our cultural norms and roles, they create, define, and reinforce them. Says Wood, "media shape our understandings of women, men, and relationships between the sexes; they tell us who we personally should be as women and men" (262). Renzetti and Curren add that media are "the definers of the important" and the "chief sources of information for most people" (145). Thus any discussion of gender, discourse, power, and classrooms would be incomplete without an examination of media—both those varieties which affect our students and us outside the classroom and those forms that inhabit our classrooms. Romaine (1999), Wood (2003), and Renzetti and Curren review and synthesize their own and others' recent gender/media studies. All agree that despite recent developments in film, television, and advertising that challenge traditional men's and women's roles, the media, for the most part, display women and men in traditional roles and reinforce gender stereotypes wherein, by "symbolic annihilation" (Renzetti and Curren 145), women are dehumanized, made sex-objects, or rendered trivial or invisible. Media prompt both women and men toward a Procrustean bed to be fitted to artificial and/or idealized roles, even if fitting means painful alterations of their bodies.

The News: Print and Non-Print. Anyone who examines newspapers and news magazines or watches national news broadcasts on a regular basis soon sees that it's a man's world out there. Symbolic annihilation occurs as women, except for entertainers or those who have recently died, are seldom featured in stories, pictured on the front page, or lauded for their accomplishments. High school student Emily Stoddard felt it necessary to remind the public that women are also soldiers in Iraq as she took exception to a *Newsweek* cover which exclaimed "Wanted: More Men and Muscle" and Virgin Radio's campaign, "Backing Our Boys" (C8). When women do appear as media subjects, they are often trivialized by references to their appearance or through the use of gender-biased language. For example, much media space has been directed toward Senator Hillary Clinton's hair. When her senatorial efforts and her recent book were reviewed in *Time*, the story was accompanied by a two-page band of eight pictures which showed her changing hairstyles over the past 30 years and linked those changes to her search for identity (Klein 41–42). When Michigan's Governor Jennifer Granholm ran for election in 2002, media made much of what they called her good looks and attractive appearance as well as her past theatrical ambitions. Seldom was her honor graduation from law school given equal press. Following her election, *Newsweek* entitled an article "Brainy, Blonde, and Ready to Rumble" and described her as having "movie-star good looks" (Clift, 62).

Despite the Granholm article, news magazines allow women few headline appearances lauding them for their accomplishments and leadership. The same *Newsweek* issue, as it reviewed 2002 and predicted "Who's Next," pictured only two women in addition to Granholm but ten men. *Time* no longer calls its end of the year cover picture the "man of the year." However, changing its title to "Person of the Year," has not resulted in greatly increased female representation. A 1952 retrospective issue, *Time Capsule 1952*, contains shots of all its cover pictures. Of the 52, only five are women; of those, two are entertainers. The December 30, 2002- January 6, 2003 issue's article titled "Person of the Year" was bordered by photo reprints of recent former persons of the year—of these many, only two are women. The article invites readers to fold out the pages and review the sorts of persons chosen in the past for this honor; there readers find four pages of "person's" pictures, only one of whom, Queen Elizabeth II of England, is a woman. As *Time* reviews 2002 and looks ahead, readers find that the "People Who Mattered 2002" were 11 men and two women (Grossman 114–131).

Network national television news reigns as the province of men: no women are cast as the anchors for the nightly news; few correspondents are female. A *New York Times* piece dubs the nightly news as "the last all-male preserve" (Rutenberg C1) as network executives state "many viewers still want the news delivered by a patriarchal figure" (C8). When cable news channel CNN named a female morning news anchor, Paula Zahn, it ran a promotional that advertised her as "just a little sexy" as in the background viewers heard what sounded like a zipper being unzipped while the words "sexy" and "provocative" flashed on the screen (Demoraes D4).

Women's and Men's Magazines. Popular women's and men's magazine articles and advertisements, through their themes, words, and images, construe women and men narrowly, often stereotyping, demeaning and sexually objectifying them. *Sports Illustrated*, with its swimsuit issue, certainly caters to the male gaze, and its counterpart, *Sports Illustrated Women*, with 36 pages of photos of "The Sexiest Men in Sports 2002," promotes women's adoption of that gaze of sexual assessment and desire (Lowry and Rosa 72–108). Many women's "homemaker" magazines—*Good Housekeeping, Woman's Day, Family Circle, House and Garden*—center on the stereotype of the woman as homemaker and woman as caretaker, cleaner, nurturer. Wood notes that while such magazines cover more issues than they did a decade ago, they still emphasize looking good, staying or becoming thin, appealing to men, and running a household smoothly (268). In women's "glamour" magazines, general themes found throughout include the need make oneself over with instructions for doing so (better hair, eyes, figure, etc.); appealing to, getting, and keeping a man via either romance or aggressive sex appeal; the logistics and techniques of sex with heterosexuality as the norm. Health and fashion articles often contain sub-theme variants of the dominant themes; advertisements reinforce dominant themes and feature models whose full-breasted, but thin bodies exemplify an ideal of beauty impossible for most women to attain (Renzetti and Curren 149).

Magazines that target adolescent women feed into the limiting and demeaning roles adult women's magazines promote. Addie L. Sayers finds a number of disturbing patterns in three magazines geared to young women—*Teen, Seventeen, YM*. Young women are often labeled in derivative and diminutive ways: *sweetie, honey, baby, princess, actress*, and *studette*. They are presented as incomplete and in competition—they never measure up; they are urged to be the best dressed, be the most noticed, have the hottest hair, buy the latest makeup or fashions. The adolescent girl is a follower, not a leader: syntactic arrangement follows old patterns—guys and girls; boys and girls, "macho movies" and "chick flicks," this latter pair stereotyping both young males and females. As they peruse these magazines, readers observe females as passive, but boys and men as active; females as non-agents or manipulated agents, but males as agents: "five clues he noticed you," "five lines that will get him talking," "he really liked you, but you stared at him too much, so now he thinks you're crazy," "He's afraid of letting you go." Girls achieve, at best, only limited agency when they shop (but in response to ads or fashion trends) and in articles that feature beauty (but in accordance with narrow cultural norms), entertainment (though more articles feature male than female entertainers), and health. They could achieve agency in career articles, but those are few to be found. Thus these teen magazines produce an overall effect: "the American adolescent girl as a full human being, as a full agent and active subject, is constantly and consistently undermined ... " (Sayers 1). They imply the best a young woman can to is compete for men's attention; obsess over her hair, body, and clothing; and play a passive, secondary, or reactive role.

In their examination of men's magazines (*Esquire, GQ, Black Men*) Renzetti and Curren note that articles give a low priority to interpersonal relationships; articles on sex—relatively few in number—emphasize sexuality over emotional attachment. Articles and advertisements feature the good life, the results of success. They conclude: The "real" man, only somewhat concerned about his appeal to women, is a free and adventuresome risk taker who

> pursues his work and his hobbies—including in this latter category his relationships with women—with vigor .... Judging from the ads, one might easily conclude that men—especially White men spend the majority of their time driving around in cars, smoking cigarettes and cigars, drinking alcohol, taking pictures with their digital cameras, much to the neglect of their personal hygiene. (151)

That final point may be changing. The *New York Times* reports that the "monstrously popular" men's magazine, *Maxim*, a publication that by self-proclamation appeals to men's "inner swine" and features "Sex, Sports, Beer, Gadgets, Clothes, Fitness," has given its name to a line of hair color products, marketed heavily in its namesake. Ads show women unable to resist these frosted and dyed, "buff" men (3 June 2002 C7). Body scents for men, like those of women, are now labeled Allure and Obsession. And the American Dialect Society chose as its 2004 word of the year *metrosexual*, defined by Word Spy as "an urban male with a strong aesthetic sense who spends a great deal of time and money on his appearance and lifestyle."

 Film, Television, Video Games, Music. Through images, actions, and word choice, non-print media—television, film, music videos, song lyrics, video games—inscribe gender stereotypes. Often they depict violence toward women and paint men as aggressors. A CBS *Evening News* story (July 7, 2003) described "Crime City," a video game in which players receive points for killing police and soliciting a prostitute, then beating her to death rather than paying her for her services. A Japanese video, "Princess," features players called "Dads," who "parent" a sexualized young female figure and program her to dress in revealing lingerie or sunbathe nude. Both mainstream films, especially horror, serial killer, and slasher films, and pornographic films regularly stage rape and other verbal and physical violence toward women. Song lyrics, MTV, and music videos films promote male dominance of women and display women, often labeled *whores* and *bitches,* as the passive victims of or willing participants in sexual violence. Alisa Valdes-Rodriguez, in "Women take a beating from violence in music," concludes that violent pop music and music videos reduce women to "punching bags, strippers, and sperm receptacles" (A6). Dr. Dre shakes beer bottles and spews beer on a stripper in a video for "The Next Episode"; Eminem raps about killing his wife and raping and murdering his mother, and rap and reggae lyrics like those noted in chapter 4 wreak hatred upon anyone whose gender does not fall into narrowly defined parameters.

 However, songs and film need not be blatantly violent, misogynist, or homophobic to promote gender stereotypes. In how many standards, popular songs, and ballads are the themes of a woman's dependence on a man or a man's love as essential to her well being addressed? In how many songs do men or women use gender-biased language as they sing about or address others? Even seemingly innocent songs can convey strong subtexts of domination. As an example, we urge readers to examine the lyrics of the well-known "Every Breath You Take" by The Police (available on many Web sites including www.azlyrics.com and www.reallyrics.com) and consider the possible emotions and motives they express.

 Television, the most accessible and most consumed non-print medium in the United States, transmits messages about gender and gender relationships similar to those discussed above. Despite exceptions such as *Judging Amy, Cold Case,* and *Crossing Jordan,* evening dramas and comedies seldom show professional women at work, actively engaged in their careers in leadership roles. Revealed as more dependent, granted less personal agency, and depicted as less important than men, television women are often thinner, more attractive, younger, less authoritative, less educated, and/or less successful than the men with whom they interact. They usually have fewer lines than male characters. If working outside the home, most are subordinate to a male boss or leader. Often women with careers, even when on the job, are more preoccupied with their relationships with men, their dress and appearance, and/or their families than they are with their careers. Male leads, often shown as very capable at work, intelligently pursue their professions. Many are single; in some shows, audiences never see them at home. In those shows, usually comedies, in which we see married men at home, we often see them as bumbling in their personal relationships and incapable of smoothly managing a home—a scenario that demeans men and reinforces the necessity of women's being responsible for maintaining relationships and running the home (Wood 2003; Renzetti and Curren).

FOR THOUGHT 5.8: Examine some of the prime time television shows that have won awards and high ratings (*Everybody Loves Raymond, Fraser, Law and Order, Without a Trace, The Sopranos, Friends, Home Improvement, CSI, CSI Miami*). How many of the above points do they exemplify? *Cold Case* counters some of the points made above. Can you name other shows that do? Which, if any, of the points made above does *Desperate Housewives* reinforce? Which, if any, does it counter?

Advertising.   Advertising's presentation of women has been critiqued in both print and DVD or video–the best of which are Jean Kilbourne's listed earlier in the chapter and *Warning: The Media May Be Hazardous to Your Health* (1990). Romaine (1999), Wood (2003), and Renzetti and Curren all offer succinct and well exemplified commentary. And anyone who takes a close and thoughtful look at ads sees that they promote the same sorts of stereotypes critiqued throughout this discussion of media. When sexualized—as is often the case—women's bodies are depersonalized and positioned to become the objects of the male sexual gaze or its female counterpart. They are often shown as vulnerable, as waif-like, as passive and often prone, inferior in size and/or dominated by the men whom they accompany. Ads prompt women to make themselves over so that their hair, lips, shape, clothing, and odors will attract men. The images and words of ads address sex—often impersonal sex—directly and by innuendo. States a Viagra ad in which Rafael Palmeiro swings a bat, "For Rafeal Palmiero and so many other guys Viagra is a home run," a play on the sex as game, getting to first base, and scoring metaphors. An ad for Virgin Mobile telephones displays a semi-clothed young woman over whom a taller man is draped; she looks up at him smiling, the antenna from his phone in her navel. The caption reads, "Set to vibrate." Ads idealize body types—thin and well-toned, the women with large breasts, the men with large chest and arm muscles—that the majority of humans do not possess and encourage men and women to achieve those ideals, sometimes by mutilating their bodies.

Radical Make-Over, in reality a feature-length advertisement for plastic surgery, encourages its viewers to achieve those body types through plastic surgery, liposuction, breast enhancement, chemical injections, or starvation dieting. Ads teach us that women are to avoid wrinkles—signs of aging—at all costs. Other ads depict the happy housewife who has discovered another effective cleaner, appliance, or cooking shortcut, or the helpless housewife who needs advice about how to clean, cook, or transport. In a single night of television, watching from 8:30 p.m.-11:00 p.m., we saw a nearly nude model advertising Victoria's Secret bras and pants; an ad for beer in which a man who must leave a drinking party early is told "don't trip over your skirts as you leave"; a K-Mart ad in which a young woman announces "cords show off my legs," and a young man states, "You can wear cords with denim." The same night a man being jailed on *Law and Order* was told sarcastically, "You were crying about going to jail? Now that's not very manly." Gender stereotypes flourish in the land of television programming and advertising.

We close this section of the chapter with a description of two advertisements which appeared on the same page in a student university newspaper. The first, a 1/4 page ad for plastic surgery, shows a young, blond, slender woman lying on her stomach, wearing a two-piece bathing suit. She is positioned so that viewers' eyes focus on her large breasts as she looks up at us. The caption reads, "Be The Best You Can Be." Diagonally, below her in an ad of equal size, is the picture of a fully clothed young man in football gear, arms up above his head, hand positions signifying victory and success. The caption reads, "Score a touchdown with ... Totally Free Checking" (*Valley Vanguard* 8).

FOR THOUGHT 5. 9: How many of the assertions about media made in this chapter do the words and images in the two ads above exemplify?

School communications and media: Applications for teachers and classrooms

Not only are our students surrounded by the media messages that promote gender bias and power asymmetries, too often their classrooms' discourse practices and educational materials reinforce the same messages. One of our students, Peter, recalls his middle school Family Life teacher announcing that his name is used to refer to the "male member." The female teacher then asked students—all male—to list all the terms they use, and Peter took harsh taunting for several weeks as his classmates combined his name with those they'd listed in class. The cartoon that heads this chapter as well as the one detailed below presents the tendency of boys to demand attention as they raise their hands to be called by teachers. Yet, the *Luann* strip below, while it initially addresses gender differences in classrooms, reinforces gender stereotypes. The scene is a classroom. Depicted are teenaged males snapping their fingers to get the teacher's attention as they volunteer to answer the question, "Who can name 3 great minds of the 18th century?" One calls out "OH!" as he snaps his fingers. Luann, a blond teenager, speaks.

Luann (to a female classmate):	Why do boys do that?
Classmate:	What?
Luann:	Snap their fingers when they raise their hands. Girls don't do that.
Classmate:	Girls don't raise their hands.
Luann:	Hm … That's true. I never raise my hand. Wonder why?
Classmate:	Because unlike boys who enjoy taking risks and aren't devastated by error, you—a typical female—fear being wrong, even when you know you're right. Therefore, you never raise your hand.
Luann:	Oh Yeah? Well watch this. (She raises her hand and snaps her fingers.)
Teacher:	Ok, Luann.
Luann:	27. (Evans 24 March 1996)

Luann sits smiling, her eyes half open. Her male and female classmates look at her with expressions that express both surprise and contempt.

FOR THOUGHT 5.10: List all of the negative messages given about girls in this *Luann* strip.

Classroom materials often reflect and sustain culturally embedded gender inequity. Recent studies of Caldecott Award winners and runner-ups reveal that "77% of the female characters were shown using household implements; 80% of the males were using work and production implements found outside the home." (Kaplan). In winners from 1972 to 1997, 61% of character appearances in the text are male, 39% female; of pictures, 60% depict males, and 40 % depict females. Interestingly, these figures show a decline in female representation since the 1950s (Davis and McDaniel). Harmon's examination of high school American literature anthologies found that relatively few selections contained were written by women and that women and girls were underrepresented as characters in selections. In selections and in textbooks' apparatus that accompany selections, women and girls are often rendered stereotypically, demeaned, or dismissed as trivial (Harmon 1993, 2000). Women and women's deeds play minor roles in those secondary history texts that aren't specifically designated as women's history texts. A look at most schools' A-V lists reveals that far more DVD/videos about male authors, scientists, and historical figures, and far more film versions of works by male authors are available to teachers. Our pre-service teachers tell us from their observations of classrooms that old practices of gender segregation and gender bias have not died out in schools, where teachers line up boys and girls separately, stage boys against girls contests, direct more attention to boys, choose reading materials and class projects with boys who do not like "girls' stories" in mind, refer to their students consistently as "boys and girls" or "you guys," and/or make blatant remarks like "throws like a girl" or "well, that's just how boys are."

Renzetti and Curren and Wood (2003) review a 1982 study done by Hall and Sandler which revealed deeply embedded discourse habits of college teachers in mixed gender classrooms. Because, as both sources amply demonstrate, a large number of studies since have found the same practices still in place at all levels of education, and because they offer a succinct summary of contentions made throughout this chapter, we list several of Hall and Sandler's findings and add commentary that extends them to K–12 classrooms.

1. Teachers maintain more eye contact and a more attentive posture when talking to male students.
2. Teachers ask more challenging questions of male students, and they draw out male students' responses and respond to or pursue their contributions more fully than they do those of female students. Additionally, teachers take more time conferring with male students than with females. Follow-up research has shown that in K–12 schools, teachers (as well as parents and the students themselves) often attribute males' academic success to intelligence and ability and females' to hard work or over-achievement.
3. Teachers call on male students more often. In K–12 schools, teachers are more likely to praise boys' contributions and to ignore boys' interruptions. Girls who call out to interrupt are more often reprimanded. Boys, while they receive more positive teacher attention than girls, are also more likely to receive negative attention and reprimands.
4. Teachers are more likely to ignore, interrupt, allow others to interrupt, or dismiss female students' contributions.
5. Teachers make comments that disparage women and their intellectual abilities.
6. Teachers comment about women's physical appearance more often than that of males.
7. Teachers use gender-stereotyped and gender-biased examples. A teacher Mary recently observed suggested that his seventh-grade boys might write about a trip they'd taken with their dads—like a fishing

trip; the girls might write about shopping with their moms or choosing make up. (Renzetti and Curren 115, 122; Wood 218).

Our final classroom exhibit demonstrates the insidious nature of deeply embedded gendered discourse practices coupled with the use of gender-biased teaching materials. Both insure that women and men learn cultural texts of gender inequity along with lessons in English language arts, history, or math. Myra and David Sadker recorded the following classroom dialogue during a grammar review in a third-grade classroom. The teaching kit that forms the basis for the teaching situation below can still be found in classrooms. In late 2004, Mary saw it posted in a middle school classroom, where she was a guest.

Teacher:	What is a noun? (More than half the class waves their hands excitedly.)
Teacher:	John?
John:	A person, place, or thing.
Teacher:	Correct. (She places a large cartoon dragon on the felt board.) What part of the definition is this? Antonio?
Antonio:	A thing.
Teacher:	Good. (She places a castle on the felt board above the dragon.) What part of the definition is this? Elise?
Elise:	A place.
Teacher:	Okay. (She puts a tiny princess in front of the dragon. The face of the princess is frozen in a silent scream.) Here is a person. Now, what is a verb? Seth?
Seth:	An action word.
Teacher:	I'm glad to see that you remember your parts of speech. (She posts a cartoon of an enormous knight riding a horse). What are some action words that tell what the knight is doing? Mike?
Mike:	Fight. What else?
Peter: (calling out)	Slay.
Teacher:	Good vocabulary word. Any others? Al?
Al:	Capture.
Teacher:	Excellent verbs. What is an adjective? Maria?
Maria:	A word that describes something.
Tim: (calling out)	Adjectives describe nouns.
Teacher:	Good, Tim. (The teacher posts a minstrel strumming a lute. A large bubble is drawn, cartoon style, showing that the minstrel is singing the words "Oh, she is beautiful.") What is the adjective in this sentence? Donna?

Donna: Beautiful.

Teacher: Now we are going to see how parts of speech can be used in stories. Each one of you will write your own fairy tale about how the brave knight slays the dragon and rescues the beautiful princess. (74)

After students write for 20 minutes, the teacher tells them that they will all have a chance to read their stories aloud to each other. The girls are directed to go into the hall to read with the student teacher, where they are to talk very softly and not bother anyone. The boys are told to stay in the classroom with her. Was the taped teacher deliberately relegating girls to a secondary status by teaching them that their contributions are not valued and by reinforcing cultural stereotypes? We doubt that to be the case. Rather, we'd suggest that this teacher, a product of the inequitable culturally embedded gender messages encoded in media and discourse practices that surround us, unwittingly reinscribed them in classroom practice.

APPLICATIONS FOR THE CLASSROOM

Throughout this chapter we have reviewed and illustrated language practices and usage on the word, grammar, discourse, and culturally embedded levels which promote gender stereotypes and gender inequity. We have argued that schools, often unwittingly, through language choices, discourse practices and curriculum, play an important role in assigning and reinforcing this lesser role to women. We readily acknowledge that some language and discourse changes have occurred. Commentary like this chapter was unavailable when Marilyn and Mary sat in pre-service teacher classes 40 years ago. We have seen change endorsed by many universities and by professional organizations such as the National Council of Teachers of English and the Modern Language Association who have both published guidelines for gender-fair discourse. Most public speakers now take care to use gender-fair language in public address. But as the examples cited in this chapter demonstrate, change has been slow and somewhat limited. Recently, Mary saw a woman directing traffic next to a "Men Working" sign. To help speed change, we have exemplified gender inequity in both the wider culture and the classroom, and we have suggested pedagogical practices that promote gender-fair discourse practices. We will close with a list of suggestions for ensuring greater gender-fairness and gender balance in classroom print and non-print media choices.

1. Choose print and non-print texts that depict women and men and boys and girls in a variety of roles and in non-stereotypical ways.

2. Choose as many texts written by women as by men and as many that feature girls/women as active and successful agents.

3. Teach students how to analyze texts—both those they read for literature and their textbooks from other classes—in terms of gender and to challenge stereotypical ways of looking at female and male gender roles. Encourage students to create alternatives to the gender presentations they find in texts. Noninclusive texts offer opportunity for discussions of gender stereotypes, gendered language, and gender expectations. Employing the following strategies as students read and discuss texts will assist in bringing gender issues to light and will encourage the sort of reading that challenges the text as it actively engages with it. The questions on p. 107 above also help.

   a. Examine the presence and absence of both men and women in texts. How many of each are there? How much space is each given? Who gets to speak? How much? What do they say? Who is silent? What roles do females and males play in the piece? Who is active? Who is relatively passive? Who leads and initiates? Who follows? What implications do the answers to these questions have?

   b. Consider what the silent person(s) in texts might say if given a chance to speak. What, for example, might Rip Van Winkle's wife, a woman negatively presented by the author, say about her husband if she were given a chance to speak? How might Marvel's Coy Mistress reply to her suitor?

   c. Examine the words used to describe female and male characters, the names or labels they are given, how they are dressed, and the amount of attention paid to their physical appearance; then, discuss the implications.

   d. Note the behaviors that are rewarded for female and male characters as well as those which are disparaged.

   e. Change the names and gender of lead characters and discuss whether those changes alter the work and its appeal.

Teachers, as they prepare lesson plans and curricula that promote gender balance, have many resources at their disposal in addition to those we cite throughout this chapter. Whaley and Dodge's *Weaving in the Women* refers teachers in 9th- through 12th-grade classrooms to a wealth of activities and to texts by a diversity of women and suggests ways in which to thematically pair texts written by women with those written by men. Mitchell lists a number of useful suggestions in her "Approaching Race and Gender Issues in the Context of the Language Arts Classroom: Teaching Ideas." Martino and Mellor detail activities and applications for examining gender in their *Gendered Fictions* as do Longmire and Merrill in their *Untying the Tongue*.

Two sets of guidelines produced by members of WILLA, NCTE's Women in Literacy and Life Assembly, *Guidelines for Gender Fair Use of Language, Guidelines for A Gender-Balanced Curriculum in English, Grades 7-12* (2002, 1999), offer secondary teachers further activities and suggestions for achieving gender-balanced curricula; the latter includes a list of book titles that can augment classroom gender balance. Both are available at www.ncte.org by typing "Positions and Guidelines" in the Search box. Both can be printed and disseminated without NCTE permission. Typing "gender" into NCTE's Search box brings up scores of resources.

Because discussions of gender and gender differences challenge ideologies and stereotypes, some of our students may wish to dismiss them. But these differences help to create cultural perspectives that sustain inequity. Words construct reality and encourage people to think along pre-ordained paths. However paths need not become ruts and can be changed. To enact such change, texts and activities which directly or indirectly query gender roles and assumptions should be interwoven into classroom discussion and curricula on a regular and ongoing basis. In time students will become more alert to both overt and covert culturally embedded evidences of gender bias and inequity. Aware, they will be better empowered to counter them in their own lives and to ensure a more gender equitable world for themselves and others.

PERSONAL EXPLORATIONS

1. Consider the word *slut* (or any other offensive and frequently used gender slur). Who gains and who loses "cultural capital" in terms of power and control from the widespread use of this term by both females and males? Gainers and losers will likely be different for different terms; for example, how do the gains and losses that occur with the word *stud* compare and contrast with those you listed for *slut*?

2. Take the quiz that begins this chapter again. Have any of your answers changed? If so, why?

3. Trace your life for 24 hours as a member of a different gender group. In your new role, how will your life be affected differently by the language and discourse practices discussed in this chapter?

TEACHING EXPLORATIONS

1. Examine the classroom texts used in your classroom or in your local school to evaluate them for gender bias. How can you counter the bias you find in classroom texts?

2. Divide the class into groups as follows: a television group, an MTV group, a song lyrics group, an advertising (TV, billboards, Internet, and radio) group, a magazine covers and articles group, a magazine advertising group, a newspaper group, a cartoon/comics group, a classroom texts group, etc. Have each group examine a selected number and variety of their targeted media for gender bias and report their findings in a show and tell multimedia presentation.

3. Observe the discourse practices in several classrooms. Try to choose classrooms in which student composition is varied in age, social class, ethnic, and gender makeup. Which, if any, of the gendered language practices and choices discussed in this chapter do you observe? How much time, if any, is spent on overt discussion of gender issues in the classrooms you observe? What conclusions for your own teaching can you draw?

4. Examine plays often taught in the secondary schools and determine if, when, and how the males and females in them do or do not follow the discourse practices of women and men discussed in this chapter. *A Doll's House, Pygmalion, A Raisin in the Sun, The Crucible, Fences, Trifles, Antigone, Macbeth, Romeo and Juliet, M. Butterfly, The Heidi Chronicles, The Miracle Worker* all work well. As students read these plays, what do they learn about gender roles?

5. List all of the lessons about gender students learn in Sadker and Sadker's taped classroom discourse (p. 140). In which ways and how many times are these lessons reinforced during the teacher's grammar lesson? Then compare your list to Sadker and Sadker's commentary on page 75 of their *Failing at Fairness*.

WORKS CITED

Anderson, Judith and Stephen Grubman. "Communicating Difference: Forms of Resistance." *Women's Place in the Academy Transforming the Liberal Arts Curriculum.* Eds. Marilyn R. Schuster and Susan R. Van Dyne. Totowa, NJ: Rowman, 1985. 221–231.

Baron, Dennis. *Declining Grammar*. Urbana, IL: NCTE, 1989.

_____. *Grammar and Gender*. New Haven: Yale UP, 1986.

Bosmajian, Haig A. *The Language of Oppression*. Washington D.C.: Public Affairs Press, 1974.

Bower, Amanda. "It's Mrs; Not Ms." *Time*. 6 June 2005: W4.

Breslau, Karen. "Welcome to Girls' State." *Newsweek* 31 Jan. 2005: 30.

Campo-Flores, Arian. "A Crackdown on Call Girls." *Newsweek*. 2 Sep. 2002: 59.

Clift, Eleanor. "Brainy, Blonde, and Ready to Rumble." *Newsweek* 30 Dec. 2002: 62.

Coates, Jennifer. *Women, Men, and Language*. 2nd ed. New York: Longman, 1993.

Davis, Anita P. and Tomas R. McDaniel. "You've Come a Long Way Baby—Or Have You?" *The Reading Teacher*. Feb. 1999: 532–536.

Demoraes, Lisa. "CNN 'outraged' over Zahn promo." *Saginaw News* [Michigan]. 8 Jan. 2002: D4.

Evans, Greg. "Luann." Cartoon. United Features Syndicate, Inc. 24 Mar. 1996.

Flagg, Fanny. *Fried Green Tomatoes at the Whistle Stop Café*. New York: McGraw, 1987.

Goldman, Irene C. "Feminism, Deconstruction, and the Universal. A Case Study On *Walden*." *Conversations*. Eds. Charles Moran and Elizabeth F. Penfield. Urbana, IL: NCTE, 1990: 120–131.

Grossman, Lev. "People Who Mattered." *Time*. Double Issue. 30 Dec. 2002-6 Jan. 2003: 114–131

Guisewite, Cathy. "Cathy." Cartoon. Universal Press Syndicate. 22-29 Mar. 2005.

"Guys." *Merriam-Webster's Collegiate Dictionary*. 10th ed. Springfield, MA: Merriam, 1994.

Harmon, Mary Rose. *A Study of Sociolinguistic Texts and Subtexts as Found in Five High School American Literature Anthologies*. Diss. Michigan State University, 1993.

_____. "Gender/Language Subtexts as Found in Literature Anthologies: Mixed Messages, Stereotypes, Silence, Erasure." *Hearing Many Voices*. Eds. M. J. Hardman and Anita Taylor. Cresskill, NJ: Hampton, 2000. 75–86.

Kaplan, Lisa Faye. "A Tale of Two Sexes." *Lansing State Journal* [Michigan]. 8 Jan. 1993: D4.

Kilbourne, Jean. *Killing Us Softly: Advertising's Images of Women*. DVD. Northampton, MA: Media Education Foundation, 2002.

Klein, Joe. "The Humanity of Hillary." *Time* 16 June 2003: 40–41.

Kosroshahi, Fatemeh. "Penguins Don't Care, But Women Do: A Social Identity Analysis of a Whorfian Problem." *Language and Society* 18 (1988): 505–525.

Lakoff, Robin. *The Language War*. Berkeley, CA: U of California P, 2000.

_____. "You Are What You Say." *The Gender Reader*. Eds. Evelyn Ashton-Jones and Gary A. Olson. Boston: Allyn, 1991: 292–298.

_____. *Language and the Woman's Place*. New York: Harper and Row, 1975.

Longmire, Linda and Lisa Merrill eds. *Untying the Tongue Gender, Power, and the Word.*. Westport, CT: Greenwood, 1998.

Lowry, Vicki and Christine Rosa. "The Sexiest Men in Sports." *Sports Illustrated Women*. July/Aug. 2002: 72–108.

Martino, Wayne and Bronwyn Mellor, eds. *Gendered Fictions*. Urbana, IL: NCTE, 2000.

McCracken, Nancy Mellin. "Re-Gendering the Reading of Literature." *Gender Issues in the Teaching of English*. Eds. Nancy Mellin McCracken and Bruce C. Appleby. Portsmouth, NH: Boynton, 1992.

MacKinnon, Catherine. *Only Words*. Cambridge, MA: Harvard UP, 1993.

"Metrosexual." Word Spy. <www.wordspy.com/words/metrosexual>.

Miller, Casey and Kate Swift. "One Small Step for Genkind." *The Gender Reader*. Eds. Evelyn Ashton Jones and Gary Olson. Boston: Allyn and Bacon, 1991. 247–258.

_____. "Women and Names." *The Gender Reader*. Eds. Evelyn Ashton Jones and Gary Olson. Boston: Allyn, 1991. 272–286.

_____. *Words and Women*. New York: Doubleday, 1977.

Mitchell, Diana. "Approaching Race and Gender Issues in the Context of the Language Arts Classroom: Teaching Ideas." *English Journal* (June 1996): 77–81.

Moses, Alexander R. "By law, Michigan's governor is a 'he'." *Saginaw News* [Michigan]. 19 May 2003: A3.

Mulac, Anthony. "The Gender-Linked Language Effect: Do Language Differences Really Make a Difference?" Eds. Daniel J. Canary and Kathryn Dindia. Mahwah, NJ: Lawrence Erlbaum Associates, 1998: 127–154.

Nilsen, Alleen Pace. "Sexism in English: Embodiment and Language." *Living Language*. Ed. Alleen Pace Nilsen. Boston: Allyn, 1999: 173–183.

———. "Sexism in English: A 1990s Update." *The Gender Reader*. Eds. Evelyn Ashton-Jones and Gary Olson. Boston: Allyn, 1991: 259–271.

Penelope, Julia. *Speaking Freely Unlearning the Lies of the Fathers' Tongues*. New York: Pergamon, 1990.

"Person of the Year." *Time* 30 Dec. 2002-6 Jan. 2003: Insert.

Petrakis, Harry Mark. "The Wooing of Ariadne." *The United States in Literature*. New York: Scott, 1991. 649–657.

The Police. "Every Breath You Take." *Synchronicity*. Interscope Records. 1983.

Prosenjak, Nancy, Mary Harmon, Sue Johnson, et al. *Guidelines for Gender-Fair Use of Language*. Urbana, IL: National Council of Teachers of English, 2002. Available at <www.ncte.org/pubs/publish/books/107647.htm>.

Renzetti, Claire M. and Daniel J. Curren. *Women, Men, and Society*. 5th ed. New York: Allyn, 2003.

Romaine, Suzanne. *Communicating Gender*. Mahwah NJ: Lawrence Erlbaum Associates, 1999.

———. *Language in Society An Introduction to Sociolinguistics*. New York: Oxford UP, 1994.

Rutenberg, Jim. "News Anchors and the Cathode Ray Ceiling." *New York Times* 3 June 2003: C1+.

Sadker, Myra and David Sadker. *Failing at Fairness: How America's Schools Cheat Girls*. New York: Scribner's, 1994.

Sayers, Addie L. "Girls Can Do Anything, but …: How the Language of Teenage Magazines Undermines Gender Equity." Unpublished paper. Organization for the Study of Communication, Language, and Gender Conference. 8 Oct. 2000, Milwaukee, WI.

Spender, Dale. *The Writing of the Sex or Why You Don't Have to Read Women's Writing to Know It's No Good*. New York: Pergamon, 1989.

Stanley, Julia P. "Gender-Marking in American English: Usage and Reference." *Sexism and Language*. Eds. Nilsen, Alleen Pace, Haig Bosmajian, H. Lee Gershuny, and Julia P. Stanley. Urbana, IL: NCTE, 1977: 43–76.

"State Constitutions Become Gender-Neutral." *New York Times*. <www.nytimes.com/aponline/national/AP-Gender-Neutral-Constitutions.html>. 21 May 2003.

Stoddard, Emily. "Women in This War, Too." *Saginaw News*. 30 Apr. 2003: C8.

Tanenbaum, Leona. "The Sleaze Factor." *Flint Journal*. 26 Jan. 1997: E1.

Tannen, Deborah, ed. *He Said, She Said*. Video. Information for the Classroom Media, 2001.

———. *Gender and Conversational Interaction*. New York: Oxford UP, 1993.

———. *You Just Don't Understand Women and Men in Conversation*. New York: Morrow, 1990.

Thoreau, Henry David. *Walden or Life in the Woods*. New York: New American Library, 1960.

Trudeau, Garry. "Doonesbury." Cartoon. Universal Press Syndicate. 27 Apr. 1992.

Trudgill, Peter. *Sociolinguistics: An Introduction to Language and Society*. New Edition. New York, Penguin, 1995.

University Of California at Berkeley. *Gender and Communication: Male-Female Differences in Language and Nonverbal Behavior*. Video. 2001.

Valdes-Rodriguez, Alisa. "Women Taking a Beating From Violence in Music." *Los Angeles Times* rpt. in *Saginaw News* [Michigan]. 29 June 2000: A6.

Valley Vanguard. 3 Dec. 2001: 8.

Warning: The Media May Be Hazardous to Your Health. Video. Santa Cruz: Media Watch, 1990.

Whaley, Liz and Liz Dodge. *Weaving in the Women*. Urbana, IL: NCTE, 1999.

Williams, Raymond. *Keywords*. New York: Oxford UP, 1983.

Wood, Julia T. *Gendered Lives: Communication, Gender, and Culture*. 5th ed. Belmont, CA: Thomson Wadsworth, 2003.

Wood, Julia T. and Kathryn Dindia. "What's the Difference? A Dialogue About Differences and Similarities Between Women and Men." *Sex Differences and Similarities in Communication*. Eds. Daniel J. Canary and Kathryn Dindia. Mahwah, NJ: Lawrence Erlbaum Associates, 1998. 19–39.

Chapter 6

Dialects: Suppression or Expression?

FOR THOUGHT 6.1: Identify the following statements as either True or False:

1. Languages that operate with double negatives are illogical because technically speaking, two negatives make a positive.
2. Some languages and dialects are structured in much more complex ways than others.
3. African American speakers operate with a strict set of language rules.
4. The dialect one speaks has nothing to do with one's intelligence.
5. Non-standard dialects are deficient linguistic systems that make complex thought difficult.

It's not uncommon to have people deny that they speak a dialect. "Oh, no," they might say, "Some folks around here speak a dialect, but I don't." Or, "We speak General American around here. We're just as standard as the rest of 'em." Or, "It's those folks at the other end of town that speak a dialect." Others appear to be deeply offended by the idea of their speech as a dialect. Still others embarrassedly admit that they might speak a dialect and say they feel ashamed of not speaking "correctly." But some bravely acknowledge their own linguistic differences and resist the prevailing attitude of dialect inferiority foisted on them by their more socially prominent neighbors.

The term *dialect* for many people suggests ignorance, lack of education, and lower social standing, an impression fostered in the media, especially television, and often promoted by the educational establishment. TV sit-coms that use dialect to insinuate intellectual inferiority, standardized tests that require knowledge of "correct" usage, and programs that label students as remedial or deficient based on their language patterns all perpetuate negative stereotypes about linguistic difference that become accepted as fact, without scrutiny or question.

In fact, many of our undergraduate pre-service teachers in our respective universities operate with attitudes toward language similar to those of the wider community. Some view language variants as polar opposites—singularly good or bad, correct or incorrect: they "know" their often deliberate, sometimes unconscious use of non-standard usages to be "bad" on a scale of absolutes; they "know" the prescriptivisms of their grammar books to be correct, and their own violations of these rules to be incorrect. Like their parents and grandparents before them, they have internalized the attitudes toward language that have permeated the American psyche. There are no class, race, or gender lines drawn here. Students from the Upper Peninsula of Michigan expect negative responses to their "yooper" dialect because it's different from so-called "standard" English. Kids from rural areas are aware that some of their language choices aren't "acceptable" in an academic community. And some of the African American students with varying degrees of African American Vernacular English features share the attitudes of their European American classmates: standard is somehow "better" than nonstandard.

In a recent class of undergraduate language students who took the survey at the beginning of this chapter, of the 33 students who responded to the survey, 18% incorrectly said that statement no. 1 was true; 97% incorrectly said that no. 2 was true; 51% incorrectly said that no. 3 was false; 15% incorrectly said that no. 4 was false; and 33% incorrectly said that no. 5 was true. If, as a student, you responded to the survey, how do your results compare?

Linguistic insecurity—speakers' beliefs that their own language patterns fall short of an ideal and therefore reflect linguistic inferiority—runs rampant in our society. Consider how often English teachers hear, "Oh, you're an English teacher. I'll have to watch my grammar" or how often individuals say, "I know my grammar isn't very good." Yet their sophisticated use of language often contradicts these self-deprecating comments. The undergraduates who hold prescriptive views of language and denigrate their own language patterns usually use language in a highly complex way, adjusting their speech patterns to meet the needs of their particular audience, shifting styles appropriately, recognizing the flexibility with which speakers of a language operate as they move from one context to another. Though they profess to believe at one level that "good" language usage always follows a prescriptive pattern of correctness, at the same time, a thoughtful analysis of their language helps them acknowledge the following:

- Language change is inevitable and occurs over time: rather than wrong, they find amusing their grandparents' use of *davenport* and *ice box*.
- Usage is variable, depending on audience: they avoid using *wife-beater* with reference to sleeveless undershirts around their grandparents or *ain't* in conversation with their professors.
- Language has the flexibility to be creative: they take great pleasure in creating usages that identify them as members of their peer groups but that restrict admission for adults.
- They modify grammatical structures as well as vocabulary as they move from one social group to another: they wouldn't be caught dead saying "With whom did you go?" to one of their roommates, even though they might feel compelled to use the construction in a more formal setting.

FOR THOUGHT 6.2: As a reflection of the creative use of language one finds among young adults, shortly after 9/11, the following terms emerged as a result of that tragedy. Match the following phrases and their intended meanings:

1. My bedroom is ground zero.	a petty concern
2. He's a terrorist.	a real mess
3. That's so Sept. 10.	out-of-style clothes
4. Is that a burka?	a student is disciplined
5. It was totally jihad.	a mean teacher

Actual language use is more variable, flexible, creative, and organic than people's assumptions about it are. What accounts for the contradiction between beliefs and actual use? Is it the inadequate and emotional nature of our beliefs that belie the reality of language? The encouragement from schools, media, and the press to believe that "correctness" is all that matters in language? The lag between linguistic knowledge and our emotional responses to language? Or is it something more?

This chapter looks at issues of *dialect* and *linguistic variation as a social phenomenon*, with all of its educational implications, and with an underlying series of political questions that reoccur:

- *Who speaks a dialect*, how do *regional and social dialects* differ, and what are the social and cultural implications of speaking *socially stigmatized dialects*?
- What does *code-switching* involve?

- What is *"standard" English* how does it develop?
- Why do speakers use *hypercorrection*?
- How does *covert prestige* affect the use of *standard*?
- How does *hegemony* operate in the imposition of a "standard" English?
- What is the *role of educational institutions* in linguistic discrimination?
- What issues are involved in the *teaching of the Language of Wider Communication*?
- How can teachers make *"linguistic contact zones"* work in the classroom?
- How does the *Ebonics controversy* illustrate issues of language and power?
- How can teachers and schools overcome the *restrictive cultural environment* usually provided for linguistically diverse students?

These questions probe the relationship between language and power, suggesting that because linguistic variation is political, not neutral, it must be studied from a critical perspective. Because a simple descriptive analysis of linguistic difference is insufficient, we need to consider the power relationships existing between those who impose the prescriptions about language use and those upon whom those prescriptions are imposed. The chapter moves beyond critical awareness of these issues to suggestions for how educators can directly address these language issues in classroom contexts and become agents of change.

DIALECT: WHAT IS IT?

Despite its negative connotations for many people, linguists use the term *dialect* to indicate a set of linguistic features that identifies speakers as members of a particular speech community representing a geographic region, a social class or educational level, an ethnic group, or, more often, a combination of these. The term, used neutrally rather than pejoratively, applies to all speakers of a language. Dialect is not exclusive to a class (working or middle) or region (southern, northern, midland) or ethnicity (African American, Native American, Pennsylvania Dutch). As a northerner born and bred, with a Dutch heritage and working-class roots, and as a member of an academic community, Marilyn speaks a particular dialect of American English that incorporates regional, ethnic, and social class features, just as her neighbor born and bred in the south, whose ethnicity is African American, and who also grew up in a working-class environment, speaks another dialect of American English. A dialect comprises a complex web of phonological, syntactic, semantic, and pragmatic features that function interconnectedly and systematically. The speaker who says, "I might could do it" uses a different system of modal verbs than Marilyn's; the African American Vernacular English (AAVE) speaker who says "She be here every day" uses a complex verb system that denotes habitual, regular activity, a form not found in other American dialects.

FOR THOUGHT 6.3: Identify the following pairs as representing either a dialect difference, or a language difference:

Chinese and Japanese

Mandarin Chinese and Cantonese Chinese

German and Dutch

Spanish and Italian

Ebonics and standard English

Spanish and Portuguese

What criteria determine the answers? If lack of mutual intelligibility is one of the criteria for determining separate languages, why are German and Dutch considered separate languages when they are, for the most part, mutually intelligible? Why are Mandarin and Cantonese referred to as dialects of Chinese even though they are not mutually intelligible? In what way do the above reflect the concept, usually attributed to Joshua Fishman, that a language is a dialect with an army and a navy?

Regional Dialect Differences

Region and geography separate one regional dialect from another. "Pahk the cah" is spoken by people east of the Connecticut River, "park the car" spoken west of the river. For reasons of geographic isolation and separation, a speech community over time develops its dialect in somewhat different directions from a neighboring community. Dialect differences exist in phonological systems, inflectional systems (word endings such as past tense markers like *ed*, or the plural marker *s*), lexical systems, syntactic systems, and pragmatic systems. Regional dialect differences occur mostly in phonology, which is what identifies a speaker as having an "accent," and in lexical systems, although some syntactic and pragmatic differences also occur. Note the following examples of regional variation, a few among the many:

R-deletion, cited above, in which *r* is deleted at ends of words or before a consonant, occurs in parts of New England, in New York City, and in some southern areas. Many southerners and midlanders make no distinction between the vowels in *pin* and *pen*, pronouncing both as "short i." In several speech communities, mergers are beginning to occur as in this example, as well as in the loss of distinction between the vowels of *cot* and *caught*. Southerners pronounce words like *fire* as one syllable (*fahr*), while northerners pronounce it more like *fi-er*. Midwesterners are known for the distinct pronunciation of *yeh*.

Lexical differences abound from one region to another. *Pop* or *coke* or *soda*; *bag* or *sack* or *poke*; *berm, boulevard, city strip,* or *devil strip* for the strip of land between the sidewalk and the street; *wicked good* in Maine and *very good* everywhere else—just a few of the lexical differences one will find as one travels from region to region. The Appalachian speaker who says, "I might could do it" operates with a different system of modal verbs, and the Pennsylvania speaker who says, "My hair needs washed" are using syntactic constructions not found in other regional American dialects.

FOR THOUGHT 6.4: Can you list other phonological or lexical features that identify your dialect as different from the dialect of another speech community? For example, what is the generic term in your particular speech community for soft drink? What does it mean to "schlep"? See how many differences you can list. What attitudes toward these kinds of language differences do you have? Are there any attitudinal differences toward a speaker who says *soda* instead of *pop*? *bubbler* instead of *drinking fountain*? *aunt* as *awnt*? Find words in your list that *do* carry different attitudinal connotations and discuss what they are.

Social Dialect Differences

Although regional dialect differences are mostly phonological and lexical, many dialect differences based on class (level of income, education, occupation) occur at the syntactic or grammatical level of language. Working class dialects, usually referenced as "vernaculars," often include changes in inflectional morphemes, which are susceptible to language variation in their inclination to become regularized (Wolfram and Schilling-Estes 76). Some speakers regularize the third person singular verb *she runs* as *she run*, to correspond with the others in the conjugation: I run, you run, we run, they run. *Had gone* becomes *had went*, in which the past tense of go (*went*) becomes the preferred form for both past tense and past participle. The tendency to regularize verb forms often results in verb use such as *she don't need it, we was wondering ...*, or *he done it*. In fact, such usages as *I seen it, I done it,* and *I have wrote* occasionally appear in undergraduate writing, a clear indication that they are not limited to oral language.

Significant inflectional change has occurred over several centuries. Old English (OE) (English as it existed before 1066) had a highly inflected verb system in which past tense and past participle were formed by changing inflections: *crowed* was at one time *crew* (the Biblical "the cock crew thrice");

helped was regularized from *hoelp*, the past tense form in OE. However, some speech communities have retained inflectional forms from earlier times. Appalachian working-class speakers have retained the prefix "a-" before some *ing* verbs like *a-huntin*, that vanished generations ago from the speech of other speakers of English. Other syntactic features include the *habitual 'be'* in African American Vernacular English (AAVE), *she done washed it*, found in a number of English vernaculars throughout various regions of the country, and *I might could do it*, found in some midland and southern vernaculars.

English dialects in the United States share far more commonalities than differences, regardless of the number of dialect differences among them. Linguists consider dialects to be mutually intelligible varieties. Despite the phonological, lexical, and syntactic differences between a Georgia dialect and a Midwestern one, between working-class speech patterns and upper-class ones, or between African American Language features and European American ones, we can all essentially understand one another. Mutual intelligibility, however, does not guarantee *productive* ability in other variations of English, evidenced by Marilyn's feeble attempts to operate productively in another dialect that make her look silly because she doesn't get the phonological features or the grammar patterns exactly right. Individuals who aren't familiar with AAVE almost always oversimplify its complex verb systems and its use of multiple negation and rarely understand the complexity of its tonal system. Bi-dialectal speakers, on the other hand, usually move back and forth between varieties of English with facility as they operate regularly in both (or several) speech communities. Code-switching, or style-shifting, in other words, occurs easily when contact with other speech communities occurs on a regular basis with ample opportunity for cross-cultural communication.

Socially Evaluated Dialects

In the discussion that follows we will shift from the label AAVE to AAL, African American Language, in order to honor the historical origins of this linguistic system and its significant patterns of difference from "standard" English.

Despite the fact that all the varieties of dialects of English are fully grammatical and rule-governed, speakers of many varieties of English suffer the stigma associated with speech patterns that veer from the standard (Delpit; Labov; Lippi-Green; Smitherman, 2000; Smitherman and Villanueva). The unfortunately all-too-frequent use of linguistic yardsticks to evaluate the worth of other social and cultural groups reflects deeply embedded language bias. The deficit notion of language—that some dialects are less well-structured, incomplete, illogical, substandard, or impoverished versions as measured against some kind of ideal language system—is patently false. No dialect limits its speakers' ability to express complex thoughts, to think critically, or to use a full range of linguistic functions and purposes. Dialects are simply different, not deficient systems of language. Nothing inherent in any particular grammatical structure makes it linguistically superior or inferior to any other structure. Some structures may be more efficient or less redundant (e.g., the deletion of third person singular *she sing* in AAL); others may carry with them specific meanings (e.g., "habitual be" in AAL as in *the coffee be cold*) that would require additional explanation in other dialects; but no structure is inherently superior or inferior to any other. Consider multiple negation, one of the more stigmatized forms in English usage. Negation in most languages is accomplished by using more than one negative marker in the sentence, unlike standard English, and before the 18th century, multiple negation was also standard in English. When Chaucer describes his knight as *doing no harm to no man no how,* his use of multiple negatives was the standard way of providing emphasis. Or when Shakespeare says, *The most unkindest cut of all,* he was operating with the commonly used double superlative. We do not denigrate Chaucer or Shakespeare for their use of language, nor do we consider language systems with multiple negation like French or Spanish as inferior. Yet many standard English speakers judge American dialects that use multiple negation as inferior. Logical? No. But language attitudes seldom are.

Many of the previous examples reflect social dialect variations—those vernacular features most often associated with working-class levels of education, income, and occupation—more likely to be stigmatized than regional differences often viewed as "quaint" or "interesting" or "amusing." But sociolinguist Dennis Preston's study of attitudes toward regional dialects in this country suggests that negative stereotyping also occurs with regional dialect features.

Several of Preston's informal assessments of regional linguistic bias have been substantiated by his qualitative studies in which nearly 150 people of European American ethnicity from southeastern Michigan, including both genders and a range of ages and social classes, rated the degree of "correctness" of English spoken in various sections of the United States (141). Residents of Michigan, on a scale of 1 (lowest opinion of who speaks "correct English") to 10 (highest) rated themselves as 8, the only area ranked this high by them, but as Preston suggests, not surprising because Michiganders tend to think of themselves as not even speaking a dialect. For these speakers, the south—Alabama in particular—received the lowest (3) rankings, followed by New York City speakers who received a 4. A group of students at Auburn University, located in the south, ranked the undifferentiated area from Michigan to Alabama as a 5, making no distinction between Michigan and Alabamian speakers, and they ranked NYC speakers even lower as 3. Southerners certainly do not rate themselves as the highest, as Michiganders do, but Preston reports an interesting twist:

Just as Michiganders found their variety "most correct," these principally Alabama students find theirs "most pleasant" (8). As one moves north, a steady disapproval of the "friendly" aspects of speech (what linguists like to call the "solidarity" aspects) emerges, leaving Michigan part of a pretty inhospitable northern area, itself a 4. (147)

Both Michiganders and Alabama college students rank NYC at the bottom for both correctness and pleasantness. Preston goes on to say, "Just as U.S. popular culture has kept alive the barefoot, moonshine-making and drinking, intermarrying, racist Southerner, so it has continued to contribute to the perception of the brash, boorish, criminal, violent New Yorker. Small wonder that the varieties of English associated with these areas have these characteristics attributed to them" (148).

FOR THOUGHT 6.5: List all the dialects spoken in your present community and in your home community. Which if any are stigmatized? If you have lived or visited in other areas of the United States, or in other English-speaking countries, what differences have you observed?

Despite these negative impressions about regional dialects, the greater stigma is reserved for vernacular or ethnic dialects, precisely because of their association with lower social status. As linguists Walt Wolfram and Natalie Schilling-Estes state,

> Regional differences are often interpreted by the American public as matters of quaint curiosity, and may even hold a certain amount of aesthetic charm, but the stakes are much higher when it comes to socially and ethnically related differences in American English. On the basis of status differences, speakers may be judged on capabilities ranging from innate intelligence to employability and on personal attributes ranging from sense of humor to morality. (151)

Negative attitudes toward other dialects rarely develop on the basis of the dialect differences themselves; rather, they form because of who *speaks* those dialects. When other ethnic or social groups are considered less deserving, less educated, less intelligent, less acceptable—these negative attitudes get transferred to those speakers' linguistic behaviors (Preston 148). Language becomes the scapegoat for racist and classist stereotypes and biases. Public discrimination on the basis of race, religion, and social class is not acceptable, but unfortunately discrimination on the basis of language difference still is (Wolfram 1999; Lippi-Green). Linguist Robert Phillipson refers to this public prejudice as linguicism, and Rosina Lippi-Green, a sociolinguist whose study focuses on African American language, says, "Accent serves as the first point of gate-keeping because we are forbidden, by law and social custom, and perhaps by a prevailing sense of what is morally and ethically right, from using race, ethnicity, homeland or economics more directly. We have no such compunctions about language, however" (64).

A case in point is the pronunciation of *ask* by some African American speakers. Lippi-Green, among others, comments on the irony of a single dialect variable as the basis for judging "the character and intelligence" of the speaker (180). An African American speaker who reverses the two consonants of *sk* in *ask* as *aks*, is often assumed to be less intelligent and less educated than speakers who pronounce the word as *ask*. Ironically, at the same time, many Americans find the dropping of the *r* among New England speakers charming. An additional irony is that the pronunciation of *ask* as *aks* stems from the Old English word *axion* (pronounced "aksion") meaning "to ask." As Lippi-Green says, "'ax' (aks) survived to almost 1600 as the regular literary form, when 'ask' became the literary preference" (179). One phonological difference can brand the speaker as using a deficient linguistic system, while another marks the dialect as prestigious which suggests that language attitudes are less a matter of the dialect variable itself than the speaker who uses the variable.

Many working-class African Americans speak varieties of AAL. Despite its severe stigmatization, it operates with a complex system of highly developed rules at the phonological, inflectional, syntactic, lexical, and pragmatic levels. Geneva Smitherman (2000), whose work on African American Language systems has become the standard, outlines a number of AAL features that suggest its African roots, evolving from African American slaves learning a system for communicating with each other, with members of other African tribes and languages, and with slave owners. Examples include *habitual be,* stressed *been,* and some phonological differences. Early forms of AAL were English creoles, according to researchers (Smitherman, Rickford), whose speakers mapped English vocabulary onto African syntactic and phonological patterns. Over the decades the language became to some extent de-creolized, with English becoming more deeply embedded in the language, but AAL today still retains a number of creolized forms that reflect African heritage in both vocabulary and syntax (Smitherman 2000, Rickford).

The following examples reflect some of the most common features found in AAL (Smitherman 2000, 22, 23):

- *Habitual Be* used to represent an action that occurs regularly: "He be working here." (meaning: he works here regularly)
- Copula (linking verb) deletion occurs when actions are happening right now: "He working." (meaning: he is working right now)
- Use of *done* for completed action: "They done been playing ball all afternoon."

- Multiple negation: "He don't never do nothing bad."
- Stressed *been* indicating an action that happened a long time ago and is still relevant: "I BEEN married" as opposed to been (unstressed), which refers to something that has already happened and may not be relevant now.
- Absence of possessive marker: "John hat."
- Absence of third person singular marker: "she sing."
- Absence of past-tense inflection markers: "He play."

A number of these features also influence the writing of AAL speakers, who may delete past-tense inflections or third person singular markers; others may use multiple negation, habitual "be," or completive *done* in both writing and speech.

A Word about Slang

The reference to AAL as mere "street slang" is made by some members of other speech communities with little understanding of AAL's linguistic complexities. As our discussion has indicated thus far, dialect variation is far more than mere slang, involving differences in phonology, lexicon, syntax, and pragmatics. All speakers, to varying degrees, use slang, which is a specialized vocabulary that is highly contextualized in terms of audience and purpose, with a specific intent to signal in-group membership. Slang generally connotes informality (*chill* rather than *relax*; *pissed* rather than *angry*). Its life span varies: some slang stays around and becomes mainstream (*cool, rip off, cram*) while other terms disappear within a few months from the groups who coined them, particularly if the terms are co-opted by other groups. Stereotypically teenagers are accused of using slang—and they often do—for the reasons cited above, but slang occurs among all populations regardless of age, gender, class, ethnicity. Current examples include *dicky fit* (emotional outburst), *sick!* (excellent or good), *bling-bling* (flashy jewelry). Much slang develops with reference to sexual acts, the opposite sex, body functions, and so on, but it can develop for any topic imaginable. (For a fuller description of slang, see Wolfram and Schilling-Estes, 62–65.)

Code-switching

Many speakers of AAL function within and between two different linguistic systems—AAL features in their personal lives and standard English in more public venues—a response to a bicultural identity whenever a speaker lives within and between two linguistic communities (McWhorter 40–42). This kind of code-switching occurs between different social levels of dialect systems, between standard and the speaker's social/ethnic vernacular.

Code-switching also occurs among many English speakers of Latino descent in this country. One form found among Latino speakers, often referred to as "Spanglish," represents a linguistic variety that maps English words onto Spanish syntax, creating a mix of the two languages. Many Americans assume that Spanglish is an adulterated Spanish, but linguist John McWhorter offers a more solid understanding of this linguistic phenomenon:

> Spanglish is nothing more or less than Spanish in America undergoing the same natural fertilization process that any language undergoes when spoken alongside another one long-term and when the dominant language's association with social and financial status exerts an irresistible pull .... What Spanglish speakers are doing is creating a new dialect of Spanish, just as English speakers created a new dialect of English while living under the sway of the French .... A thousand years from now, if Latinos preserve Spanish in this country, it will be—indeed could only be—in a form loaded with English vocabulary ... This will be considered simply an alternative variety of Spanish in the same way as Canadian French is an alternative, but not invalid, variety of French. (45–46)

Spanish spoken by Latino speakers in this country could evolve into alternative varieties of Spanish as McWhorter suggests, or it could undergo a similar kind of transformation that AAL underwent as it moved from a creole to a variation with a greater degree of English influence. Only time will tell. Regardless of its trajectory, however, the Spanish/English varieties spoken by large numbers of Latinos, including not only Cubans, Mexicans, and Puerto Ricans, but also Dominicans and Central and South Americans who live in the United States, are valid linguistic systems used for communicating the full range of needs, ideas, philosophical considerations that any other dialect is capable of doing. The only difference is that this linguistic system is in the process of potentially dramatic change.

Code-switching also occurs among speakers who more consistently use two language systems without mixing them. A Mexican woman may speak fluent Spanish to her family in Mexico and fluent English at her job in the United States, or she may be much more comfortable in her native Spanish but perform adequately in English at work. Many code-switchers, then, speak their native languages perfectly and their adopted language fluently or at least adequately. Code-switchers are not deficient users of language but persons efficiently using two linguistic systems. Consider the grocery clerk who speaks English to one person in line and fluent Spanish to the next person, or who, in the middle of his English conversation with Mary, yells to the clerk in the produce section in Spanish for a check on the cost of bananas. And then consider politicians who speak one way on the House or Senate floor but another way to their constituents at home.

Sometimes code-switchers will switch within the same speech turn, sometimes even within the same sentence. Mary has had numerous experiences while in Austria and Germany trying to communicate with her sketchy German, and the folks there use a combination of German and English to talk to her. McWhorter claims that speakers switching between Spanish and English codes almost always keep the rules of each language straight. They don't tack the inflectional endings of one language onto the words in the other; the switching usually occurs at neutral points between phrases or clauses. McWhorter says, "most code-switchers are committed to keeping the languages separate on at least a broad level; no code-switchers simply gaggle along in a mad stew of the two languages" (42).

Inherent Variability in the Use of English

Code-switching can best be explained by understanding the social implications of language use. Speakers who freely, willfully, sometimes unconsciously, change their patterns of speech as they move from one speech community to another do so because they have an inherent sense of their audience's expectations for language use. The AAL speaker who moves between her ethnic dialect and standard English adjusts her language to meet the perceived social expectations of her audience, often with ease and little self-awareness, adjusting usages, pronunciations, word choice, and grammar as the situation demands.

All speakers of English, however, including standard speakers, use the rules of English in variable ways. No speaker, vernacular or mainstream, operates 100% of the time with the features of his dominant dialect (Wolfram and Schilling-Estes 10–11; Rickford 9). For example, the deletion of a consonant in a cluster of consonants, often used in AAL, occurs in the speech of most standard speakers, as in the deletion of the *ts* in the cluster *sts* in *breakfasts* as *breakfas* or as *breakfases*; *iced tea* as *ice tea*. Both pronunciations occur among speakers who consider themselves to be standard speakers. Most speakers, regardless of dialect affiliation, delete the *t* in *westside* or *the west side of town* and in *softball*. Speakers who fail to see their own speech features objectively may, in fact, deny that they alter their pronunciations from "standard." Similar phenomena occur with the pronunciation of *ing* words in which all speakers alternate occasionally between *in* and *ing*, depending on the degree of formality of the conversation, and with the choice of *who* or *whom*, most speakers preferring *I don't know who to send it to*, rather than the prescriptive *I don't know to whom to send it*. Even in the most formal settings, the latter seems unusually stilted, despite the prescriptions of grammar books. Because speakers and writers whose home language differs from standard English shift structures toward "standard" patterns on occasion, teachers can use the students' own work as models of correctness. When a student uses both *had gone* and *had went*, a not uncommon occurrence, the standard form can be used in that student's writing to help him understand how to modify the non-standard one.

"STANDARD" ENGLISH

Our discussion of language differences suggests that defining "standard" English is no mean feat, given the breadth and complexity of linguistic variation. It is not as simple as finding a list of standard features in Warriner's *English Grammar*—because no such list exists. Rather, "standard" is defined in almost all cases by its negatives—what it is NOT—that list in Warriner's of usages to avoid, that list of grammatical features that mark the speaker's dialect as "non-standard." As linguists Wolfram and Schilling-Estes claim, "The vast majority of socially diagnostic structures exist on the axis of stigmatization rather than the axis of prestige" (158). The speaker who consciously avoids *ain't* and double negatives, who avoids using habitual *be* or deleting consonants in a cluster (*walked* rather than *walk* for the past-tense form), who avoids using a singular verb with a plural subject (we was), is accommodating his dialect in the direction of some kind of perceived "standard." In fact, the term *standard* itself is problematic because it implies for many people that all variants are "substandard."

"Standard" is never an either-or phenomenon. Wolfram and Schilling-Estes (10–12) distinguish between informal standard and formal, the latter based on written edited English, the rules perpetuated in schools that are conservative, highly prescriptive, and resistant to change; the former found in much public speech and writing. Informal standard avoids the most stigmatized linguistic patterns but may still use some colloquialisms, and it varies from region to region.

Sociolinguist James Stalker prefers to consider "standard" as an attitude toward language based on accommodation (465) rather than a list of features. Speakers often accommodate their language to audience expectations and purposes of the discourse—linguistic moves that suggest "language in use, in process, dynamic, not a ... steady state" (466). Usually they accommodate in the direction of the assumed language of their audience (wanting to impress the boss by careful choice of words and structures), though occasionally it is in the opposite direction in order to signal social distance (not wanting to buddy up to someone they perceive to be of lesser importance, or of inferior economic status). The degree to which speakers avoid stigmatized structures and move toward greater standardization will depend on what they want speech to accomplish. Speakers jettison double negatives and verbs that don't agree in number with their subjects when it is socially advantageous to do so. They make rhetorical choices for a number of reasons—to impress their listeners, to make them feel comfortable, to become part of a group, to suggest distance from the group, to reveal who they are, or to conceal who they are—shifting language patterns from moment to moment, from one conversation to the next, depending on audience, purpose, and the set of social circumstances in which language is embedded. "Hey, what's cookin'?" Marilyn says to her daughter as she prompts her to tell her what she's been up to. To her colleagues she is more likely to say, "So, what's been going on with you these days?" When she wants to impress an audience, Marilyn tends not to pronounce -ing words as *in'* rather than *ing*, avoids the use of colloquial language, and pays more attention to subject/verb agreement.

FOR THOUGHT 6.6: Pay attention to your own variable language use. How do you "code-switch" or switch styles when talking about the grade you're earning in a class with a peer and with the professor? How do you request a loan from a parent, and how does that request differ linguistically when you ask your roommate for a short loan? In your own classroom, how do you imagine your speech style changing from discussing a classroom problem with a fellow teacher to discussing the issue with the child's parents? Think of other scenarios in which your language changes depending on the audience, even while remaining on topic. Why do you think these differences occur? And how can you use your own examples and those of your students to help your students understand that phenomenon?

Figure 6.1, adapted from Wolfram and Schilling-Estes, suggests a continuum of language use rather than a binary system based on correctness or incorrectness. It characterizes three major points on the continuum ranging from formal standard to informal standard to non-standard. Formal is reserved for the most formal kinds of written and spoken English, but most writers/speakers more likely use a version of informal standard, which includes conventional public English that avoids most of the stigmatized forms. Particularly in speech there is variation from region to region and in what is considered "standard." Informal standard, in other words, is considerably more flexible than is the "textbook" English of formal standard.

So ... What IS "Good English"?

If we wish to counter traditional views of "good English" with a more nuanced understanding of the characteristics of effective language, we might start with the following considerations. "Good" English is not a list of prestigious forms, nor is it categorically jettisoning all non-standard features; it is rather a process of accommodation in language use that fulfills our purposes with language and meets the needs of our audience. Linguist Paul Roberts describes it in the following way:

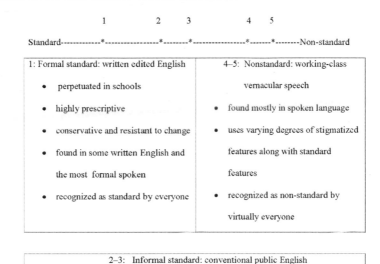

FIG. 6.1. Standard and non-standard vernacular English: A continuum. Adapted from Wolfram and Schilling-Estes, *American English*, 10–12.

As a practical matter, good English is whatever English is spoken by the group in which one moves contentedly and at ease. To the bum on Main Street in Los Angeles, good English is the language of other L.A. bums. Should he wander onto the campus of UCLA, he would find the talk there unpleasant, confusing, and comical. He might agree, if pressed, that the college man speaks "correctly" and he doesn't. But in his heart he knows better. He wouldn't talk like them college jerks if you paid him .... This is not to say that correctness and incorrectness do not exist in speech. They obviously do, but they are relative to the speech community—or communities—in which one operates. As a practical matter, correct speech is that which sounds normal or natural to one's comrades. Incorrect speech is that which evokes in them discomfort or hostility or disdain ... (274–5)

Roberts further suggests that some features of language *can* be labeled good and bad: clarity vs. obscurity, precision vs. vagueness, but people rarely mean this when talking about good and bad language. Educator Robert Pooley says, "'Good English' is marked by success in making language choices so that the fewest number of persons will be distracted by the choices" (5). Both teachers and students need to understand that approval or disapproval depends on the speech community. The fact that we alter our language as we move from one speech event to another—from talking with friends in our baseball jargon to talking with our adviser about transferring credits; from discussing philosophical issues in a college classroom to talking about jazz with our buddies—suggests that we use language creatively and flexibly. It is important, as Leah Zuidema, a secondary English teacher and graduate student, says, that students hear English teachers "acknowledging that a nonstandard register or even another dialect or language is sometimes the most appropriate and effective choice" (672).

Appropriate, however, is a loaded term. Who determines what is appropriate on any given occasion? Does it suggest, as Pennycook maintains, that there is a static social order? (52) And if so, is *appropriateness* just a less objectionable term for *correctness*? Missing from discussions of *appropriateness* is the notion of agency, a point we return to later.

The Evolution of Standard English and Its Political Implications

"Standard" English did not spring fully formed from the omnipotent minds of the grammar gods but evolved over several centuries for a variety of reasons. Standard expectations of language use are determined by those with the greatest sociopolitical/economic power, a fact that has been demonstrated historically and globally in many languages. Old English dialects a thousand years ago went in and out of fashion as different dialect regions of England came to have greater or lesser degrees of economic power. West Saxon, the dialect in which *Beowulf* was written, was the most prestigious of four dialects in Old English. But it was on the basis of the East Midland dialect that a standard English began to develop near the end of the Middle English period, gaining ascendancy in prestige because London, located in this region, became the economic and educational center of England (Baugh and Cable 53).

Eighteenth century English grammarians, who were steeped in the myth of the inherent superiority of one form of English over another and who saw language as a means of sorting and labeling people, wrote several prescriptive grammars whose mandates we still follow. In earlier centuries, the variability in language remained happily unencumbered by social evaluation, but in the 18th century, grammarians began imposing their belief that since English was an impoverished version of Latin, English structures should more precisely match Latin ones. Eighteenth century rationalism and its admiration of antiquity encouraged a world view that valued logic and order (no double negatives because two negatives make a positive), that encouraged the structures of English to be molded within the structures of Latin syntax. If Latin didn't end sentences with prepositions or split infinitives, neither should English. In a total disregard for the very different syntactic structures of the two languages, grammarians attempted to impose Latinate structures on English. Hence, the birth of prescriptivism. Eighteenth century grammars eventually found their way into classroom practices, including the current ones in use today.

The attempt to impose prescriptive usage rules on English speakers would have been difficult to accomplish except for the fact that an emerging middle class during the 18th and 19th centuries saw opportunities for language choice as a means of achieving upward social mobility. People striving to become part of the middle class were more susceptible to the language fiats of the prescriptivists, believing that changing their speech patterns would be a means of gaining access to that class and its power (Thomas and Tchudi 178). If speakers wanted to be thought of as members of the elite, they had better act like them, dress like them, and sound like them. Language as gate-keeping is very much in evidence today: "If you want to get a good job, you've got to learn standard English," the English teacher says to her students. The assumption that language used "properly" will imbue them with cultural capital affording them special privileges and setting them apart from the lower classes they consider to be their social and intellectual inferiors powerfully motivates some people to acquire standard dialect forms.

George Bernard Shaw's *Pygmalion* and the 1983 film *Educating Rita* both speak directly to the political issues of language and social status. In Shaw's play, Eliza Doolittle must replace her cockney dialect with Received British Pronunciation, all accomplished with the help of Professor Henry Higgins and his lessons in correct pronunciation. Both works raise the issue of giving up one's identity and language in order to become a legitimate member of another class. This prescriptive stranglehold on the population, this "200-year-reign of terror, administered by grammarians and prescriptivists and usage busybodies, left speakers of non-Standard English with an unshakable inferiority complex," (H4) says William Grimes in his review of David Crystal's book, *The Stories of English*. This inferiority complex is too often perpetuated in English classrooms by teachers unaware of the politics of language, power, and identity.

Important to note is that non-standard dialects are not "sub" dialects of the standard. Colloquial or vernacular dialects developed, not FROM standard, but along WITH standard through the same historical processes of language change (McWhorter 7). Standard is just one variant of the language among many others. Those others may not have the same degree of prestige, simply because they are spoken by people with less economic and political power. In the United States, if southern dialects currently have less social prestige than the northern, it has less to do with the features of southern dialects than with the fact that southern areas, until recently, did not emerge and remain the primary centers of economic and educational power in this country.

Another complication in "standard English" is that different regions of the country regard different features as standard. The standard in Mobile, Alabama, differs from the standard in Moline, Iowa; both variations, however, are considered standard because of the absence of socially stigmatized features. Both communities, of course, also have vernaculars, but the point is that different regions of the country have different assumptions of "standardness."

And, the features we associate with *standard*—or rather the lack of features we associate with non-standard—shift with changing social attitudes. What was once considered non-standard usage may now be considered standard, and vice versa. Eighteenth century grammarians prescribed careful distinctions between the use of *shall* and *will*, rarely followed today in either informal or formal standard usage. *Ain't* and the use of double negatives were common English-speaking practices until the 18th century, spoken by the rich and powerful and common laborers alike. Distinctions between *who* and *whom* have been standard practice since the 18th century, although the fine distinctions between them are no longer always observed either by those in power or by working-class speakers. Attitudes, styles, usages shift over time—and with the circumstances of our talk.

And finally, as we consider the spread of English across continents and around the world, we find that the English spoken in England and the United States, as David Crystal suggests, is only a tiny minority dialect of World English. Other countries have their own alternative form of English: Irish English, British English, Scottish English, Australian English, Jamaican English, the English spoken in Hong Kong and Singapore, among many others. The "standard" varieties of these Englishes may differ dramatically from country to country, thus weakening a highly prescriptive and narrow view of what "standard" is.

FOR THOUGHT 6.7: Make predictions about the kinds of linguistic changes that you expect to see occurring over the next few years, based on current practices. For example, the distinction between *like* and *as* is waning in some language situations. Can you identify two or three other changes that might be occurring? How do you feel about these changes? Do you see them as a decline? A useful simplification? Or, as a part of attitudinal change, are we becoming more tolerant of certain language features?

Hypercorrection and Attempts to Use "Standard" Forms

FOR THOUGHT 6.8: Identify which in the following pairs of sentences is the "correct" usage:

1. This argument is between you and me. This argument is between you and I.
2. Give it to whomever arrives first. Give it to whoever arrives first.

One sentence in each of the pairs exemplifies the concept of "hypercorrection," the rejection of a familiar speech pattern in favor of the perceived "correct" pattern. Linguistic insecurity—the feeling of inferiority about our use of language that Crystal discusses—sometimes results in unsuccessful attempts at using structures that are thought to be more prestigious. The use of *I* instead of *me* in sentences like "This argument is between you and I" frequently occurs because the speaker is aware of the proscription against the use of the objective pronoun *me* in the subject position ("Me and him are going to the movie") hammered home by teachers and parents who want their children to use "good grammar." The push for using *I* in the subject position becomes overgeneralized in its use in the object position as well: "This argument is between you and I." Another example is the attempted use of *whom* as a form of *who*. If the who/whom distinction is not part of the speaker's unconscious, internalized rule system for language, the form may result in use of the redundant *to* along with the *to whom* construction, as in "I didn't know to whom to give it to." In written language, the ubiquitous apostrophe has increasingly been the victim of hypercorrection as well. It has begun to appear in strange places, almost always when an "s" appears at the end of a word: "Don't forget to pick up the egg's," the note says, or, "They divided the money according to the stipulation's of the will." The linguistic insecurity associated with this item of punctuation has escalated to such a point that, as educator Anca Nemoianu says, "When it comes to the apostrophe, many of today's writers are in a state of total disorientation, sprinkling the little orthographic marks over a sentence in the hope that they might fall in the right places" (96).

Covert Prestige and the Learning of "Standard" English

Despite the numbers of linguistically insecure Americans overly eager to use "correct" English, and the speakers of vernaculars who see their linguistic systems as inferior, a good number of speakers, refreshingly, use their vernaculars proudly without exhibiting signs of linguistic insecurity. As we discussed in chapter 5 relative to gender and language, the motivation of solidarity with one's own speech community is a compelling force working against the motivation of status and accommodation (Gee 91). Wolfram and Schilling-Estes claim that covert prestige allows many speakers to elevate their own views of their dialect above the views expressed by the wider community—that speakers positively evaluate the linguistic features of their socially-stigmatized dialects (159). The North Boston young adult in the videotape *American Tongues* (Alvarez and Kolker) prides himself on his working-class dialect and sees it as an advantage among his peers. The AAL speaker on the "Oprah" show who applauds his dialect as part of his own self-identity values the very features that the wider society stigmatizes. Dialect is a powerful tool for ethnic and so-cial solidarity. This solidarity makes some speakers resist learning standard English and is the reason that slang can be a very powerful linguistic tool for establishing an identify with a particular group that effectively prevents out-siders from entering. Not all vernacular dialect speakers want to change their speech and take on the linguistic features and the cultural trappings that ac-company the standard dialect. "Talking white" is not necessarily the goal of AAL speakers, even if they may see it as advantageous in some abstract ac-knowledgment of the "job market."

Clearly, while we want both teachers and students to understand the complexity of language attitudes and how those play out in the learning of a standard variety of English, we want all students to respect one another's di-alects, and we want all students to maintain their home dialects, even while they become more proficient in a wider repertoire of language patterns and styles—including standard English patterns.

Hegemony and the Teaching of "Standard" English

The Italian linguist/philosopher Antonio Gramsci argues that human be-ings feel compelled to shape their identities to fit the particular context in which they operate, which is a kind of non-coercive, invisible cultural power (Corson 18). Educational institutions to some degree exert pressure to con-form linguistically by playing on speakers' fears of linguistic error and so-cial embarrassment, a form of power that encourages people to shape their language for social and cultural reasons in order to build greater linguistic cultural capital. Educator/linguist David Corson describes this hegemony as power that "penetrates consciousness itself, so that the dominated be-come accomplices in their own domination" (18).

Is the teaching of "standard" English to vernacular English speakers a form of hegemony? To the extent that schools' language policies promote one form of language as superior to another, to the extent that vernacular speakers accept as "natural" the negative values imposed on their non-stan-dard speech patterns, the teaching of "standard" English likely is a form of hegemony, an agent of reproducing the existing culture rather than work-ing for positive change. When schools insist that speakers of vernacular dia-lects undergo linguistic change, and the speakers themselves accept the denigration of their language patterns as legitimate, schools are participat-ing in hegemony. Speakers who accede to the linguistic demands placed upon them by the dominant culture without questioning the imbalance of power or their right to their own language are unwitting participants in the process, a phenomenon that helps explain why stigmatized features of speech are very often judged more harshly by the very people who are most likely to be using these features (Labov 11).

Lippi-Green cites the contributions of popular culture to a standard language ideology that is primarily White, middle class, and Midwestern (64–65). Several Disney animated films as well as TV sitcoms and movies use dialect and accent to contribute to the viewers' assumptions about character. In *The Lion King*, for example, Whoopi Goldberg, the voice of one of the evil hyenas, slips in and out of AAL, and yet AAL is not used by any of the other African American actors whose voices represent the other characters, including James Earl Jones as the father (94). Says Lippi-Green, "In general, children who have little or no contact with African Americans are exposed to a fragmented and distorted view of what it means to be black, based on characterizations which rest primarily on negative stereotype linked directly to language difference" (95).

Researcher and educator Victor Villanueva refers to this phenomenon as colonization, the dominance of one cultural-ethnic group by another, in which the dominated accept the standards of the dominant group (31). This form of hegemony, says Corson, allows "schools to feel more legitimate when they stigmatize different features of speech, non-standard varieties, languages, or other aspects of people's identities" (18–19).

FOR THOUGHT 6.9: How have you seen linguistic hegemony enacted in your upbringing and in your schooling? Do your own attitudes toward your use of language suggest the kind of linguistic hegemony we are describing here? Why or why not?

THE EDUCATIONAL INSTITUTION AS A SOURCE OF LINGUISTIC DISCRIMINATION

Teacher Assumptions and Classroom Practices

Mary Louise Pratt's discussion of "linguistic contact zones" delineates the kinds of "social spaces where cultures meet, clash, and grapple with each other ..." (qtd. in Harmon *Contact* 198). Classrooms are linguistic contact zones where power and language get played out in a variety of ways: insistence on "standard" English in all circumstances; little understanding of students' linguistic capabilities in their own dialects; a demeaning of other linguistic varieties. Many students quickly come to see the importance of playing the language game. And for those who don't—who object to the imposition of a set of linguistic and cultural values from the middle-class teacher—or who object to the de-valuing of their own linguistic systems—the educational system retains its power over them. Cultural reproduction insures that the people who already possess linguistic capital retain that power at the expense of those without it (Bourdieu 80–83).

Leveling the linguistic playing field involves more than teaching standard English. Several studies over the past three decades that look at the conflict between teachers' assumptions about language and students' language behaviors have identified culturally different patterns of classroom behaviors among linguistically diverse children. They reveal different interactional styles with peers and with teachers and different assumptions about functions of language and literacy that don't always match educational expectations. Susan Philips' studies of Native American children and their differing expectations about eye contact and classroom interaction suggest the kind of difficulty Native Americans and other ethnic groups experience in middle-class classrooms. When teachers expect direct eye contact from students when being talked to, and when they assume that silence signals lack of cooperation, they may be misunderstanding the culture of the students for whom direct eye contact and verbal response are signs of disrespect for those in authority (129). Sarah Michaels's study of sharing time (cited in Gee, 116–120) points out the differences between the narrative structures of AAL speakers and those of middle-class White children. African American children used a topic associating or episodic style not valued by most middle-class teachers, while the White children were more likely to use a topic-centered, teacher-approved style. S.B. Heath's study of three culturally different communities in the Piedmont areas of the Carolinas suggests that children's differing expectations of literacy, depending on the cultural assumptions they bring with them to the classroom, can impede their acquisition of literacy if their assumptions differ from the teachers' (235). When the dominant culture's assumptions about language and literacy become the standard by which teachers measure all children, middle-class discourse patterns become the naturalized norms—rarely questioned and always reified as normal and common sense, the way things are and ought to be.

Educator Lisa Delpit argues that some African American students' resistance to standard English results from the responses they encounter to their dialects:

> I propose that the negative responses to the children's home language on the part of the adults around them insures that they will reject the school's language and everything else the school has to offer .... Since language is one of the most intimate expressions of identity, indeed, "the skin that we speak," then to reject a person's language can only feel as if we are rejecting him. (47)

Teaching standard discourse patterns is not the innocent, objective task it is often considered to be but is actually a highly charged political activity. Rather than providing an access to the culture of power, schools too often reserve that access for those who already possess it. As Corson says,

Historically, schools have supported [an] ideology of correctness, because it seems to offer an objective benchmark [that gives] special status to some dominant language variety or other, partly because this simplifies the task of ranking and sorting students .... And because some children start out in schools with more of the valued linguistic resource than others, and are consistently rewarded for its possession, an injustice results for the many who arrive in schools with less of the standard variety. (71)

The Larger Institution and Linguistic Discrimination

While our previous discussion has centered on the need for teachers to become more aware of cultural and linguistic differences and to value them, we must also consider the broader curricular role played by educational institutions in linguistic discrimination. Schools in the business of teaching standard English often have misguided notions of how this can be accomplished. Learning the forms of discourse of the dominant culture for those not acculturated into them from an early age is complicated, says sociolinguist James Gee, first, because discourse is more than simply learning a few grammatical structures and avoiding others. It also involves learning the discourse rules that govern the appropriateness of expressions, the pragmatic rules of conversation, and the knowledge, attitudes, and behaviors that accompany these language patterns, which are difficult to learn as secondary discourses if they have not been acquired as part of a speaker's primary discourse. Speakers must take on a whole different "identity kit" (Gee 127).

At the same time, schools may use the "hammer" of standard English as a means of gate-keeping. When learners don't have full exposure and experience with the target discourse, when they lack familiarity with the intricacies of the discourse, and when those in control of the target discourse are unwilling to share the knowledge about how the discourse operates, standard English can be used to maintain control over entrance and participation. When placement into college prep classes is denied on the basis of language "deficiencies," or when high-stakes writing tests "weed out" test-takers not fully in control of "standard English" features in their writing, classifying students based on language results in limited access to the forms of power already enjoyed by those with the "right" linguistic credentials. Isn't it curious that basic skills classes often are most heavily populated by linguistically diverse students and college prep classes by middle-class White students?

Schools operating with deficit models of language get their force from a culture of fear and distrust of the "other." If cultural differences are viewed as abnormal and unnatural, the linguistic patterns represented in other cultures are considered not merely different, but inferior. An easy, though false, leap then assumes that some dialects preclude complex thought and learning, that students must acquire a "standard" dialect that will allow them to think—and to function at a higher cognitive level.

Deficit assumptions about language permeate educational policies and practices. One of the most celebrated cases involving placement is the court case over two decades ago in which the parents of African American children attending King Elementary School filed a lawsuit against the Ann Arbor, Michigan, school system, arguing that their children were being discriminated against because of their dialect. On the basis of their AAL speech patterns, interpreted by the school as language deficiencies that prevented them from learning, the children had been assigned to special education classrooms or put into lower academic groups. The parents sued on the basis of inadequate instruction and denial of full educational benefits afforded other children—and won their case (Wolfram and Schillings-Estes 264; Smitherman 1981). Equating linguistic difference with linguistic deficiency and cognitive deficiency limited the students' access to the programs provided for standard English speakers—a blatant example of gate-keeping that enforced a standard but withheld the benefits for language diverse students.

Dialect has also been used regularly for the placement of elementary students into reading programs or groups. While dialect difference does not in and of itself result in interference of comprehension in reading, interference *can* occur because of institutional bias. Children with non-standard dialects are more likely to be placed in lower reading groups than standard speaking children, and once there, they have more difficulty moving from a lower group to a higher group (Shannon 131; McDermott and Gospodinoff 223). Furthermore, reading groups tend to get differentiated instruction. Teacher interruptions for correction of oral reading miscues occur much more often in lower groups than in higher, regardless of the quality of the miscue or the reader's level of comprehension. Corrections of high-quality miscues that do not change the meaning of the text can, in fact, impede comprehension rather than enhance it. Particularly troubling, researchers find, is the tendency to correct the miscues caused by variations in the reader's dialect. Dialect miscues (inserting a double negative, for example, or deleting a past-tense inflection of a verb) do not interfere with meaning and need not be corrected. Reading "there were a lot of goats" as "there was a lot of goats" doesn't lessen the reader's comprehension. Calling attention to such a high-quality miscue—one that retains the essential meaning—during the oral reading process merely suggests to the reader that the purpose of reading is more to read perfectly without error than to comprehend the passage. Readers in lower groups also do less reading in context and have fewer opportunities for sustained reading and silent reading that help build reading fluency (Cazden; Shannon; Allington; Gambrell et al.). As educators Dornan, Rosen, and Wilson suggest, "when one's dialect, social class, or cultural group in part determines the placement, many Hispanic, Native American, or African American kids, regardless of initial ability, start out behind and frequently never catch up" (64).

High-stakes testing, too, with its powerful ideologies about linguistic difference, may unwittingly disenfranchise students whose language patterns veer from standard forms. Lawyer and psychologist Martin Shapiro of Emory University critiques the high-stakes TAAS exam in Texas. For norm-referenced tests, in order to achieve higher consistency and technical reliability, according to Shapiro, items with the greatest gaps between high and low scorers are the items that will be used. "Because minority group students typically perform less well on the test as a whole, the effort to increase reliability also increases bias against minorities" ("Racial Bias Built into Tests" 1). Other research also reports that the kinds of test items that are most useful for reliability are those that unintentionally favor non-school learning and the social backgrounds of white middle-to-upper class children ("Racial Bias Built into Tests" 2).

How else do schools validate standard English and disparage other variants of English? In some cases, through the choice of materials; in other cases, by ignoring the critical issues of language while focusing on the superficial. In her study of high school literature anthologies, Mary Harmon found that one anthology focused exclusively on the relationship between dialects and humor as it introduced the works of Mark Twain:

> "dialect speakers amuse"; "dialect calls for laughter" are the messages students and their teachers are sent and may well receive. Yet the anthology never asks, "amusing to whom?" or "why amusing?" (*A Study* 104)

In this anthology's discussion of dialect related to Arthur Miller's *The Crucible*, dialect is defined as "the distinctive manner of speech of people living in a particular region" used to "capture the flavor of a particular region" (qtd. in Harmon 104). Harmon states:

> After being told its features, students are directed to find examples of dialect in the play. One wonders if they notice that farmers and common villagers speak using dialectal features, but preachers and judges do not. No questions concerning dialect as a marker of social class distinctions occur in the anthology. (105)

Harmon suggests the following patterns emerging in anthologies' references to dialect variation:

- Limited space is given to discussions of dialects.
- Much of the dialect discussion centers on the works of Mark Twain.
- Anthologies tend to emphasize regional aspects of dialect.

- Passages that define, describe, or illustrate dialect often have a negative tone.

Harmon (117–118) concludes:

> I wonder what it is like to be the speaker of a nonstandard dialect in classrooms that use anthologies that repeatedly link dialect with humor and describe it as *peculiar* or *queer* or *deviations*. As a source of humor or as the speaker of a dialect not "acceptable at all times and in all places," the dialectal speaker may be made to feel as Smitherman suggests, that "the value assigned to nonstandard speech is tantamount to the difference between going to the front door and going to the back door." (Smitherman, in Harmon 118).

Teaching the Language of Wider Communication

A liberatory language curriculum should provide students with opportunities for preserving their vernaculars along with expanding their repertoire of language use in order to help them negotiate their way through the linguistic maze within and between speech communities, a policy that Geneva Smitherman describes as teaching the U.S. Language of Wider Communication (*Talkin* 20). In adopting this policy, teachers clearly understand that an attempt to teach all the structures that theoretically comprise "standard" English is an impossible task for the reasons detailed above. On the other hand, becoming aware of which non-standard forms are most important to avoid in more formal circumstances is a more realistic goal. Avoidance of multiple negation, "habitual be," or subjects and verbs not agreeing in number may be necessary for individuals to assimilate fully into the wider linguistic community, but it is by no means a sufficient condition for doing so. Teaching a standard form of language without recognizing the legitimacy of dialect variations in American culture is always counter-productive. Providing options for students, on the other hand, suggests the legitimacy of language varieties and acknowledges the role of various speech communities in language use. Enforcing standard forms that are heard and used only in the classroom provides limited scaffolding for learners. Teaching must be augmented by an authentic context in which standard forms are heard frequently and the learner operates in that speech community with some regularity to enable the learning to occur naturally and with ease.

To have successful language programs for linguistically diverse students, school systems will need to confront the issue of hegemony and their own complicity in promoting middle-class assumptions and values to the exclusion of others, including their assumptions about language. To what extent do their language policies provide options for students rather than limitations? Which voices are encouraged, and which ones are ignored? Which language policies value the voices of all speakers, which ones are used as a means of power, control, and limitation?

Some specific instances: For years, English teachers have attempted to eradicate non-mainstream dialects by insisting on replacement forms of standard English, at least in writing, and often in classroom speaking. Yvonne Cofer, a veteran African American teacher in the Detroit Public Schools, reports that one of her principals a few years ago systematically culled books from the library written in dialect. Another teacher in a mid-Michigan school system who asserted the legitimacy of AAL with her students was forced to defend herself at a public School Board meeting. And a *New York Times* article reports on Professor Kirk Hazen's discussions with groups of students in local middle schools and high schools in Appalachia in an attempt to change negative public attitudes about Appalachian dialect. Legitimizing the local dialect is a point not everyone wants to hear:

> His redeeming message is that there is no "good" or "bad" version of the mother tongue. "In general, I think people's spoken language should go unmolested. All living language is change." The professor explained this basic tenet of linguistics even as complaints and demands for his resignation pile up at his supervisor's offices at West Virginia University. "They want my head," he said in an interview, amazed that critics consider him a threat to proper education ... The only real problem with dialect, Dr. Hazen said, is the prejudice of outsiders who rate some people as inferior and deny them opportunities because of the way they talk. (Clines A12)

And yet, we should not be amazed by his critics' reaction. Language is power. Legitimizing non-mainstream varieties gives voice to people who have historically been voiceless, and many fear that doing so sets a dangerous precedent and undermines their own power.

The Ebonics Issue

The controversy stirred up in 1996 by the Oakland, California, school district and their policy regarding Ebonics dramatically exemplify the negative values associated with some non-standard dialects and its speakers. The term Ebonics dates back to the mid-70s but came to public attention only as a result of the Oakland language policy. "Ebonics" historically connects the word *ebony* and the phonics/sounds of the dialect, but it actually suggests much more than the sound patterns of its speakers. It also embraces the linguistic patterns as well as the cultural experiences and language styles of most African Americans. The term is preferred over *African American Vernacular English* by some linguists because it is a language spoken, particularly in its stylistic features, by many African Americans, not just working-class members (Weaver 233).

The controversy emerged when the Oakland School District published its language resolution recognizing the existence of Ebonics and its historic and cultural roots, urging the acceptance of Ebonics as a legitimate form of communication, and establishing policies for the teaching of English that would honor the students' language systems. (Weaver 238). Their intent was to teach students about Ebonics and to use their awareness of the structures of Ebonics to understand the structures of standard forms of English—a kind of contrastive analysis approach to language study often used in English as a Second Language classrooms. The public, encouraged by incomplete reporting by the press, unfortunately too easily assumed that it was an either-or situation. Either Ebonics or standard English forms would be taught. It was inconceivable to many Americans that a non-standard dialect could or should be taught, for whatever purposes. In fact, many Americans, with little understanding that Ebonics had any structure whatsoever, believed that it was merely street slang and bad grammar. Rather than recognizing the teaching of Ebonics as a strategy for helping students become bilingual and bicultural, the public as a whole used it as a target of ridicule and derision. Newspapers around the country derided the Ebonics movement with such headlines as:

Ebonics makes Learning Standard English Difficult—*Ann Arbor News*
Ebonics Won't Make Blacks Smarter—*Baltimore Sun*
Ebonics? No Thonics—*U.S. News and World Report*
The Ebonic Plague—*New York Times* Op Ed Page
Hooked on Ebonics—*Newsweek*
Why Ebonics Is Irrelevant—*Newsweek*

And one newspaper included a political cartoon with the headline "Hooked on 'Ebonics'" that presented a caricature of a young African American male wearing a T-shirt reading "Oakland Publik Skools," his left arm replaced by a hook with a pencil attached, his eyes half shut, standing near the paper he has written with the words in childish letters, "We be bad in English" (with the E in *English* reversed).

Who benefits from an insistence on a standard language ideology model? It can hardly be those speakers of non-mainstream dialects whose primary discourses are denigrated on a regular basis. While it is true that access to more standardized forms may be important for social and educational purposes, should speakers choose to adopt those forms, it is *not* true that assimilating into middle-class culture will be accomplished on the basis of shifting dialect patterns. Lippi-Green says:

Right now people attempt to conform and to assimilate because they are inundated with promises and threats if they do not. The threats are real .... The promises, however, are not so real. Because discrimination on the basis of language has not to do with the language itself, but with the social circumstances and identities attached to that language, discrimination will not go away when the next generation has assimilated. Mainstream U.S. English is a flimsy cover to hide behind in the face of serious intent to exclude on the basis of race or ethnicity .... Language subordination is about taking away a basic human right: to speak freely in the mother tongue without intimidation, without standing in the shadow of other languages and peoples. To resist the process, passively or actively, is to ask for recognition, and acknowledgment. It is a demand for the simple right to be heard. (242–243).

The real beneficiaries are those in power who, even while attempting to enforce a "standard" English, use language difference as a means of discrimination, as a means of controlling who gets to talk and who gets listened to. It dis-empowers students from marginalized cultural backgrounds. This cultural stripping, insidious and demeaning, effectively shuts down cultural values that critique mainstream assumptions about class, race, and ethnicity. The handling of the Ebonics issue reflects the colonialism still rampant in social and educational institutions.

APPLICATIONS FOR THE CLASSROOM

The Students' Right to Their Own Language

Helping students develop agency must be a goal of all language programs. If speakers are to unburden themselves from the weight of incorrect, demeaning, and damaging assumptions about language variation, educational institutions and the teachers within them must begin to reshape language programs. As Smitherman suggests, armchair philosophizing about the legitimacy of all dialects does little good if there are no institutional changes in the policies regarding dialect variation. One of the agents for change is the Conference on College Composition and Communication, a part of the National Council of Teachers of English, which adopted its now well-known policy, *The Students' Rights to their Own Language*, two decades ago:

> We affirm the students' right to their own patterns and varieties of language—the dialects of their nurture or whatever dialects in which they find their own identity and style. Language scholars long ago denied that the myth of a standard American dialect has any validity. The claim that any one dialect is unacceptable amounts to an attempt of one social group to exert its dominance over another. Such a claim leads to false advice for speakers and writers, and immoral advice for humans. A nation proud of its diverse heritage and its cultural and racial variety will preserve its heritage of dialects. We affirm strongly that teachers much have the experiences and training that will enable them to respect diversity and uphold the right of students to their own language. (qtd. in Smitherman 2000, 376–7)

Although the impetus for this resolution was the denigration of language patterns related to race and ethnicity, it is clear that the intention touches on dialects of any social class, irrespective of race or ethnicity, that suffer the stigma associated with linguistic difference. Responses to the resolution have been varied. On the whole, the result is an increasing awareness of the needs of student writers, the legitimacy of their language patterns, and the ethical issues that emerge from an insistence on replacing one dialect system with another, more standard one. Few teachers who have remained active in the profession haven't changed their approaches and attitudes toward linguistic variation. Yet they often feel in a bind, struggling between the demands of public insistence on standardization and of their own professions who see these issues in highly complex ways. The struggle will continue as long as structures of power in the United States shape educational institutions and use language variation as a means of gate-keeping.

While educating people about language variation is important, we must not be so naïve as to assume that education alone will do it. Until we question those in authority who make the language tests and policies that determine who gets into the club and who doesn't, and until we acknowledge that language issues often disguise racial and social issues, we'll have a nation divided on the basis of language and social class.

Linguistic "Contact Zones" at Work

How can classroom teachers provide support for the Students' Right to Their Own Language? When we asked our students to generate a list of activities for use in an English language arts classroom that would help students maintain their home languages and dialects while affording them opportunities to learn the Language of Wider Communication—"standard" English—they offered the following list:

- Frequently allow for writing situations that emphasize fluency.
- Provide rhetorical situations in which a variety of dialects and social registers are appropriate: journals, letters, fiction, poetry, drama, advertisements, some speeches, some personal essays.
- Provide reading, listening, viewing materials in a variety of dialects, discourse genre, discourse styles.
- Provide for the discussion of situations in which "standard" English is not appropriate as well as those in which it is.
- Actively affirm dialect differences, assisting students to recognize and value their own dialects as well as those of others.
- Provide for instruction about language—its social and political importance, its relationship to power.

- Explore the arbitrary nature of "standard" English as well as the power associated with its use.
- Know and point out distinctions between students' languages and the language of wider communication. Help students hear those differences as well as acknowledge them in writing.
- Eliminate labels such as *good, proper*, or *bad* English. Speaking and writing "standard" English is not next to cleanliness and godliness; it should have no special moral implications.
- Offer reading materials, when available, in both students' dialects and the language of wider communication.
- Be sensitive to the identify conflicts code-switching may cause for some students who may encounter oppositional hostility in their home communities.
- Strive to overcome culturally embedded attitudes toward language use and recognize that attitudes toward language are often a veneer for attitudes toward the people who speak those languages or dialects.
- Avoid correcting students' grammar and syntax publicly. Students have the right to their own dialects.
- Avoid the English teacher tendency to hyper-correction. Point out patterns of error in written work.
- Concentrate on what students already do well; build on their inherent linguistic competency.

CONCLUSION

Breaking the cycle of social and cultural reproduction must start with attitudinal change on the part of classroom teachers, which is clearly beginning to happen as these student responses suggest. Rather than eradicating dialects, educators are affirming the need to embrace all linguistic systems, even while providing support for acquiring the language of wider communication. The two are not mutually exclusive. Smitherman suggests:

> It is crucial to have organizational positions as weapons which language rights warriors can wield against the opponents of linguistic democratization. "Students' Right" .... provide[s] the necessary intellectual basis and rhetorical framework for waging language debates and arguments (*Talkin* 397).

Such policies do have an impact on educational practice. No longer are there many principals or librarians who cull books from the library written in dialect or teachers who must defend themselves for suggesting that non-mainstream dialects are legitimate linguistic systems. Many educators understand the political implications of language assumptions and use, but they must also begin helping students see the relationships between language and power by critiquing anthologies that ignore the politics of language and literature and by resisting attempts to see language diversity as a problem rather than as a resource. Policies must begin to change on a curricular level. Corson suggests the need for language discussions to occur in a "genuinely *critical* context," in which students become "critically aware of the social and historical factors that have combined to make one variety of the language more appropriate in contexts resonant with power and prestige, while allotting non-standard varieties a status of appropriateness only in marginalized contexts" (77). Pennycook argues that we must analyze our notions of what communicative competence is and begin to question whether those notions are based on a "static and unquestioned version of social order," and then begin to develop notions of language that have a "more transformative social agenda" (53).

We hope this chapter will help educators see themselves as agents for social change rather than as agents of cultural reproduction. Language variation and the attitudes about dialects should become a focal point of any language arts classroom. In that spirit, we offer the following strategies for teachers to consider as they work with their own students in the linguistic "contact zones" of their own classrooms to open up possibilities for discussion and critique.

PERSONAL EXPLORATIONS

1. Have you ever been in a situation where your speech was marked or denigrated, or where your speech made you feel like an outsider? Have you heard the speech of others denigrated? Have YOU ever denigrated the speech of others? Why? How will the insights you have gained from reading this chapter affect your linguistic assumptions, perceptions, and teaching?

2. Imagine that you are this 9th grade student's English teacher. What AAL features described in this chapter appear to carry over into this student's writing? Can you find patterns of dialect use in the writing? If so, how could you use these patterns to help the student understand differences between his home dialect and the school dialect? Find uses of standard patterns used in the writing that can serve as models.

"The Five Dollars"

Once when I was 7, I saw my mother bag on the drawer. So I went to the drawer and look in the bag and seen a roll of money. I got five dollar out and told my boy and sister that I had got it. So we went to the store and bought lot's and lots of candy. We eat most of the candy. Went we got home my mother was sitting on a chair she told us that she want to speak to us. We went over were she was and she ask use did we take five dollar out of her bag we said we didn't so she said OK. It was lunch time when this happen. So we went back to school and went we got home she ask us again we said no we didn't see the five dollar. Then she said that when she went to the store she asked Mrs Heard did we bring five dollar and she said yes we did. She told use to go upstairs. We went up stair and she beat use. While she was beating use my sister and brother was said they didn't take the money but she said you two went with him to spent the money. After she beat use I told her that I was going to run away. So I went out side and walked around the block and went back to the house. When I got in my mother was up stair in bed and my brother told me that my mother said I would come back home. So I did. So I did. (Daniels and Zemelman 136)

3. Collect some grammar books used in middle schools and high schools. Do they acknowledge the legitimacy of dialect variation, or is any variation from "standard" something they assume must be corrected? Are there particular groups of speakers they target for language change?

4. Check out some Ebonics Web sites on Google to see the kinds of attitudes being expressed. Relate the content of these Web sites to the discussion of Ebonics in this chapter, as well as to the issues discussed in "The Power of Words" chapter and the "Hate Language" chapter.

TEACHING EXPLORATIONS

1. Have students interview grandparents and great-grandparents to see which vocabulary words they used "back in the day" that contrast with current usage. Discuss with them the nature of language change and its legitimacy.

2. Ask your students to collect newspaper/magazine articles or cartoons over a period of time that comment on various aspects of language. Political cartoons and the "funnies" work well for a variety of comments on language issues. Collect as many examples as you can—10–15 perhaps—and with your students analyze these artifacts in terms of what people's perceptions about language are.

   a. What issues of language and its use are being written about? Provide categories of what you are finding.
   b. What is the perspective on language being taken in these artifacts? Prescriptive, descriptive?
   c. How do these issues relate to issues of language you're discussing in class?
   d. Does your analysis suggest that people/newspapers/readers are likely to be conservative or liberal when it comes to language issues?

3. Ask your students to view *American Tongues* or *Do You Speak American?* as a way of coming to understand language variation and its legitimacy.

4. Experts and theorists repeatedly tell us that literary texts are language texts and that in literature one finds a repository and reservoir of language. Find three pieces of literature that would serve as literary selections that reflect language issues for the students you will be teaching. They may directly address language and language use and users—or they may demonstrate critical aspects of language use. Ask your students to consider how each piece presents a set of attitudes about language, conveyed through the characters' use of language or through the language issues that underlie the linguistic elements of the text.

For example, George Bernard Shaw's *Pygmalion* addresses the issue of language and class as it relates to the rise of the middle class in England at the beginning of the 20th century. One of the characters says to Eliza Doolittle, the lower-class flower girl whose dialect represents her working class roots,

> A woman who utters such depressing and disgusting sounds has no right to be anywhere—no right to live. Remember that you are a human being with a soul and the divine gift of articulate speech: that your native language is the language of Shakespeare and Milton and The Bible; and don't sit there crooning like a bilious pigeon. (27–28)

What does this passage tell us about dialect attitudes and language use as they relate to social class issues? What do you perceive Shaw's attitudes to be?

Zuidema suggests using chapter 6 of *A Lesson Before Dying* by Ernest J. Gaines or chapter 12 of *To Kill a Mockingbird* by Harper Lee for linguistic exploration.

5. Ask your students to view a Disney feature-length cartoon such as *The Lion King* and do an analysis of the dialect spoken by a variety of characters. What are the characteristics of those characters who use AAVE in the film? What are the characteristics of those who use "standard" English? What is the message these examples convey about the relationship between dialect and character?

6. In the poem "Words," Vern Rutsala (30–31) lists two kinds of words—one list that he describes as words that as a boy in school "embarrassed" him because they represented experiences not possible for working class poor folks: *dining room, study, lobster thermidor*—and a second list of words that were familiar but not sanctioned by the school: *ain't* and *he don't*. Rutsala states that even though he knew they were "incorect," he preferred

to use the unsanctioned words because they more closely fit his working class life, i. e., their "cold linoleum," their "outhouses."

Find a copy of the poem online or in *A Geography of Poets: An Anthology of the New Poetry*, edited by Edward Field. Discuss this poem as a class, in small groups. How could you use this poem with secondary students to help them understand the relationship between language and identity?

7. Investigate language attitudes by tape-recording four speakers who speak different dialects and who read identical short passages. They may be from other regions of the country, other ethnic groups, other social classes. Make sure they are approximately of the same age and are either all men or all women so as to control for the effects of age and gender in your study. Play the tapes to 10 different people, making sure they are the same gender and approximately the same age of the four people you've recorded. Ask these people to rate your recordings according to the following:

a. How pleasant they find the accent/dialect: very pleasant, pleasant, neutral, unpleasant, very unpleasant.
b. How prestigious the dialect was (using the same gradient sale).
c. How intelligent the speaker was.

You can ask them to include some open-ended questions as well, such as, "What kind of job do you think this person has?" What do their responses suggest about linguistic profiling? (adapted from Thomas, Wareing et al. 208).

8. Consider using some of the activities recommended in the "For Thought" sections with your own students as a way of helping them come to understand the variability and range of English usage: collecting language data, interviewing people to discern attitudinal issues related to language variation, analyzing pieces of popular culture that are imbued with negative linguistic stereotypes, and so on.

WORKS CITED

Allington, Richard L. "The Reading Instruction Provided Readers of Differing Reading Abilities." *Elementary School Journal* 83 (1983): 548–559.

Alvarez, Louis, and Andrew Kolker, producers. *American Tongues*. New York: Center for the New America Media, 1987.

Baugh, Albert, and Thomas Cable. *A History of the English Language*, 5th ed. Upper Saddle River, NJ: Prentice, 2001.

Bourdieu, Pierre. *Distinction: A Social Critique of the Judgement of Taste*. Cambridge: Harvard UP, 1984.

Cazden, Courtney. *Classroom Discourse: The Language of Teaching and Learning.* Portsmouth, NH: Heinemann, 1988.

Clines, Francis X. "Linguist Encourages Pride in Appalachia's Dialect." *New York Times* 7 Feb. 2000: A12.

Corson, David. *Language Diversity and Education.* Mahwah, NJ: Lawrence Erlbaum Associates, 2001.

Crystal, David. *The Stories of English.* Overlook, 2004.

Daniels, Harvey, and Steven Zemelman. *A Writing Project: Training Teachers of Composition from Kindergarten to College.* Portsmouth, NH: Heinemann, 1985.

Delpit, Lisa. "No Kinda Sense." *The Skin that We Speak: Thoughts on Language and Culture in the Classroom.* Eds. Lisa Delpit and Joanne Kilgour Dowdy. New York: The New Press, 2002. 31–48.

Dornan, Reade, Lois Matz Rosen, and Marilyn Wilson. *Multiple Voices, Multiple Texts: Reading in the Secondary Content Areas.* Portsmouth, NH: Boynton, 1997.

Gambrell, L., R. Wilson, and W. Bantt. "Classroom Observations of Task Attending Behaviors of Good and Poor Readers." *Journal of Educational Research* 74 (1981): 400–404.

Gee, James. *Social Linguistics and Literacies: Ideology in Discourses*, 2nd ed. London: Falmer, 1996.

Grimes, William. "Standard English? Piffle." Rev. of *The Stories of English*, by David Crystal. *Ann Arbor News* 12 Sep. 2004, E4.

Harmon, Mary. "Contact, Colonization, and Classrooms: Language Issues via Cisneros's *Woman Hollering Creek* and Villanueva's *Bootstraps*," in Wolff, Janice, *Professing in the Contact Zone: Bringing Theory and Practice Together.* Urbana, IL: NCTE, 2002. 197–212.

———. "A Study of Sociolinguistic Texts and Subtexts as Found in Five High School American Literature Anthologies." Diss. Michigan State University, 1993.

Heath, Shirley Brice. *Ways with Words: Language, Life, and Work in Communities and Classrooms.* New York: Cambridge UP, 1983.

Labov, William. *The Social Stratification of English in New York City.* Washington D.C.: Center for Applied Linguistics, 1966.

Lippi-Green, Rosina. *English with an Accent: Language, Ideology, and Discrimination in the United States.* New York: Routledge, 1997.

McDermott, R.P., and Kenneth Gospodinoff. "Social Contexts for Ethnic Borders and School Failure." *Culture and the Bilingual Classroom: Studies in Classroom Ethnography.* Eds. Henry Trueba, Grace Guthrie, and Kathryn Au. Rowley, MA: Newbury, 1981. 212–230.

McWhorter, John. *Spreading the Word: Language and Dialect in America.* Portsmouth, NH: Heinemann, 2000.

Nemoianu, Anca. "In Front of Our Eyes: Undergraduates Reflecting on Language Change." In *Language Alive in the Classroom.* Ed. Rebecca S. Wheeler. Westport, CT: Praeger, 1999. 89–99.

Oprah Winfrey Show, 1987.

Pennycook, Alastair. *Critical Applied Linguistics: A Critical Introduction.* Mahwah, NJ: Lawrence Erlbaum Associates, 2001.

Philips, Susan. *The Invisible Culture: Communication in Classroom and Community on the Warm Springs Indian Reservation.* New York: Longman, 1983.

Phillipson, Robert. *Linguistic Imperialism.* Oxford: Oxford UP, 1992.

Pooley, Robert. *The Teaching of English Usage.* Urbana, IL: NCTE, 1974.

Preston, Dennis. "They Speak Really Bad English Down South and in New York City." *Language Myths.* Eds. Laurie Bauer & Peter Trudgill. London: Penguin, 1998. 139–149.

"Racial Bias Built into Tests." *FairTest Examiner*, Winter 1999–2000. <www.fairtest.org>.

Rickford, John R. *African American Vernacular English: Features, Evolution, Educational Implications*. Malden, MA: Blackwell, 1999.

Roberts, Paul. "Speech Communities." *Language: Readings in Language and Culture*, 6th ed. Eds. Clark, Eschholz, and Rosa. New York: St. Martin's, 1998. 267–276.

Rutsala, Vern. "Words." *A Geography of Poets: An Anthology of the New Poetry*. Ed. Edward Field. New York: Bantam, 1979.

Shannon, Patrick. "Reading Instruction and Social Class." *Becoming Political: Readings and Writings in the Politics of Literacy Education*. Ed. Patrick Shannon. Portsmouth, NH: Heinemann, 1992. 128–138.

Shaw, George Bernard. *Pygmalion*. New York: Penguin, 1985.

Smitherman, Geneva. "The Historical Struggle for Language Rights in CCCC." In *Language Diversity in the Classroom: From Intention to Practice*. Eds. Smitherman and Villanueva. Carbondale: Southern Illinois UP, 2003. 7–39.

_____. *Talkin that Talk: Language, Culture and Education in African America*. New York: Routledge, 2000.

_____. *Black English and the Education of Black Children and Youth: Proceedings of the National Invitational Symposium on the King Decision*. Detroit: Wayne State University, Center for Black Studies, 1981.

Stalker, James. "A Reconsideration of the Definition of Standard English. *Linguistics for Teachers*. Ed. Linda Miller Cleary and Michael Linn. New York: Mc Graw-Hill, 1993. 465–473.

Thomas, Lee, and Stephen Tchudi. *The English Language: An Owner's Manual*. Needham Heights, MA: Allyn, 1999.

Thomas, Linda, "Attitudes to Language." *Language, Society and Power: An Introduction*. 2nd ed. Eds. Linda Thomas, Shan Wareing, Ishtla Singh, Jean Stilwell Peccei, Joanna Thornborrow, and Jason Jones. New York: Routledge, 2004. 193–209.

Thomas, Linda, Shan Wareing, Ishtla Singh, Jean Stilwell Peccei, Joanna Thornborrow, and Jason Jones, eds. *Language, Society and Power: An Introduction*. 2nd ed. New York: Routledge 2004.

Villanueva, Victor, Jr. *Bootstraps: From an American Academic of Color*. Urbana, IL: NCTE, 1993.

Weaver, Constance. "Ebonics and the 'Parsley' Problem." In *Lessons to Share: On Teaching Grammar in Context*. Ed. Constance Weaver. Urbana, IL: NCTE, 1998.

Wolfram, Walt, and Natalie Schilling-Estes. *American English: Dialects and Variation*. Malden, MA: Blackwell, 1998.

Wolfram, Walt. "Dialect Awareness Programs in the School and Community." *Language Alive in the Classroom*. Ed. Rebecca S. Wheeler. Westport, CT: Praeger, 1999. 47–66.

Zuidema, Leah. "Myth Education: Rationale and Strategies for Teaching Against Linguistic Prejudice." *Journal of Adolescent and Adult Literacy* 48 (2005): 666–675.

Chapter 7

English Language Learners, Bilingualism, and Linguistic Imperialism

Consider the irony: despite its increasing diversity, the United States remains an underdeveloped country when it comes to language skills. Immigrants are importing other tongues at record rates. Yet the vast majority of native-born Americans remain stubbornly monolingual. Our ignorance of other languages and cultures handicaps us in dealing with the rest of the world. U.S. trade, diplomacy, and national security all suffer. (English Plus Web site)

I am chairman of U.S. English, the nation's oldest and largest organization fighting to make our common language, English, the official language of government at the federal and state levels. Why? The high uncontrolled rate of immigration to the U.S. is rapidly changing the face of our great country. From culture to politics, the way we function as a society is under stress .... English, the greatest unifier in our nation's history, is under assault in our schools, in our courts and by bureaucrats. (Mauro Mujica, U.S. English Website)

A billboard on a Lansing, Michigan, street reads:

POOR ENGLISH

(but great Oriental food)

Asian Buffet

Language issues have always been political issues, as we've discussed in earlier chapters. English as a Second Language Programs and bilingual programs are no exception. The quotes above represent two very different views of bilingualism in this country, and the billboard suggests, in part, a relationship between authenticity and "broken" English. But the sign is even more tellingly an example of linguistic colonization and hegemony at work that even many immigrants themselves buy into: the assumption that immigrants aren't fully part of American culture until they can speak "good" English.

This chapter brings together many of the issues of language and power in its discussion of *English language learners and the politics of schooling in the larger society*. It addresses the lingering *monolingual policies* still in place in most speech communities in the United States, related largely to the *role of language in nation-building and nationhood;* the promotion of *English Only legislation* at the federal and state levels and the ideological underpinnings of these movements. We then move on to discuss the range of *programs for English language learners* and review the research on the *importance of maintaining the first language* for preserving one's identity and for achieving academic success. We conclude the chapter with the discussion of *instructional strategies for English language learners* for teaching students in mainstream classrooms.

Two terms used with some frequency in this chapter need explanation. *Assimilation* is the process by which an individual begins to comprehend, produce, and operate within a cultural and linguistic context that is different from the home language and culture. Obviously this term suggests a continuum, ranging from total assimilation in which the home language/culture is virtually replaced by the target language/culture, which is a rare phenomenon, to varying degrees of assimilation while retaining some part of one's first language and culture. While some individuals, indeed, may shuck off their previous lives and existences and absorb American mainstream culture and language, thinking and functioning within the system with little apparent reference to or use of the first language/culture, vestiges of one's original language and cultural background always remain, although they are not always fully acknowledged. For all practical purposes the individual sees himself as an American. Period.

During some phases of American history, near the end of World War I, when the linguistic diversity of the 19th century was replaced by linguistic intolerance in the early 20th, school became the tool for eliminating languages and cultures other than English (Cadiero-Kaplan 32). *Assimilation* came to mean just that—total absorption of the home language and culture into the adopted one, with the rejection of the first language and culture in favor of the second. Most schools have adopted a perspective of getting students "Americanized" as quickly as possible, even if it means directly or indirectly suggesting the rejection of the home language. On the other hand, many educators, anthropologists, and political scientists (Cadiero-Kaplan; Crawford; Gonzalez, Moll, and Amanti; Ricento and Burnaby; Schmidt), who have studied bilingual issues are currently encouraging a different understanding of *assimilation*—one that considers it much more broadly, to mean something akin to "an accommodation of the majority ideology within an overall ideology of pluralism; cultural [and linguistic] maintenance within partial assimilation" (Baker, qtd. in Ricento and Burnaby 14 [bracketed information mine]). This suggests accommodation rather than full assimilation, a much more realistic goal.

Bilingualism is the condition in which speakers operate with two language systems. Bilinguals, as we discussed in chapter 6, have the ability to move between the two linguistic systems with ease and comfort, sometimes using one, at other times the other, depending on the contextual rhetorical needs. We aren't implying that speakers must be able to speak like natives or be totally literate in the target language but that they have enough fluency in both languages to use them effectively for a variety of purposes in their respective domains.

MONOLINGUAL LANGUAGE POLICIES IN THE UNITED STATES

The old joke goes:

What do you call someone who speaks two languages?
Bilingual
What do you call someone who speaks three languages?
Trilingual
What do you call someone who speaks one language?
American.

Historically the impetus to learn a second language for native speakers of English in U.S. schools and for the public in general has not been strong. The United States has periodically gone through phases of political isolationism, partially reflecting our history as a democracy and reinforced by the fact of our relative geographic isolation from other countries, unlike western European nations that are in close proximity to one another. Although this is changing to some extent, a majority of U.S. citizens still do not have the advantage of living and working closely with different cultural groups speaking different languages, an irony given our history as a country composed largely of immigrants. Until recently, there has been little reason economically for encouraging the learning of a second language, and in fact, large numbers of U.S. citizens harbor attitudes about other languages and cultures that are embarrassingly ethnocentric. Asserting our dominance and control in global politics, we have implicitly suggested that the United States is the center of the universe, language included.

Related to the concept of bilingualism is *pluralism,* a view that favors the enhancement and status of minority languages in the United States and stands in sharp contrast to the assimilationist position that favors supporting English as the sole public language over all other languages (Schmidt 4). This chapter considers the range of educational and political issues found within these differing perspectives on language use in this country.

Because the notion of the United States as part of the global community has largely been a foreign concept, no pun intended, it is not surprising that for much of the last century and into the 21st, U.S. classrooms have been dominated by monolingual teachers who speak only English and by curricula that use English as the only medium of learning and instruction. Our history as a nation and the strength of our military, political, and economic position in the world have made most U.S. citizens satisfied to remain monolingual, reflected in the under-funding of second/foreign language programs, still considered a frill in many school districts. Foreign language classes still enroll a relatively small percentage of the student population. While enrollments in modern-language courses in U.S. high schools have increased over the last 20 years, largely due to stiffer college entrance requirements, a very low percentage of either high school graduates or college graduates reach a proficiency level in a second language (English Plus Web site, quoting an American Council on the Teaching of Foreign Languages [ACTFL] Newsletter). Despite the recognition that students must prepare for a multicultural, multilinguistic world, researchers/educators Bruce Horner and John Trimbur claim that American educational institutions still overwhelmingly operate with a uni-directional monolingual language policy that privileges English above all other languages.

Ironically, despite the existence of these monolingual educational tendencies, the U.S. workforce has become increasingly diversified, a change that compels the learning of a second language for many citizens in the business community. As part of the global community, U.S. business and industry has had to adjust practices to accommodate the diversity of languages in use. In Battle Creek, Michigan, with the Japanese acquisition of an automotive parts manufacturing company, programs have been initiated to teach English to Japanese workers and to teach Japanese to American workers. Even in inland states such as Kansas, the increase in the Hispanic population in one county alone jumped 110% during the last decade, and many English speakers are taking courses to learn workplace Spanish. One employee of a propane company says, "It's amazing how much more valuable you are as an employee in Garden City if you can speak two languages" (Sharp 1). And police departments around the country are hiring bilingual personnel, though they are often in short supply. The Dearborn, Michigan, Police Department, for example, has been recruiting bilingual police officers and interpreters to help them do their jobs, according to *The Saginaw News* ("Language Diversity" 19 June 2002), and interpreters have been used in several criminal investigations in southeast Michigan to work with the dozens of languages spoken in the area.

American military and intelligence organizations, in great need of personnel who speak Arabic languages, are discovering the problems that monolingualism brings. In the Persian Gulf War, the Department of Defense was able to identify only 45 U.S. military personnel with any Iraqi language backgrounds, and only five of those were trained in intelligence operations (Congressional finding of the Foreign Language Economic Enhancement Act, qtd. in English Plus Web site). The situation had changed little by 9/11 and the Iraqi war of 2003. Military and intelligence forces were once again scrambling to find individuals fluent in Arabic as a result of several missteps in identifying terrorist activity. Ironically, monolingualism, championed by English-Only groups, has become a danger to U.S. security.

When learning a second language *is* valued in our school systems, the languages that represent "high culture" are considered the premium, academic languages: French, German, and other northern European languages rather than southern European, Asian, or African languages (Moll, "Literacy Through Two Languages")—the languages more readily recognized for acceptance into graduate school, for laying claim to "knowing another language." In spite of the increased need for speakers fluent in Asian and Arabic languages, these languages are rarely valued as foreign languages offered in schools. Rather than seeing these languages as resources and opportunities for both immigrant students and non-immigrant students, many schools assume a subtractive policy of first-language eradication in which English is learned at the expense of the home language.

FOR THOUGHT 7.1: Did you study a foreign language in high school? College? For how many years? Which language did you study? Why? How much speaking experience did you receive? Are you fluent? How did you become so? If you are not fluent, why aren't you? What are the advantages of being able to study and speak a second language? For whom in the United States is doing so becoming increasingly important? Why might it be important for all teachers to have had at least some experience learning a second language?

Nationhood and Patterns of Belief

Some resistance by majority Americans to learning other languages results from the strong connection between language and identity, as Horner and

Trimbur claim: the use of spoken and written English that "forms … an imagined community and a sense of nationhood" (607) that serves as the unifying element of our country. That concept, coupled with the assumptions first, that English is becoming a world language, and second, that cultures and languages of the "other" are to be feared or avoided, encourages the continuation of monolingual policies for a large population of citizens. Strong opposition to bilingualism manifests itself most clearly in how immigrants are treated in this country. When one's belief about nationhood centers almost exclusively on the English language and culture, potential conflict arises with the increasing numbers of speakers of other languages coming into our schools and our society. The number of immigrants has nearly tripled from 1970 to the end of the 20th century, from under 10 million to over 26 million at the end of the century (Corson 104), and the number of students with limited English proficiency has doubled in the last 10 years to five million in the last decade, according to data from the U.S. Department of Education (Zhao A8 A11). The 2002 census sets the number of Spanish speakers above the age of five at 28 million, the number of Chinese speakers at 2 million, and the number of English speakers at 215 million (Kellogg B5). As of 2001, 10% of all students in public elementary classrooms are English language learners (Shanahan). And Garcia (qtd. in Cadiero-Kaplan, xix) predicts that by 2030, 70% of the students in California schools will be English language learners. Even in small midwestern communities, second language learners are rapidly increasing in number. In the Lansing, Michigan, public schools, for example, the 15% of students who speak a first language other than English represent over fifty languages (Range B1). It should be noted that, while many immigrants are members of the working class in this country, immigrant populations extend across the spectrum of social classes, with the more affluent likely being fully bilingual in both languages and feeling comfortable operating with two languages for appropriate contexts (Corson 101).

Unfortunately, with demographic change in schools and communities come resistance and animosity. Xenophobia, a fear of the "other" and the "other's" linguistic, ethnic, and cultural differences, is caused by a number of factors:

1. Linguistic—the fear that we will not be understood, or that we will not understand, and that other languages/dialects/cultures are deficient.
2. Social—a fear that our own worlds and communities will be changed by those who are "invading" our territory.
3. Cultural—the fear that one's own culture will be "contaminated" by other cultures with different attitudes, habits, belief systems.
4. Economic—the fear of immigration policies that increase competition for jobs, and the fear that increased immigration will result in an increase in a state's welfare expenditure.

5. Educational—the fear that money for educational programs will be absorbed by non-native speakers in special programs.
6. Political—the fear of a loss of power, both personal and public.

While many U.S. citizens see these changing demographics as positive and embrace language programs to reflect the changing population, most Americans still see them as negative (Horner and Trimbur 609). Second-generation Cuban-American citizens in Florida, for example, regularly attest to the negative reception their or their families' use of Spanish receives from monolingual English speakers. And a bumper sticker on a Michigan car reads, "Welcome to America. Now speak English."

Although the following episodes occurred several years ago, they illustrate that animosity toward speakers of languages other than English prevails in too many parts of the United States. In Union Gap, Washington, a sign over the bar at the Old Town Pump read, "In the U.S.A. it's English or adios amigo" The bar owner stated, "This is America, where English is supposed to be the main language. We don't want Spanish gibberish here, and we mean it" (Brandt A4). In the Texas panhandle during a child custody case, Judge Samuel Kiser warned Martha Laureano, a Spanish speaker,

> If she starts first grade with the other children and cannot even speak the language that the teachers and the other children speak and she's a full-blooded American citizen, you're abusing that child and you're relegating her to the position of housemaid. Now get this straight. You start speaking English to this child because if she doesn't do good in school, then I can remove her because it's not in her best interest to be ignorant. The child will hear only English. (*Ann Arbor News* 30 Aug. 1996: A6)

Ultimately these negative attitudes toward other languages and those who speak them are accompanied by assumptions that these languages and cultures—deficient and inferior—are going to adversely affect the "purity" of American cultures and language. John Tanton, the co-founder of U.S. English, expressed the kind of hatred toward immigrants we address in chapter 3:

> Will the present majority peaceably hand over its political power to a group that is simply more fertile? Is apartheid in Southern California's future? As whites see their power declining, will they simply go quietly in the night? Or will there be an explosion? ... Perhaps this is the first instance in which those with their pants up are going to be caught by those with their pants down. (Hacker, qtd. in Smitherman, 1990, 112–113)

As his comments indicate, John Tanton, also the founder of the Federation for American Immigration Reform, supports Horner and Trimbur's theory that immigrants are considered a "threat to the health of the nation's cultural, social, economic, and physical environment" (608), diluting the purity of the American system and imposing negative changes on American culture. The "immigrant problem" becomes a language problem, most easily dealt with by eradication. Rather than seeing monolingual U.S. citizens as linguistically limited, these individuals see the "foreigner" as deficient.

FOR THOUGHT 7.2: How many languages are spoken in your home area? What are they? Are the speakers of these languages also speakers of English? Have you heard others make either complimentary or disparaging remarks about any of these speakers?

The Ideology of Labels

Like the language ideologies described in earlier chapters, the language ideologies related to English language learning play a major role in attitudes toward immigrants and non-native speakers of English (Crawford xx), and, in fact, often become national myths upon which educational policies are formed. Many of those ideological perspectives are fueled by linguistic labels that have become "loaded" terms for public consumption such as "foreign," "immigrant," "those" people, and their use of English as "broken"—terms that too quickly reduce, essentialize, and pigeon-hole. A U.S. English political advertisement opposing "bilingual education" that appeared in major news magazines in 1996 played to the public's suspicions of immigrants and bilingual education as it stated, referring to immigrants of the 19th century, "They knew to survive they had to learn English. How come today's immigrants are being misled?" Ignoring the facts of first generation immigration history, the ad continues, "They learned without bilingual education. And without government documents in a multitude of languages." The ad ignores what and how "they learned," the kinds of employment they found, their exploitation by U.S. capitalism, and the low wages at which "they" worked (*U.S. News and World Report* 1 Aug. 1996, 87).

Essentialized language ignores the complexities of immigrant situations. Some learners of English are immigrants whose first language they bring with them to the classroom; others, American-born of immigrant parents may be bilingual and yet classified as "immigrant"; and still others may be American-born but not proficient in English. Horner and Trimbur ask, "How many years or generations must have elapsed for an individual or family to shed 'immigrant' status?" (610). Essentialized language is also used to describe immigrants' use of English as "broken" English. We rarely speak of our "broken French," or "broken Spanish," yet immigrants get branded regularly for their "broken English," as if, says Amy Tan, "it were damaged and needed to be fixed, as if it lacked a certain wholeness and soundness" (394–395).

Finding a positive, unambiguous term for speakers for whom English is not their home language is an important part of undermining xenophobia. Researchers have struggled with terms and labels, seeking terms that don't essentialize, that don't unfairly label, that aren't negatively construed. "Limited English Proficient" emphasizes what students are missing, not what they bring; and "Non-English Proficient" also ignores the positive in students' capabilities. One California school system coined the phrase "Linguistically Gifted Persons" because the students already spoke one language and were learning another (Loveless 74). Whether a positive term like this will have any credence beyond this particular school system remains to be seen, but it is clear that labels do matter because of what they imply and what they ignore. The preferred term is "English language learner," a term far less pejorative, although admittedly so general a term as to potentially include native speakers of English as well.

The facile use of categories and labels also ignores the complex relationship between language and culture, a relationship that is fluid and changing from situation to situation. "The language identity of those named foreign, immigrant, or native is no more easily fixed than is their national identity," suggest Horner and Trimbur (611). And because many people commonly move back and forth between the U.S. and the land of their birth, they identify at different times with different languages and nations. Binary categories force students to "categorize their identity into an either-or sort of framework, when in fact they may not perceive it in such clear-cut distinctions" (Chiang and Schmida 90).

Contributing to the problems of language ideology may be assumptions growing out of personal family history such as the fact that a family member learned another language without the aid of bilingual education. Language ideologies may also be based on a political principle that immigrants coming to the U.S. have a patriotic obligation to speak English, or on an ethnic paranoia that suggests that even though English is spreading throughout the world, Spanish is taking over the United States (Crawford 62). These ideologies often take on mythic proportions that fly in the face of political realities.

ENGLISH ONLY: EFFORTS AND EFFECTS

Supported by U.S. English, the English Only movement fuels the fire of resistance to immigrants, their languages and cultures, and complicates the educational decision-making about programs for English language learners. English Only attempts to mandate English as the official language, with serious implications for speakers whose first language is not English. Although its stated goal is American unity through a common, mandated language, English Only exploits xenophobic tendencies in its attempts to limit immigration and to restrict the political power of non-English speakers.

Spanish is often the unstated target of U.S. English supporters. The increase in the numbers of people living in the United States for whom English is not their first language has given rise to a growing fear of Spanish as the largest minority language in the United States and its potential influence on American culture and society.

English is our national language, but to date no federal laws have been enacted mandating English as the official language. Much of that legislation occurs at the state level. By late 2003, nearly half of the states—23—had legislated some version of an English Only law (Crawford 153), the number accelerating with the increasing numbers of immigrants entering this country. A March 2003 news release from U.S. English proclaimed that because there are 329 different languages spoken in this country, a figure established by the 2000 census, it is important to have a common language that "can spread unity." The news release went on to extol the virtues of H.R. 997, a bill proposed in the House of Representatives referred to as the "English Language Unity Act of 2003." The bill, if it becomes law, would mandate that "all laws, public proceedings, regulations, publications, orders, actions, programs and policies" would be conducted in English (U.S. English Web site), both to encourage national "unity" and to save money on printing materials in other languages and in hiring translators for various official purposes. Exceptions would be made for "public health and safety services, judicial proceedings (although actual trials would be conducted in English), foreign language instruction and the promotion of tourism" (U.S. English Web site). The bill, to date, has, however, not been released from committee for a vote.

Many Americans appear to agree with this bill, according to U.S. English polls, and on the surface it seems innocuous enough because of the symbolic nature of the English Only laws in many states (Sharp 1). But the political ramifications of this proposed law are troubling. The United States has a rich history of multicultural/multilingual governmental policies going back to the Constitution. Our nation's founders, in their wisdom, did not declare English the official language because they saw no reason to do so. In fact, in the early years of our democracy, many official documents were published in both German and French to accommodate speakers of those languages. Even though the percentage of people not speaking English then was considerably higher than at the beginning of the 21st century, our country's founders did not feel that English was threatened, nor did they fear that non-English-speaking citizens would not learn English (L. Thomas B4).

The current push for English as the only official language not only seems unnecessary but may, in fact, severely limit the rights of citizens or those attempting to gain citizenship. If all official government business is to be conducted in English exclusively, how many people are going to be disenfranchised by their limited ability to use English, and how many programs are going to be eliminated unless their business is conducted in English? Whose ends does it serve to treat immigrants as a "financial burden, a cultural threat, and a potential source of division"? (Crawford 2). Note the following restrictions that the H.R. 997 bill would impose:

- A Uniform Language Testing Standard for naturalization that all applicants would need to meet;
- The conduct of all naturalization ceremonies in English.
- The repeal of bilingual provisions of the Voting Rights Act, which guarantee minority-language voting materials in certain jurisdictions.

Mauro Mujica, the head of U.S. English, argues that making English the only official language is the way to enforce the learning of English. He goes on to question even the teaching of Spanish to Whites, "if it creates the notion that those who speak Spanish needn't learn English" (Sharp 1).

This concerted push for a single language as the only language to be used for public purposes limits linguistic possibilities and disadvantages English language learners—and strongly suggests a form of linguistic and cultural imperialism that some of the founders of this country would have found repulsive.

FOR THOUGHT 7.3: List all of the state and federal government agencies and services that would be affected if H.R. 997 were to become law. How would your own school district or community be affected by such a law?

English Only: Assumptions Versus Facts

Just what are the assumptions on which U.S. English bases its arguments, and what are the responses of linguists and educators who have studied the issue? These considerations are important because of the many state and federal educational policies that have evolved from them. Linguist Lee Thomas provides an overview of four major assumptions of English Only, along with evidence that counters those assumptions:

1. Mandated English for all citizens will promote national unity.
   Evidence seems to suggest that mandated language policies privileging the dominant language over minority languages are, in fact, more divisive than unifying. Linguistic coercion simply doesn't work. In

Puerto Rico, English was strongly resisted when it was mandated in schools; in Ireland, Irish is dying out despite the mandate to teach it. People tend to resist the imposition of language policies that often fail to consider political realities. In Spain, there were more people speaking Catalan at the time of Franco's death than before he attempted to ban it. Learning English is more likely to be the consequence rather than the cause of seeing the educational, economical, and political value of English. As L. Thomas suggests, tolerant policies unite and promote nation-building through inclusiveness, and intolerant attitudes force separatism and resentment (131).

Proponents of English Only believe that the United States is the great melting pot, where assimilation into mainstream culture and language on the part of immigrants is both natural and normal; retaining one's native language and culture, the argument goes, impedes one's ability to become part of U.S. culture. Expressing loyalty to this country can be demonstrated only by giving up one's native language, an act considered by many to be the obvious solution to linguistic diversity (Crawford 67). Most immigrants coming to the U.S. are eager to assimilate—at least to the extent that they wish to learn English quickly and become part of U.S. society—to "fit in" and enjoy the benefits of their adopted homeland. On the other hand, many immigrants are resistant to giving up their native languages and cultures, believing it possible and preferable to retain their ethnic cultures/languages even while becoming acclimated to the culture and linguistic system of the country they are now living in. Any policy that encourages immigrants to acquire the linguistic and cultural systems of their adopted country at the expense of their native languages and cultures is likely to be detrimental to their acculturation of English and to their academic success, as research by Wayne Thomas and Virginia Collier shows, a point to be discussed later in this chapter.

2. Language diversity is inherently divisive and will lead to ethnic conflict. Language diversity as the cause of divisiveness is greatly exaggerated. The French language spoken in Quebec has often been blamed as divisive; however the lack of equal economic opportunities has often marginalized speakers of French. The language issue has become a convenient scapegoat (L. Thomas 131–132). In Switzerland, citizens speak German, French, or Romanash, depending in which part of the country they live. In addition, many Swiss speak second and third languages, English and Italian among them. All of this multilingualism has done little to divide a very unified country. In fact, in the United States, divisiveness occurs more often when laws of English Only are enacted. In Arizona, for example, where all bilingual programs have been eliminated in favor of shorter immersion programs, Native

Americans see English Only policies as an affront to their attempts to revitalize their tribal languages and contend that the law promotes the same kind of monlingual policies in schools that resulted in the loss of many of their tribal languages in the first place (Zehr 1).

3. Current immigrants learn English much more slowly than immigrants in past centuries because non-English speakers can get by too easily without learning it.

The myth that immigrants are not learning English at the rate they used to is contradicted by James Crawford's evidence that "Anglicization rates are probably higher today than at any point in U.S. history, even as linguistic minority populations expand, because of a rapid shift to English among second-generation immigrants" (59).

Currently immigrants are becoming speakers of English within one or two generations, no less quickly than in earlier times. A study based on recent census data has found that 92% of second generation Latinos speak English "well or very well even though 85% speak at least some Spanish at home," while 96% of second generation Asians are proficient in English (Sanchez 6A). Clearly English is in no danger of being overtaken by Spanish or by Asian languages. As L. Thomas argues, the percentage of Spanish speakers today is no greater than the percentage of German speakers before World War I (Thomas 134).

What *is* being lost, too often, is a speaker's first language. In Arizona, according to researcher Luis Moll's longitudinal study of bilingualism in the U.S., 85% of second generation Mexican immigrants have lost fluency in their home language, and they overwhelmingly (94%) prefer to speak English. Says Moll, "If you close the doors to English, they break a window to get in" ("Literacy Through …"). Clearly, there is little need for an official mandate to learn English when, in fact, it is being acquired voluntarily at a very steady and fast rate.

4. Bilingual programs don't work.

Bilingual programs have had their difficulties: too few teachers who speak the home languages; the complexity of administering programs; and the expense of such programs. But to claim that they should be disbanded in favor of other types of ESL programs makes little sense. Xenophobia, when coupled with concerns about adequate funding for education in general, complicates and politicizes educational policymaking. For example, the passage of Proposition 227 in California in 1998 that mandated the end of bilingual programs and instituted one-year English immersion programs instead was less a matter of deciding the educational effectiveness of bilingual programs than a matter of saving money by withdrawing support from programs that appeared to be costlier (Crawford 50–51). Our discussion below examines this issue at greater length.

It is clear that English-Only policies or the policies of U.S. English are more about restricting other languages than about promoting English. As Crawford, foremost authority on English Only, suggests, "The English Only movement is … about scapegoating immigrants for many of this country's social problems. It's about limiting the rights of language minority groups. And it's about manipulating ethnic fears and animosities for partisan advantage. So, for anyone who believes in the principles of democracy, tolerance, and equality, there are plenty of reasons to oppose English Only laws" (2). U.S. English provides almost no financial support for ESL programs, despite their claim that their purpose is to promote the speaking of English. Instead, the money from this organization is used for political influence to promote their cause of immigration control and anti-immigrant sentiment rather than providing opportunities for learning English (L. Thomas 136).

Recently a backlash has emerged against the restrictiveness of English Only laws. According to Crawford, "The more common it is to encounter minority languages in public places or popular culture, the less threatening they become" (70). "There's nothing foreign about Spanish anymore," says Sam Slick, the founder of Command Spanish, a firm specializing in the teaching of Spanish in the workplace (Sharp 1). Many places of business provide information in both Spanish and English, particularly in the southwest and in California, and Spanish is working its way into everyday use across the nation, from Spanish-language media to magazines, music, and other forms of popular culture. Changing demographics of the population have increased the need for Spanish programs, but often there aren't enough Spanish-speaking teachers to meet the increased demand (Johnson 1). More and more marketers prepare ads and product information in Spanish as well as English, and Spanish and Asian television stations are readily available on cable. The Iraqi war has underscored the vulnerabilities of the United States in its overwhelmingly monolingual policies, and training programs have recently been developed that provide instruction in Arabic languages to speakers of English.

Ideological Views of Language and Literacy Education

Readers might wonder why we have focused so heavily on issues related to the English Only movement in this country. That movement is, after all, something happening in state legislatures, not in school systems or educational institutions. Yet, the very governing bodies who vote on issues of mandating English as the official language also make decisions about educational programs for English language learners—and the educational implication for English language learners is immense. The irrationality of some of the legislation, based on fears of linguistic and cultural change, has had a profound effect on educational policies. In California, for example, by a state referendum in 1998, the voters themselves abolished all bilingual programs, to be replaced by immersion programs. Too often any potential debate about the merits or demerits of programs based on solid research gives way to the irrationality of fear and prejudice. As Schmidt claims " … at the heart of the dispute over justice and equality for language minorities in the United States is a fundamental conflict … over the role of non-English languages and cultures in the U.S. society," a debate, he says, that "cannot be resolved without coming to terms with the nature of our national identity in relation to language and ethnic diversity" (162). Is the U.S. fundamentally monolingual with the result that it should remain monolingual in its policy-making, or should its policies reflect its multi-cultural and multi-lingual nature?

Programmatic decisions about the education of English language learners are inevitably tied to the ideological views of policymakers. Do legislators and the public in general see literacy in English as needing to provide basic skills and perpetuating American cultural values, or do they see literacy as a more highly nuanced set of abilities that allow learners to operate with linguistic and social agency? Researcher and educator Karen Cadiero-Kaplan outlines four ideologies of schooled literacy summarized below:

1. Functional literacy that is skills-based, which enables an individual to complete job applications, read at a minimal level to conduct the basic business within a given society, and operate at a fourth to sixth grade competency level. While little attention is paid to critical thinking, much attention is focused on basic skills that provide the mechanisms for reading and writing in English but require less personal agency.
2. Cultural literacy that focuses on core cultural beliefs and knowledge—"What Every American Needs to Know"—as E. D. Hirsch subtitles his book on *Cultural Literacy*. Designed to promote the core understandings and values of upper-middle-class culture, such an ideology results in programs that advance "American values," some of which evolve into advanced placement courses and college prep programs that are more likely to serve students who already have considerable cultural capital according to Cadiero-Kaplan (8–9). Such programs rarely reach those who have been educationally disenfranchised, including second language students, who are instead more likely to populate functional literacy programs.
3. Progressive literacy, in contrast to functional and cultural literacies, that encourages the inclusion of student voices and cultures. Such literacy practices include student-centered approaches that assume students as constructors of knowledge, not mere recipients of

it—practices that allow for more student decision making in the classroom and for personal discovery.

4. Critical literacy, which goes a step further than progressive literacy, to question the political and ideological underpinnings of given knowledge, to promote critical thinking, to transform curriculum and instruction to meet the interests and needs of all groups of students, including minority and second language students, and to see literacy as social action. (Cadiero-Kaplan, 13–14)

These sets of assumptions, particularly the first two, operate to varying degrees in most school systems. Progressive and critical views of literacy operate less regularly, however, particularly in this era of "educational reform" and concern about school failure often attributed to "progressive" forms of education. The 80s and 90s saw a growing focus on phonics and skills-based programs emerging from the publication in 1983 of *A Nation at Risk: The Imperative for Educational Reform* (National Commission on Excellence in Education, 1983). All this culminated in the No Child Left Behind legislation of 2001. If progressive forms of education, critical thinking, and student-centered approaches are in use, they are more likely to be operating in majority classrooms and middle-class school systems, not in minority or second language classrooms (Cadiero-Kaplan 13). In the section that follows, we consider varying programs, their underlying assumptions within the framework provided by Cadiero-Kaplan, and their implications for secondary English classrooms.

A RANGE OF PROGRAMS FOR ENGLISH LANGUAGE LEARNERS

While programs for English language learners have existed for some time in school systems whose student populations are more heavily international, the changing complexion of schools across the country is forcing the issue for many districts that have been until recently entirely monolingual. It is not uncommon to find English language learners in rural districts in Michigan and Ohio and in larger cities throughout the Midwest. As a result, rural and urban districts across the country have begun to consider policy and program changes addressing the needs of a changing population of students.

School systems are approaching English language instruction in various ways, each with its own set of assumptions about the relationship between the learner, the learner's culture, and the dominant culture. Programs range from short-term English submersion programs with their sink-or-swim approaches all the way to bilingual programs that include cultural and social awareness issues for both English speakers and English language learners (Corson 99–151; Thomas and Collier 7). Most schools have adopted an assimilationist model whose goals are to help children become assimilated into American culture, but there is wide divergence in the degree to which "assimilation" can also accommodate the maintenance of one's own linguistic and cultural systems. One argument for assimilation is that many negative attitudes toward speakers learning English dissipate as they begin to assimilate themselves into mainstream American culture and as they lose their foreign accents. However, assimilation programs can have detrimental effects if home languages are not valued, as we discuss below.

Figure 7.1, adapted from Crawford (42) and Thomas and Collier (7), illustrates the range of English language programs with varying degrees of first-language involvement: from submersion programs that all but ignore the student's first language, to immersion programs and pull-out programs that work with direct instruction in English, to sheltered instruction pro-

Program	Language	Components	Duration	Goals
Submersion (sink-or-swim)	100% English	Mainstream instruction; no special help		Assimilation
ESL pull-out	90-100% English	Mainstream instruction; ELLs pulled out 30-45 min./day for social English instruction	As needed	Assimilation
Structured immersion	90-100% English	Sheltered subject matter instruction in English	1-3 years	Assimilation
Transitional bilingual education	10-50% L1; 50-90% English	L1 and sheltered subject matter instruction; daily ESL	2-4 years; ELLs exit on becoming English proficient	Assimilation; L2 acquisition without falling behind academically
Two-way bilingual; dual language/two-way immersion	10% English in early grades; more English in later grades	Taught subject matter in both languages	5-6 years	Bilingualism and bi-literacy; long-term academic achievement in English; gradual transition to all classes in English

Key

ELL: English language learner(s)
ESL: English as a second language
L1: First language
L2: Second (target) language

FIG. 7.1 Programs for English language learners.

grams in which subject matter is taught for a period of time in the learner's first language, and to more long-term bilingual programs that use the first language for instructional purposes until the learner is capable of working with English as the language of instruction. The chart indicates that linguistic assimilation is the goal of most of the programs, but readers need to keep in mind that the meaning of assimilation can vary from one school to another even within identical programs. Those programs in the last category—bilingual programs offering instruction in the first language—have been at the center of much debate in this country.

Maintaining First Languages: What the Research Suggests

The controversy surrounding bilingual programs raises the following questions: Do bilingual programs work? Do they coddle students and delay the learning of English unnecessarily? Are there less expensive ways of working with English language learners? Are there enough bilingual teachers fluent in the students' first language to support bilingual programs? These are not insignificant questions.

The discussion of the virtues and limitations of bilingual programs that follows must be placed within the context of the recent events in Arizona (2000) and California (1998) that disbanded all bilingual programs in those states and replaced them with immersion programs designed to teach English in a matter of months rather than years. With the passage of Proposition 227 in California, the goal of programs for English language learners has become learning English as rapidly as possible in a structured immersion program, with little attention focused on first-language maintenance. Opponents to bilingual programs claim that children cannot learn English with the bilingual approach because their English learning will be delayed, resulting in failure later on, but the underlying issue may be economic rather than educational. Of the three million English language learners in the United States, almost half reside in California (Cadiero-Kaplan 47).

Programs that deny the value of the first language too often promote cultural and linguistic conformity over cultural and linguistic diversity (Cadiero-Kaplan 49). What sets bilingual programs apart from immersion programs is the value placed on the home language. Recognizing the important relationship among language, culture, and identity, bilingual programs encourage the maintenance of home languages to prevent the dehumanization that occurs when immigrants are stripped of their cultural and linguistic connections. Teaching English at the expense of a student's home language is not only shortsighted; it is demeaning and unethical. If an immersion classroom or a submersion classroom goes so far as to forbid anything other than English spoken in the classroom, that prohibition can result in silencing students' use of language as was the case with Native

American children in the mid-20th century who were forbidden to speak their native languages while attending White schools. Not only were they silenced and their native cultures demeaned, they were sometimes physically punished for using their home languages. Some Asian students in this country have reported similar experiences.

Research strongly supports linguistic pluralism and multilingualism for English language learners. The best programs, says Luis Moll, alluding to strong bilingual programs, are those whose teachers are certified bilingual teachers; where there is mutual trust and respect for each other's culture; where social networks are constructed for exchange of cultural and linguistic knowledge; where there is ideological clarity about the goals and purposes of bilingual education; where education occurs outside as well as inside the regular school day through after school programs and events; and where the community feels in control of its language behaviors. Stephen Krashen's expertise in bilingualism and second language acquisition leads him to suggest that the maintenance of the home language is particularly important for academic success. First, the knowledge that children get through their first language helps them comprehend English, and second, a strong literacy background in the native language greatly enhances their ability to become literate in English. In other words, the kind of knowledge children develop in their first language—both content and literacy skills—transfers to the second language (Krashen 4). He also suggests that students do not necessarily have the ability to transition to full English programs even when they appear to be functioning well in social situations. The development of academic English always takes longer than the development of conversational ability.

The academic benefits of literacy in students' native languages are realized in their increased ability to become literate in English. Some evidence demonstrates that children in immersion programs who reject their first language, and whose English is weak, have the potential to become "semi-literate" (Schulte 3D). These children, unlike immigrant children from more literate homes, usually need the support of a bilingual program. True bilinguals, Moll claims (*Literacy Through Two Languages* 2004), based on his longitudinal study of Mexican immigrants in Arizona, are more successful academically than those who have lost their first language as they acquire English; they have higher self-esteem and greater academic achievement. And as educator Stephen Cary suggests, "students who develop a strong foundation in their primary language in multi-yeared bilingual programs consistently outperform second language learners in all English programs" (105).

Researcher Danling Fu's study of Chinese students in English classrooms provides a case in point. Her belief is that allowing English language learners to write in their own languages while they are learning English will enable them simultaneously to develop their thinking abilities, and literacy development must be accompanied by the learner's development of thinking. If writing is severely curtailed by the limitations of the learner's understanding of the target language, unnecessary delays may occur in the acquisition process. Says Fu, "If we let them wait until their English is good enough, their thinking and writing skills will not only have stopped developing but will have diminished—especially damaging for those students who don't yet have good writing skills in their first language" (74). That kind of transfer from L1 to L2 is critically important, as Fu's study on the writing of Chinese students demonstrates. Giving students options of writing in Chinese or English or both usually results in the following progression: much writing in the initial stage is in Chinese; the interim stage always has a mix of the two languages; and gradually English begins to take precedence over Chinese. Such an approach honors the first language and uses it as a means of thinking and writing development in both languages.

Equally important is not delaying the study of content until the student gains fluency in English. The recommended procedure for English language learners suggests first placing them in content classes taught in the home language, with some instruction in English and lots of social contact with speakers of English. In the intermediate stages, they can move into some courses taught in English and remain in some taught in their home languages. In advanced stages, English language learners can join mainstream classes but need continued work in ESL instruction. As Richard Rothstein argues, "Good bilingual programs do not delay the learning of English but begin it right away, while keeping children from falling behind in social studies, literature, math or science" through their instruction in the first language (*New York Times* 8 Nov. 2000). Requiring children to focus exclusively on the learning of English while putting other subjects on hold will result in their falling far behind their English-speaking counterparts.

Thomas and Collier's recent longitudinal study reviewing the research in U.S. public schools in 23 school districts in 15 states from 1985 to the present provides strong evidence that supporting English language learners in their home languages is critical to their cognitive development and academic success. Enrichment programs (dual language programs) that provide English instruction along with instruction in the home language and support of home language and culture are vastly superior to pull-out ESL programs and English immersion programs when the data are looked at longitudinally. Test scores in California in 2002 in the first three grades did climb under the structured immersion programs. By the end of the third grade there appeared to be little difference between programs. But by the end of the 11th grade the differences were striking. The fewest dropouts came from dual language programs, and they were the only programs, according to Thomas and Collier's study, "that assist[ed] students to fully reach the 50th percentile in both L1 and L2 in all subjects and to maintain that level of high achievement, or reach even higher levels ... through the end of schooling" (2).

Moll argues that the outlawing of bilingual education in states like Arizona and California without giving any real consideration to its educational merits, renders it a criminal activity. And even more important, he says, such outlawing severely limits teachers' abilities to build on the linguistic and cultural experiences of students, "their most important tools for thinking" (276). Prohibiting the use of Spanish for instructional purposes, he says,

> also imposes a (de facto) pariah status on both the language and its users, including teachers, students, families, and community, and is a continuation of the historical subtractive conditions for learning that have come to characterize, whether in English or in Spanish, the schooling of working-class Latino children in the United States. (276)

While true bilingual programs are ideal if circumstances are conducive to them, we also recognize the educational realities. We are not suggesting that bilingual programs are the only useful and educationally valuable ones. True bilingual programs are complicated by the paucity of teachers who can speak other languages, particularly the less common languages, and by the large number of languages represented in some districts that make that kind of instruction impossible. Even in schools that view the home language as an important part of the speaker's culture and learning—linguistic capital, in a sense—language maintenance/bilingual programs are often underfunded, expensive to run, and complicated to administer. Horner and Trimbur further point out other institutional problems that arise regarding English language learners: large class sizes and under-prepared teachers; classmates who isolate themselves from non-mainstream students and students who do not speak English fluently; curricular structures that are not conducive to serving English language learning populations of students; and assessment measures that ignore language differences and therefore marginalize these students even further.

We advocate, however, that regardless of the program, teachers and administrators begin to develop a set of understandings about English language learners that recognizes the value of their linguistic and cultural backgrounds, that encourages learners to incorporate those backgrounds into their learning of English, and that sees the learning of English as an additive process rather than a subtractive one. Assimilation into the mainstream language and culture becomes less a matter of replacing one set with another than of operating within two or more cultural groups with two or more language systems, depending on the rhetorical situation. It suggests a fluidity of movement, an ease in going back and forth, and a high comfort level in each and all.

No program—bilingual or immersion or any variation of—need deny English language learners the right to use their first languages for the purpose of learning English and understanding content, but bilingual programs make this inherently more doable because they operate with the premise of the need to maintain the first language. Immersion programs, on the other hand, must work much more diligently to provide these opportunities. Because they are based on the premise of learning English quickly, often at the expense of the first language, the impetus to discourage the use of the first language is strong. Only if educators are aware of the importance of maintaining the home language and are committed to that philosophy can they begin to overcome the limitations of immersion programs.

Furthermore, we strongly advocate for a set of classroom practices that don't underestimate the intelligence of the English language learner simply because of a lack of fluency in English. Like other students, English language learners must be given opportunities to develop critical literacy abilities, to question and critique, and to use the language for social action and transformation. It is not enough for them to be able to function only at basic levels. Additive bilingual programs that expect the continued use of the mother tongue rather than its replacement recognize the strong and important connection between language, culture, and identity.

Educators must be particularly careful in their teaching of English not to use English for the colonizing of English language learners by enforcing the use of English as a means of cultural control, while simultaneously withholding it as a means of critique and agency. Researchers like Michael Apple, Karen Cadiero-Kaplan, and Alastair Pennycook have argued that majority students in middle-upper class schools are often provided with critical literacy skills that lead to greater social power, but that working class students and minority language students are more likely to be provided with a "practical" curriculum that focuses on functional literacy skills: good work habits and patterns of behavior and thought that support existing political structures. The disparity between student opportunity manifests in tracking and ability grouping, as we discussed in chapter 6 for speakers of minority dialects. Reductive programs, sociolinguist Cathy Mazak suggests, assume that "second language learners are blank slates—or worse, that their first languages inhibit their learning—and that if they were just given the right tools (i.e. grammar rules and memorized vocabulary items), they could become readers and writers of decontextualized chunks of their L2" (21). Functional literacy skills focus more on developing good citizens whose minimal competencies enable them to become willing consumers of the dominant culture rather than individuals who use literacy for critical thought and action.

NATIONAL LANGUAGE POLICY

Many changes regarding the instruction of second language learners can occur in individual classrooms, as we outline in the next section, but changes must also begin occurring from the top—from the level of policy-making. The Conference on College Composition and Communication, an organization within the National Council of Teachers of English, passed a resolution in 1988, the National Language Policy, calling for approaches that affirm students' language rights in response to the English Only movement:

Background

The National Language Policy is a response to efforts to make English the "official" language of the United States. This policy recognizes the historical reality that, even though English has become the language of wider communication, we are a multilingual society. All people in a democratic society have the right to education, to employment, to social services, and to equal protection under the law. No one should be denied these or any civil rights because of linguistic differences. This policy would enable everyone to participate in the life of this multicultural nation by ensuring continued respect both for English, our common language, and for the many other languages that contribute to our rich heritage.

CCCC National Language Policy

Be it resolved that CCCC members promote the National Language Policy adopted at the Executive Committee meeting on 16 March 1988. This policy has three inseparable parts:

1. To provide resources to enable native and non-native speakers to achieve oral and literate competence in English, the language of wider communication.

2. To support programs that assert the legitimacy of native languages and dialects and ensure that proficiency in one's mother tongue will not be lost.

3. To foster the teaching of languages other than English so that native speakers of English can rediscover the language of their heritage or learn a second language. (qtd. in Smitherman, *Talkin That Talk* 394–395)

The resolution, in short, advocates for programs that provide opportunities for strengthening and enhancing all students' linguistic options. English Plus, a movement that supports the principles of 4 Cs National Language Policy, currently attempts to educate Americans about the virtues of multilingualism as it argues for a U.S. language policy that views linguistic diversity as an asset and that encourages the maintenance of home languages even while supporting the learning of English. Rather than viewing minority languages as a source of problems and a threat to America's future, English Plus sees them as resources and opportunities that can enrich all students' educational experiences. Schmidt, in fact, advocates for two-way bilingual programs for all students:

> ... it is wasteful folly for U.S. educators to strip language minority students of their native languages in the elementary grades, only to try to reinstill them in other students in high school. Would it not be to the common good to establish "two-way" bilingual education programs for *all* U.S. students, so that every American high school graduate would have mastered both English and another language? The benefits of such a policy would accrue to the United States in terms of not only our national linguistic resources for political and economic interaction but also our openness to and understanding of the cultures, values, and identities held dear by the many peoples with whom it is in our interest to interact productively (175–176).

Schmidt's recommendation is aligned with that of the CCCC advocacy of a National Language Policy, a position that all educators and policy-makers should consider before making instructional decisions about policies for English language learners.

APPLICATIONS FOR THE CLASSROOM

Most teachers will not find themselves teaching entire classes of English language learners; much more likely is the possibility that they will have several English language learners mainstreamed into their English or social studies or science classes, and many teachers will find themselves in school systems with minimal support for special programs for these learners. What are teachers to do to help them achieve fluency in English, even without the support of a well-funded ESL program? We are suggesting the following strategies:

1. Establish some basic principles upon which to make decisions regarding the work you do with English language learners. Virginia Collier suggests the following principles:

   a. students who are learning English, already fluent in another language, are resources rather than problems: use students as experts;
   b. learning a second language is a natural process, a developmental process, a gradual process, and a long-term process: give students time and opportunity to learn;
   c. social issues are closely integrated with language issues through the learning process: view the learning of English within a broad social and cultural context that involves the student's own culture as well as U.S. culture;

d. there is a strong relationship between L1 academic/cognitive development and L2 academic/cognitive development: encourage maintenance and use of the student's native language;

e. the learning tasks should promote active, discovery learning that is cognitively complex;

f. changes in the sociocultural context for English language learners must occur in order to ensure their integration with English speakers;

g. bilingual programs need to be promoted as gifted and talented programs;

h. enrichment, not remediation, must be the focus in working with English language learners.

2. Because not all teachers have bilingual educational resources at hand, Stephen Cary suggests these *specific classroom applications* for teachers with mainstreamed English language learners in their classrooms:

a. Assessing students' English language abilities. Do not assess students' English proficiency until they have had a couple of weeks to acclimate to their new schools and classrooms. Use formal assessment measures sparingly because they are unable to provide the kind of authentic language assessment that is necessary to assess authentic language. Use instead a wide-ranging, observational model of assessment that includes portfolio work and observational data, along with more formal assessment measures.

b. Gathering information on the cultural and linguistic background of students. Use available materials on the cultures and home languages of your students from the World Wide Web, reference books, trade books, school and public libraries, family members, etc.

c. Getting reluctant speakers to speak English. Providing students with lots of time to talk and reason to talk is essential. Talking in small groups or with one other speaker of English is less intimidating than talking in front of the whole class. Engaging activities also contribute to an interest in talking and using the language, particularly when the activities are related to the English language learner's own realm of experience and interest.

d. Making difficult texts more readable for English language learners. Use visuals, role-playing, plot situation simulations, and videos to aid comprehension, along with more conventional comprehension strategies to make texts more accessible for all readers. The teacher modeling reading strategies helps all learners, including English language learners. Helping learners connect ideas in stories and texts to their own experiences makes the reading more accessible. The use of dual language textbooks when available is an excellent means of providing information that the reader can glean from either language. Dual language trade-books are increasingly available, such as *The Treasure on Gold Street, El Tesoro en la Calle Oro* by Lee Merrill Byrd.

e. Improving English language learners' writing in English. Authentic writing tasks that go through the processes of drafting, revising, and editing are likely to get better results than a skills-based model for writing in which students usually don't write for real audiences or purposes. Writing tasks that have a direct impact on students' school or home lives especially engage writers. Collaborative writing is also useful and gives students oral language practice as well enhancing their writing skills. (And I would add, using Danling Fu's suggestion to allow English language learners to use their home language in their writing as they develop fluency in English.)

f. Teaching grade-level content to English language learners. Design lessons that are engaging, and use real artifacts to increase interest in authentic learning and texts.

g. Supporting students' first language. Teachers can encourage home language maintenance by establishing a classroom community that values all languages; by allowing students to use their first language and encouraging their parents to maintain their language, even while learning English; by offering support through community volunteers, peers, cross-age tutors, etc.

This list of strategies recommended for English language learners is equally important for students for whom English is their first or only language. Although it may be necessary to use some direct instruction and some guided activities with English language learners, they also benefit from "whatever is good for mainstream students, such as reading aloud, interactive learning, inquiry projects, book talks, reading response journals, and writer's notebooks" (Fu 156).

FOR THOUGHT 7.4: Stephen Cary says that "Giving students permission to get language wrong goes a long way in helping them get it right" (Cary 59). Which of the strategies listed above encourage language experimentation, English language use in authentic contexts, language learning in communicative contexts?

---

3. Educators and researchers Pat Rigg and Virginia Allen advise teachers to surround their students "in a rich bath of language" in classrooms where talk and group work are encouraged, rather than offer them "a string of language beads, one bead at a time" (xi). Other specific strategies that help English language learners include the use of:

a. picture books, picture dictionaries, and books with repeating patterns of language;

b. music and singing;

c. story telling and show and tell;

d. charting and mapping;

e. photographs and photograph collections which tell stories;

f. a buddy system in which English speaking students pair with the English language learner;

g. class members deciding on the critical words English language learners need to "survive" in school and together devising ways to teach these words;

h. labeling key items in the classroom in English and in the English learners' languages;

i. taking a projects-approach to learning;

j. artwork, including painting and drawing.

4. As part of program-building, Rigg and Allen offer suggestions for considering English language learners as individuals, not as "the other(s)":

a. Teachers who work with English language learners must understand that these learners are people first and learners second; they must be treated with respect and compassion and must be placed in grade level classrooms appropriate to their age.

b. Teachers need to remember that many of these students have had little say in the disruption in their lives that has placed them in U.S. classrooms; many miss their homes and friends; many are frightened; some may come from war-torn countries where they have experienced horrors; many may be reluctant to learn English, as their home language not only is critical to their identity and sense of heritage, but also because their home language may seem to be their last crucial link with all they have lost—they certainly do not want to lose it too.

5. Classroom teachers can broaden their students' (and their own, if need be) attitudes toward other languages and the people who speak them by asking them to read, explore, and discuss literature about:

a. English learners who have learned English and maintained their first language

b. English speakers who have learned English at the sacrifice of their home language

c. Non-speakers of English as they encounter an English speaking environment

d. Native English speakers' attitudes toward speakers of other languages

A wealth of literature exists that will help foster linguistic empathy and, perhaps, the acceptance of bilingualism and language maintenance. *The Indian Wants the Bronx* by Israel Horovitz, a play that won three Obie awards, records the hostility and cruelty two men from the Bronx display toward a man from India who speaks no English. Poems which present the conflicts, longings, memories, and triumphs of bilingual speakers include Li-Young Lee's "Persimmons," Derek Walcott's "A Far Cry From Africa," Gustavo Perez-Firmat's "Limen," Czeslaw Milosz's "My Faithful Mother Tongue," Lawson Fusado Inada's "Kicking the Habit," Pat Mora's "Elena," and Lorna Dee Cervantes' "Refuge Ship." M. Nourbese Philip's book of poetry, *She Tries Her Tongue, Her Silence Softly Breaks*, considers language issues; particularly pointed is her "Discourse on the Logic of Language" that emanates from an edict of slavery that says, "Every slave caught speaking his native language shall be severely punished. Where necessary, removal of the tongue is recommended. The offending organ, when removed, should be hung on high in a central place, so that all may see and tremble" (32).

Two very different prose pieces that take opposing stances on the maintenance of one's native language and present the dilemmas of the English learner are "Learn! Learn!" by Hugo Marinez-Serros and Richard Rodriguez' "Aria: A Memoir of a Bilingual Childhood." Amy Tan's "Mother Tongue" reveals the conflicts and humiliation her mother faced as an immigrant English language learner. Many of these pieces can be found anthologized in *New Worlds of Literature* edited by Jerome Beatty and J. Paul Hunter. Others are widely anthologized. A look through any anthology of U.S. Latino literature will reveal many selections that examine bilingual issues. Three excellent anthologies are:

e. *U.S. Latino Literature Today*, edited by Gabriela Baeza Ventura
f. *Herencia: The Anthology of Hispanic Literature of the United States*, edited by Nicolas Kanellos, et al.
g. *Hispanic American Literature: A Brief Introduction and Anthology*, also edited by Kanellos.

Novels that directly and indirectly examine the complexities of monolingualism and bilingualism include Rosario Ferre's *The House on The Lagoon*, which among many other issues traces the Spanish versus English disputes on Puerto Rico; Sandra Cisneros' recent border novel *Caramelo*; Amy Tan's *The Joy Luck Club*, and Chang Rae-Lee's *Native Speaker*.

Funding and Resources

In this chapter we have reviewed the controversy that surrounds bilingual education and have advocated for the support of students' first language even as they are learning English, detailed English-Only policies and posited reasons for their inception, offered the alternatives of English Plus and the CCCC National Language Policy, and suggested ways teachers can work with English language learners in their classrooms. What we haven't addressed is the need for additional funding and resources for schools and communities with increasing populations of English language learners. At the community level, the *New York Times* ("Bilingual Education" Oct. 9, 2002) reported that 850,000 speakers of English as a second language were in bilingual education programs in 2000, another 987,000 were in immersion programs, and more than two million were in programs that combined the two approaches. But L. Thomas reports that thousands of immigrants each year are turned away annually from ESL classes because of a serious lack of classes to meet the demand. In New York City, for example, the areas of the city with the highest concentrations of immigrants have few classes to accommodate the need (Bernstein 1920).

The problem is particularly acute in the nation's public schools—and not just in systems like Los Angeles, New York City, Miami, or Houston. Schools in all communities work with a level of linguistic and cultural diversity unknown fifty years ago when the Brown v. Board of Education outlawed school segregation in an attempt to insure equal access to educational opportunity for all (Hajela). As journalist Deepti Hajela reports:

> It's an issue in every part of the country. In Lexington, Nebraska, where the majority of the factory town's 2,800 students are Hispanic. In Minneapolis, which has the largest community of Somalis in America. And at Newtown High School in the Elmhurst section of Queens, where students come from all over the world and speak dozens of languages. (1)

Not providing educational opportunities for English language learners runs the risk of creating two nations—those who have linguistic capital and access to power—and those who do not. The scarcity of monetary resources for classroom instruction and for work with parents—and the scarcity of qualified teachers—are huge barriers to realizing the goal of educating all students (Hajela 1). In this age of diminishing resources and a diminishing will to provide funding that will ensure equal education for all, we are falling far behind the promise that Brown v. The Board of Education envisioned.

It is our job as teachers to welcome all of our students and to provide the best possible education for them all, regardless of whether they are native speakers of English or English language learners. But teachers can't do it alone. A commitment from the public and from the federal government is fundamental to making this a reality. Teachers can advocate for better programs, for greater understanding, and for better classroom instruction. Teachers can and must become agents of change.

PERSONAL EXPLORATIONS

1. You and your class have nearly and successfully made it to Thanksgiving break. The Tuesday before Thanksgiving, your principal comes to your room to announce that on Monday you will have two new students in your room. They are both from Iran, and they speak no English. Neither do their parents. Members of a nearby church are both families' sponsors in the United States; however, no members of the church speak Persian.

After Thanksgiving in your middle school English/social studies class, you're about to begin a new unit on the 1920s in the United States, which has a strong English language arts component: reading both creative and informative texts, writing, speaking, listening, viewing; the unit is interdisciplinary.

How will you welcome and integrate your two new students into your classroom? What strategies will you use to:

a. Help these students adjust to daily life in your classroom among your other students?
b. Find out information on the students' cultural background?
c. Make your language more understandable to these two new students?
d. Help them to overcome their reluctance to speak English? Make difficult texts more readable?

2. Peruse the Web site of U.S. English <us-english.org> and read the information in the "resource room" promoting the reasons why federal and state legislation to mandate English as the official language is an important issue. Read the site critically—between-the-lines—and list some of the tacit examples of xenophobia, often disguised as concern for the immigrant.

3. Go to James Crawford's website on language issues: <http://ourworld. compuserve.com/homepages/JWCRAWFORD/> What are his counterarguments to English Only? What information does he use to support his arguments? Cite three negative effects on the education of children that he argues will occur if English Only becomes federal policy.

4. Interview three non-native speakers of English at your university to find out about any difficulties they have encountered learning English, the attitudes of native English speakers toward them, and positive and negative experiences they have had as non-native speakers living in the United States and being educated or teaching in English. Now do a series of three interviews of non-native speakers in your community, asking questions about the same topics. What have you learned from the interviews?

5. What sorts of programs, if any, exist in your local schools to assist non-native English speakers? Where do they fall on the continuum on p. 203 Interview two teachers in your local schools who have worked with non-native speakers in mainstream classes. What strategies did they use to assist these students? How do you assess the effectiveness of their strategies?

6. Read "Aria" and "Learn! Learn!" How are the stances of the two pieces different? Similar? Rodriguez is a critic of bilingual education that enables children to learn in their own language as they are learning English. As he recalls his childhood, what losses did he experience as he moved into the mainstream world of English? How did Richard's and his siblings' learning English distance them from their family? Their heritage? How did their doing so silence their father?

TEACHING EXPLORATIONS

1. Examine some of the literary pieces suggested above and some of the anthologies. How might you use three to five pieces to help your students become more aware of the personal issues that emerge as non-English speakers become English learners?

2. Develop a set of lessons for the English language learners you might have in your classroom that incorporates the principles and strategies outlined in this chapter. How will your work with these students differ from the work you do with native speakers of English?

3. Describe how your own thinking about English language learners in mainstream English classrooms has changed. How will your classroom teaching be modified as a result?

4. For further strategies specifically developed for working with ELL students in reading, writing, and language and literacy assessment, see Maria Brisk and Margaret Harrington's book, *Literacy and Bilingualism: A Handbook for ALL Teachers*. Their suggestions for teaching ELLs are also applicable and relevant for students whose first language is English.

WORKS CITED

Ann Arbor News 30 Aug. 1995: A6.

Apple, Michael. *Ideology and Curriculum*. Boston: Routledge, 1979.

Beatty, Jerome, and J. Paul Hunter, eds. *New Worlds of Literature*, 2nd ed. New York: Norton, 1994.

Bernstein, Nina. "Problems with Speaking English Multiply in a Decade." *New York Times* 19 Jan. 2005: A20.

"Bilingual Education on Ballot in Two States." *New York Times* 9 Oct. 2002: A18.

Brandt, Aviva L. *Ann Arbor News*, 5 Jan. 1996: A4.

Brisk, Maria, and Margaret Harrington. *Literacy and Bilingualism: A Handbook for All Teachers*. Mahwah, NJ: Lawrence Erlbaum Associates, 2000.

Cadiero-Kaplan, Karen. *The Literacy Curriculum and Bilingual Education: A Critical Examination*. New York: Lang, 2004.

Cary, Stephen. *Working with Second Language Learners: Answers to Teachers' Top Ten Questions*. Portsmouth, NH: Heinemann, 2000.

Chiang, Yuet-Sim and Mary Schmida. "Language Identity and Language Ownership: Linguistic Conflicts of First-Year University Writing Students." Eds. Harklau, Linda, Kay M. Losey, and Meryl Siegal. *Generation 1.5 Meets College Composition: Issues in the Teaching of Writing to U.S.-Educated Learners of ESL*. Mahwah: Lawrence Erlbaum Associates, 1999. 81–96.

Corson, David. *Language Diversity and Education*. Mahwah: Lawrence Erlbaum Associates, 2001.

Crawford, James. *Educating English Learners: Language Diversity in the Classroom*. Los Angeles: Bilingual Educational Services, Inc., 2004. English Plus Web site: <http://ourworld.compuserve.com/homepages/JWCRAWFORD/engplus.htm>.

Fu, Danling. *An Island of English: Teaching ESL in Chinatown*. Portsmouth, NH: Heinemann, 2003.

Gonzalez, Norma, Luis Moll, and Cathy Amanti, Eds. *Funds of Knowledge: Theorizing Practices in Households, Communities, and Classrooms*. Mahwah, NJ: Lawrence Erlbaum Associates, 2005.

Hajela, Deepti. "Language Issues Challenge to Brown's Promise." MSNBC, 10 May 2004, 1–4.

Hirsch, E. D. *Cultural Literacy: What Every American Needs to Know*. Boston: Houghton-Mifflin, 1987.

Horner, Bruce, and John Trimbur. "English Only and U.S. College Composition." *College Composition and Communication* 53 (2002): 594–630.

Johnson, Doug. SFGate.com. 25 May 2002. <http://www.sfgate.com/cgi-bin/article.cgi?file=/news/archive/2002/05/25/national>.

Kanellos, Nicolas, et al. eds. *Herencia: The Anthology of Hispanic Literature of the United States*. New York: Oxford UP, 2002.

Kanellos, Nicolas, ed. *Hispanic American Literature A Brief Introduction and Anthology*. New York: Longman, 1995.

Kellogg, Sarah. "Language Diversity Is Low in State." *Ann Arbor News* 15 Aug. 2004: B5.

Krashen, Stephen D. *Under Attack: The Case Against Bilingual Education*. Culver City, CA: Language Education Associates, 1996.

"Language Diversity Helps in Policing." *Saginaw News* [Michigan] 19 June 2002: A8.

Loveless, Jan. "Language Policy and Teachers: The Wider Implications of Changing from a Deficit to a Positive Model in a Multicultural School Community." Diss. Michigan State University, 1996.

Mazak, Cathy. "Negotiating el dificil: English Literacy Practices in a Puerto Rican Community" Diss. Michigan State University, 2006.

Moll, Luis. "Literacy through Two Languages: Problems, Practices, and Possibilities." NCTE Conference, Nov. 19, 2004, Indianapolis, IN.

———. "Reflections and Possibilities." In *Funds of Knowledge: Theorizing Practices in Households, Communities, and Classrooms*. Eds. Norma Gonzales, Luis Moll, and Cathy Amanti. Mahwah, NJ: Lawrence Erlbaum Associates, 2005. 275–287.

Pennycook, Alastair. *Critical Applied Linguistics: A Critical Introduction*. Mahwah, NJ: Lawrence Erlbaum Associates, 2001.

Philip, M. Nourbese. *She Tries Her Tongue, Her Silence Softly Breaks*. London: The Women's Press, 1989.

Range, Stacey. "Schools Struggle to Meet Children's Needs." *Lansing State Journal* [Michigan]. 28 March 2005: B1.

Ricento, Thomas, and Barbara Burnaby, eds. *Language and Politics in the United States and Canada: Myths and Realities*. Mahwah, NJ: Lawrence Erlbaum Associates, 1998.

Rigg, Pat, and Virginia Allen. *When They Don't All Speak English*. Urbana, IL: NCTE, 1989.

Rothstein, Richard. "Debunking Double Talk on Bilingual Ed." Editorial. *New York Times* 8 Nov. 2000: 5.

Sanchez, Mary. "Americans Wrongly Fear Languages." *Lansing State Journal* [Michigan]. 1 Jan. 2005: 6A.

Schmidt, Ronald, Sr. *Language Policy and Identity Politics in the United States*. Philadelphia: Temple UP, 2000.

Schulte, Brigid. "More and More U.S.-Born Kids Need Help Speaking English." *Lansing State Journal* [Michigan]. 28 July 2002: 3D.

Shanahan, Timothy. "Highlights from the National Reading Panel Report: Implications of Literacy Research for Second Language Learning." Teachers for a New Era Conference. 8 Sep. 2004. Michigan State University, East Lansing, MI.

Sharp, Deborah. "Those Who Don't Speak Spanish May Be Left Behind." *USA Today* 19 June 2001. <http://www.usatoday.com/news/nation/2001-05-09-spanish-usat.htm>.

Smitherman, Geneva. "The Mis-education of the Negro." *Not Only English: Affirming America's Multilingual Heritage*. Ed. Harvey A. Daniels. Urbana, IL: NCTE, 1990. 109–120.

Smitherman, Geneva. *Talkin that Talk: Language, Culture, and Education in African America*. New York: Routledge, 2000.

Tan, Amy. "Mother Tongue." *Patterns for College Writing*. Eds. Laurie Kirszner and Stephen Mandell. New York: St. Martin's, 1998. 393–397.

Thomas, Lee. "Language as Power: A Linguistic Critique of U.S. English." *The Modern Language Journal* 80.ii (1996): 91–101.

Thomas, Wayne P. and Virginia P. Collier. "How to Close the Academic Achievement Gap for Linguistically and Culturally Diverse Learners." Teachers for a New Era Conference. 8 Sep. 2004. Michigan State University, East Lansing, MI.

U.S. English website: <http://www.us-english.org/inc/about/chairman.asp>.

Ventura, Gabriela Baeza, ed. *U.S. Latino Literature Today*. New York: Longman, 2005.

U.S. News and World Report 1 Aug. 1996: 87.

Zehr, Mary A. "Tribes Oppose Arizona Bilingual Ed. Measure." *Education Week* 13 Sept. 2000. <http://www.edweek.org/ew/ew_printstory.cfm?slug=02ariz.h20>.

Zhao, Yilu. "Wave of Pupils Lacking English Strains Schools." *New York Times* 5 Aug. 2002: A8+

Afterword

Whenever we ask our students to write papers, we always tell them to be sure to include the "so-what" factor. As you digest the thoughts, suggestions, theories, and resources you have just read, we hope the "so-what" factor is readily apparent to you. Language unifies and divides; it hurts and heals; it names and defines. Language constrains and suppresses some people while it advances and expresses others. It can serve as an equalizer, or it can sustain and replicate inequity. It can enlighten and free or manipulate and control. And it can enhance us as humans or dehumanize us. Thus, language has amazing power. Its power permeates society as a critical tool through which societies and persons' roles in them are constructed and maintained.

Yet societies and roles are not absolute. Inequities need not be permanent. If we, in our roles as citizens and teachers, wish to be agents of the sort of social change that leads to lesser, not greater inequity, we must increase our own and our students' knowledge of language and its use and broaden our own and our students' attitudes toward its variants and the speakers of those variants. We must observe our own linguistic behaviors to determine their positive or negative impact on our students. We must expose language use and attitudes that bespeak and underlie hatred, fear, or mockery of others and that render them humiliated, denigrated, or dehumanized, whether those persons are women and girls, boys and men, homosexuals, speakers of non-prestige dialects, English language learners, or persons in any minority—social class, ethnic, age, handicapped, religious. We must help our students understand that language use and choices are never innocent; they are always invested with power that either heightens or lessens speakers' and listeners' cultural capital.

Once we recognize the centrality of language in cultural construction and in the mediation of all learning, we will want to ensure that our classrooms and our schools are not environments in which what students learn fosters greater cultural capital for some and less for others. Rather, we will want to help our students realize that addressing their language use and attitudes is a means to root out and redress the inequities within classrooms, communities, the United States, and the world.

Throughout, we have promoted moving the study of language well beyond that of traditional grammar and vocabulary to include social and political study about language and the roles language plays in power production and maintenance. We have encouraged such study on an ongoing basis in classrooms and have provided many activities and resources for teachers to do so. We are confident that as they adapt and apply many of the FOR THOUGHT sections and EXPLORATIONS projects to their own classrooms, they will find, as we have, that the study of language is filled with "Aha!" moments for themselves and their students. As they regularly bring in news events and clippings, cartoons, comic strips, films, CDs, videos and literary pieces that directly or indirectly comment on language use and make these an everyday part of their classrooms, they will soon find, as we have, that their students have become actively engaged in classroom discussion about language and more alert to language use. Soon their students will voluntarily bring in language exhibits themselves.

This book was written to provide a context for studying the social and cultural issues embedded in language use, to consider these issues within the context of the classroom as they apply to the teaching and learning of language, and to encourage teachers to engage in study about language with their students. We are all producers and consumers of language. Our production and consumption can either work toward greater societal health and a fuller realization of personal potential, or they can result in the stunted growth or decline of both. It is our hope that the materials in this book nudge teachers, students, and classrooms, as well as the society they all inhabit and create, toward greater equity and toward personal and public growth for all.

Author Index

221

Subject Index